The Historical Critique of Career and Technical Education in California from 1900 – 2000 and the Status of California Community Colleges in the 21st Century

The Historical Critique of Career and Technical Education in California from 1900 – 2000 and the Status of California Community Colleges in the 21st Century

Henry O'Lawrence

California State University Long Beach

Informing Science Press

Historical Critique of Career and Technical Education in California

ISBN: 1-932886-68-0
        978-1-932886-68-9

Published by

Informing Science Press
publishing arm of the Informing Science Institute:

131 Brookhill Court
Santa Rosa
California
95409
USA
Phone: +1 707 531 4925
Fax: +1 480 247 5724
ISPress.org
InformingScience.org

Printed in the US

Dedication

To Dr. Thomas M. Bogeticvh, former executive director, California Advisory Council on Vocational Education from 1972-1988 and the Executive Director, California State Board of Education from 1988-1992, and thanks to my former department chair, Dr. Paul Bott from whom I took over as department chairman when he retired. Special thanks to my great mentor, and the former Dean of College of Health and Human Services, Dr. Ronald Vogue; Dr. Thomas Coaxum, Director of Institutional Research at Alabama A & M University, Dr. Ruby Rodney, Winston Salem State University in North Carolina; and Dr. Edgar Farmer, Penn State University. And to all my Friends and Colleagues in the field of Workforce Education and Development.

O'Lawrence, H. (2013)
The Historical Critique of Career and Technical Education in California from 1900 – 2000 and the Status of California Community Colleges in the 21st Century
Santa Rosa, California: Informing Science Institute

CONTENTS

O'Lawrence, H. (2013)

The Historical Critique of Career and Technical Education in California from 1900 – 2000 and the Status of California Community Colleges in the 21st Century

Santa Rosa, California: Informing Science Institute

Preface

This book should provide the reader with an overview of the evolution of career and technical education in California over the 20th century and provide some insight as to its strengths and weaknesses as well as what challenges it faces in the new millennium. For those who are privileged to be a vocational education professional, much of this story will be familiar to you. However, for those of you unfamiliar with vocational education, let me briefly share with you why career and technical education/vocational education or, as we call it today, workforce education and development (corporate training and human resources development) is so important and needed in California's public schools. Vocational education, career and technical education/occupational studies, and workforce education and development are used interchangeable throughout the book.

What is vocational education? By its very nature vocational education, or career technical education as it is currently defined in state law, ideally can be defined as an integrated process that provides students the opportunity to select, prepare, secure, and progress in a job or career. The key words in the definition are "integrated" and "process." Integrated mean that vocational education is part of the total educational process and should be available to all students regardless of their educational objectives or ability. Process means that all the educational components—basic academic skills, career and job counseling, vocational exploration, job skill training, internships and paid or unpaid work experience opportunities—are sequentially linked so that youth can transition from school to work and become productive workers.

What are the benefits of vocational education, and in particular, to the student? There are many benefits including these outcomes:

Vocational education makes the 3Rs and science come alive. Vocational education is a vehicle to teach and reinforce basic academic skills. For some students vocational education can be utilized to teach the 3Rs and science. Through direct application of job skills, students see a direct relationship to the real world and, in particular, the world of work. We know from an understanding of psychology that all students don't learn at the same rate or by the same teaching methods. For a number of students vocational education brings a sense of reality to why school is important to them. For others, it is the motivational force that keeps them in school and helps reduce the dropout rate.

Develops the work ethic. An important aspect of job success is how well a worker demonstrates certain basic employability skills and work ethic. This includes being to work on time, giving eight hours of productive labor for eight hours of pay, and the ability of working as a member of a team or independently. This work ethic is not the exclusive domain of vocational education. It is something that can be gained through the entire educational process, if in fact it is integrated throughout the curriculum.

Students must understand that all learning that takes place in school relates to the real world and not just the educational world. Vocational education helps bridge that gap by providing real world applications that reinforce the 3Rs and science as well as providing simulated as well as on the job work experiences. All of these help develop positive attitudes toward and for work.

Employment. The bottom line for vocational education is the ability of a student to secure and advance in a job or career field of their choosing. National longitudinal studies tell us that vocational education graduates that find employment are happier on the job, and stay longer on the job than students without a vocational education background. In other words, vocational education provides students with a competitive edge. State and national longitudinal studies tell us that a large number of vocational education graduates continue their education and training beyond high school. Basically, they have made the connection that to reach higher up on the job ladder requires more schooling and/or training.

Rewarding careers and job mobility. This outcome is very much related to employment. Many students utilize vocational education skills to pay their way through college. Statistics tell us that very few, about one-out-of-three who graduate from high school, graduate with a four year degree. For the two out three that enter college and don't make it through, the students with vocational education skills have a competitive edge over their academic counterparts. They have a fall back position and can get employed in a career field of their choice at a step or two lower than would have been reachable with a B.A. degree. On the other hand, when a student with a general or academic background (with no specific job skills) fails in college, their fall back positions are often not as promising or rewarding as those of their counterparts who took vocational education in high school. When compared, the competitive edge goes to the student with vocational education experiences.

Why does California need vocational education? The primary reasons are economic. The U.S. Department of Commerce tells us that there is direct relationship between the availability of education and training opportunities, the quality of life, and the economic well-being of a region or state. Career and technical education provides economic benefits to the individual, society and the business community. First and foremost, it benefits the individual—the student. There is nothing better than a job to give a person a feeling of self-worth, dignity, and most important self-reliance. For society, a productive self-reliant worker is a contributing member pulling his or her own weight, paying taxes, buying goods and services, and is probably less likely to be on welfare or involved in crime. As a rule, the investment made in vocational education is generally returned to the community within six months after a person enters the job market. Finally, employers benefit by having a steady flow of well prepared and productive workers. This increases their profits, and in many instances reduces the cost of a product or service to the consumer.

The importance of vocational or career and technical education or workforce education and development can be summed up in this old Chinese Proverb: Give a person a fish and they will have a meal, and teach them to fish and they will eat the rest of their life.

How this book is organized. Section one of this book discusses the historical foundation of career and technical education in California starting from the beginning of 1900 to 2000. This section is devoted to historical, philosophical, and social concepts of career and technical education in California. Four chapters cover historical and current issues in career vocational education in California. The uniqueness of the section is the fact that chapters are written based on document review, memo, and collections of materials obtained from Dr. Thomas M. Bogeticvh and compiled for editing and analysis at the Department of Professional Studies by the author.

Part two of this book including chapter four contains research on the 21st century workforce and the community college's CTE programs and role in the economy completed over the years and published in tier one research journals in the country. For example, chapter six of the book is a result of a thesis project completed by my former student, Renah Wolzinger and co-authored for publication. Renah is now the department chair of Design Arts, Digital Media, Design and

Computer Science at Golden West College. Chapter eight was a research completed and edited by my colleague, Dr. Martinez, who was the Distance Learning Director under my leadership when I was a department chairman of Professional Studies.

Major accomplishments of this book are that it provides a forum and voice for scholars in California. This book allow us to learn and understand how career and technical education was viewed at the beginning of foundation, the curriculum and the impact it has on California labor force today. We can also see in part two of this book the labor market disadvantages we are facing due to lack of proper structures in the CTE programs across the State.

O'Lawrence, H. (2013)
The Historical Critique of Career and Technical Education in California from 1900 – 2000 and the Status of California Community Colleges in the 21st Century
Santa Rosa, California: Informing Science Institute

Section 1: Career and Technical Education in California – 1900 to 2000

Chapter One

The Formative Years: 1900-1975

Introduction

The words Vocational Education, Career and Technical Education, or Workforce Education and Development are used interchangeably throughout this book. Career and Technical education is a major factor contributing to the economic wellbeing of California. As the fifth largest economy in the world, California has a continuous need for workers with work skills, understandings, and attitudes that are closely aligned with job market needs. Without an adequately prepared work force California would not be able to compete in today's global economy. However, the issue has been and continues to be (1) when job preparation should begin and (2) what should be the role of the public schools. Thousands of dedicated vocational educators believe California's claim to success and a competitive edge in the world economy is due, in part, to having initiated the process of job preparation in the public schools starting around 1900. Therefore, it is essential to sustain vocational education's position as an integral part of the public schools system.

This historical review primarily focuses on the progress, accomplishment, and issues confronting vocational education from 1975 through 2000 in the K-12 system. However, in order to understand the significance of California's decision to include vocational education as a part of the public school system, one must first understand how this came about during the time period preceding the body of this review.

The Early Years of Vocational Education in California

Although the first signs of vocational education did not appear in the public schools until about 1900, the need for vocational education was stimulated by at least two influences. First, it is fundamentally recognized that vocational education has always been influenced by practical needs. Vocational education did not originate, nor persist, by chance or accident. It began and progressed because of choice, not chance. Vocational education was created because of economic and social necessity. Vocational education's existence has depended on how well it has addressed those needs.

Second, the need for attaining occupational competencies through training can be traced as far back as 1854, the first establishment of the Mechanics Institute in San Francisco after California became a state in 1850. The Institute was dedicated to the accumulation of library materials pertinent to the mechanic's craft, the dissemination of the lore through series of lectures, the staging of annual industrial exhibits, and the organization of classes in such areas as drawing, mathematics, wood carving, and metalworking.

In 1866 the California legislature established the Agriculture, Mining and Mechanical Arts College. It became the University of California in 1868. A founding principle of the University was to provide *"practical education of the classes in the several pursuits and professions of life"* (California Department of Education 1982-84 Report). In 1901, the California Legislature authorized the establishment of a "polytechnic school" to be located near San Luis Obispo. By its action, the Legislature registered its concern for providing a practical education for work and careers in the public schools. The school featured instruction adapted to the high school level in agriculture, mechanics, and household arts. The instructional schedule consisted of one-half classroom work and one-half laboratory. Some 100 students were enrolled in 1906 (67 boys and 33 girls).

Career and technical education, as we know it today, was virtually absent in the high schools until after the turn of the century. In 1906, Los Angeles High School reported six courses of study, three of which were occupationally oriented. The courses included the following classes: classical, Latin, mechanics, mining, civil engineering, and chemistry; architecture (mechanical drawing, mathematics through trigonometry, drafting); fine and applied arts. Also, in 1906 San Jose built a new high school patterned after the University. It was composed of five buildings two of which were identified as domestic science and manual arts buildings.

In 1910, Superintendent of Public Instruction, Edward Hyatt, noted a significant decrease in student enrollment between grades one and eight - 68,000 down to 27,000. He saw a solution to this problem-- vocational education. His remedy was *"the introduction of practical subjects and practical methods which will hold boys, particularly, in school until they have a fair education"* (Area VI County Office Assistant Superintendents Vocational Education Committee Working Papers). A privately endowed vocational school was established in San Francisco in 1912, the Lux School for Industrial Training exclusively for girls. It was intended for girls interested in occupations related to cooking, dressmaking, millinery, marketing, housekeeping, laundering, dyeing, home decorating, home nursing, and the planning and furnishing of homes.

State Leadership Established. In 1913, the State Board of Education appointed Dr. Edwin R. Snyder as Commissioner of Industrial and Vocational Education to identify vocational education that would serve as a significant and important component of California's public schools. In 1915 the Stockton school system opened a prevocational school for average boys in grades six through eight. Special attention was given to exploration of a variety of occupations. In the same year, a full-fledged vocational school supported with public funds was established in Oakland.

Federal Role Initiated. The major stimulus for vocational education occurred during and immediately following World War I when the need for skilled workers was fueled by the war effort. Vocational education was acknowledged as an indispensable part of the nation's capacity for a national defense. Following several years of debate on whether the federal government should have a role in the support of the public schools, Congress passed the Smith-Hughes Vocational Education Act on February 23, 1917. This Act set several precedents. First, it established a permanent appropriation for federal support of vocational education that has been augmented numerous times-the most recent being in 1998. Second, it opened the door for federal aid to other parts of public education.

The California Legislature moved quickly to accept the Smith Hughes Act. On March 31, 1917, and it then became state law. The consequences of this action were the shaping of vocational education as an integral component of California's public schools system. In 1917,

California's high schools enrolled approximately 125,000 students of which nearly 8,000, or 6 percent, were enrolled in vocational education. In contrast there were 1,675,393 students enrolled in high school in 2000. In 1999, when the most recent figures available, a total of 1,078,886 students were enrolled in secondary vocational education classes and 424,263 in vocational education adult classes in the K-12 system (California State Department of Education and Chancellor's office of the California Community Colleges, 2000). Although these vocational education enrollment figures appear significantly large, they do not represent an accurate count of individuals participating in vocational education. This will be discussed further in this review. Vocational education programs suffered during World War I1 as many vocational education teachers were involved in the war effort. Entire programs were shut down. However, following the war, vocational education was called upon to phase out the remnants of war training programs and establish retraining programs for thousands of veterans and men and women requiring new skills for peace time jobs.

The 1950's found public education concerned over the effectiveness of the high schools serving the diverse needs of all students. Approximately 20 percent of high school youth were prepared for higher education, 20 percent for employment and 60 percent were relatively under-served or ill-served. Vocational education undertook a self-evaluation while the rest of the educational community directed their efforts to infuse "relevance into all subject matter."

Forces of Change. Vocational education was the sole curricular area benefiting from federal aid to public education for 41 years of its establishment. Funding provided to the state was primarily for capacity building. This included support for state leadership, program development, and teacher training. Stimulated by the launching of Sputnik I, passage of the National Defense Education Act in 1958 marked a significant change in federal support for education. It had been long held that federal aid would result in federal domination which would interfere with the constitutional provisions of education in the states. Almost overnight, vocational education became a minority within the arena of federally sponsored programs. The urgency of national interests set aside concerns about federal aid for education. Immediately, states, including California, launched efforts to extend and improve (1) public school curricula in science, modem foreign languages, and mathematics, and (2) supportive counseling and guidance services.

In the 1960's a large infusion of federal aid for various aspects of education at the K-12 and the university level was initiated A large portion of these funds were directed to stimulate innovation and change with a significant portion going to ensure access and success to underserved and under-represented or special needs students. Vocational education was not exempt from the new thrust in federal support. The emphasis changed from supporting the infrastructures-capacity building (equipment, staff support, construction, etc.) to providing access and support to special populations, i.e., the disadvantaged, handicapped, and out of school youth. Vocational education's role was no longer defined as simply preparing students for employment; it took on a social responsibility to provide equal access to those students who may have been previously excluded from vocational education.

In 1961, the federal government attempted to do something about the problems of unemployment with the passage of the Manpower Development and Training Act, MDTA. The act was jointly managed by the State Employment Agency and the State Department of Education. MDTA ran its course for 12 years and claimed an 80 percent employment record after completion of the training of its clients. This was the first of several federal acts to address the problems of unemployment.

The Vocational Education Act of 1963 stimulated the growth of vocational education. It also brought new responsibilities as noted above. Federal support increased dramatically, and by 1975 state funding had increase from approximately $3 million to $44 million.

Legislative Impact: During the ten-year span of 1960-1970 the California Legislature was very active in vocational education legislative policy. A special vocational education subcommittee was established and hearings held in the Assembly. The advocacy of vocational education was not uncommon as evidenced on the platforms of several legislators seeking reelection. The result of this interest was a series of statues designed to remove existing barriers inhibiting vocational education. This included a statutory provision supporting vocational education as a "primary purpose" of California's public school system. So there would be no doubt, the Legislature added to the required courses of study for the secondary schools the area of:

> *"applied arts," including instruction in the areas of home economics, industrial arts, business education, or agriculture, for general education or prevocational education or occupational training."* (Little, 1970)

In 1963, the Legislature enacted a law entitled County Vocational High Schools. The law was summarily rejected by the educational community. The existence of such institutions dated back to the 1920's and were ultimately phased out in the 1950's. The public schools elected to retain an existing policy adopted by the State Board of Education, endorsed by the Department of Education and accepted by the California Legislature. That policy stated:

> *"that any organizational structure that provided for the physical segregation of public school students into specialized schools on the basis of sex, economic status, national origin, race, or career objectives was not in harmony with best interest of the state's youth, economy or society.* "(Little, 1970)

The County Vocational High School statute was amended in 1966, 1968, and again in 1969. The modification allowed county superintendents and school districts to establish Regional Occupational Centers and Programs (ROCPs) to serve both youth and adults. By 1970, 24 ROCPs were operational.

During the 1960's, giant strides were made to provide direction for work experience education programs which were developed during the 1950's. California was one of the first states to recognize the value of this experimental program to meeting the career and vocational needs of students. At the direction of the Legislature, the State Board adopted regulations to govern this program to assure safeguards for students so that child labor laws meshed with the educational purposes of work experience education.

In 1967, the Legislature removed a long-existing restraint on state aid for vocational enrollments. State aid to secondary school districts had been given to the schools determined by average daily attendance (a.d.a.), which was based on a minimum school day of four hours. The consequence of this formula was that by the time students enrolled in their basic required courses, the four hours were accounted for. Thus, vocational education was completely a district cost. The a.d.a. formula was changed allowing districts to receive augmented a.d.a. support for vocational programs. In 1967, the community colleges were separated from the jurisdiction of the State Board of education resulting in a variety of issues. These issues included governance, coordination, delineation of function, financial support and delivery of vocational education to youth and adults under the State Plan for Vocational Education and state statutes. Under federal and state law, the State Board of Education is designated as the sole state agency responsible for the receipt and expenditure of federal funds. In addition, state law allows the K-12 adult schools, ROCPs, and the community colleges to serve adults. In addition, there are approximately 2,000 private postsecondary institutions providing vocational training to adults. This raised a very big issue in the Legislature. They were concerned about unnecessary duplication and delineating program responsibilities for serving adult students. This issue has yet to be fully resolved.

Comprehensive Study: In the spring of 1967, a $400,000 contract was awarded by the State Board of Education to Arthur D. Little, Incorporated, to conduct a comprehensive study of vocational education in California. The charge given by the Board was to give them "a visionary goal for the future." At the same time they were asked for a response to these questions:

- Why are we importing European toolmakers when men in our cities are unemployed?
- How do we know we are training people for the right jobs?
- Should there be vocational education in the high school?
- What special efforts are being made to educate persons from poverty areas, persons from minority groups and others who have special needs in education for meaningful work?

The two-year study was bold and all encompassing. Its vision was far reaching, calling for major reforms throughout education to support the vocational training needs of students. The report was summarily rejected by state vocational leaders. They noted implementation of the recommendations would require such extensive modifications of public education that they were impractical to implement. The report offered a framework for organizing "education" in a way that cut boldly across constraints and made recommendations for improving program elements such as guidance, community involvement, teacher training, a management information system, area planning, and the organization of education. There were some similarities in the report recommendations to recent changes in federal policy and current state educational reform efforts. Several of the Report's recommendations were initiated in statute by the Legislature. These will be discussed in further detail.

Citizen Advisory Councils

Passage of the Vocational Education Act of 1968 created a National Advisory Council on Vocational Education and state councils in the respective states. The Act augmented the Smith Hughes Act and went into effect July 1, 1969. However, the California Advisory Council on Vocational Education and Technical Training, CACVE, was activated months before the Act became law and enabling state statutes were approved by the Legislature and Governor. The sole purpose of CACVE was to provide citizen oversight on the use and effectiveness of the state program of vocational education. The national council served in a similar capacity to provide oversight and direction at the national level.

Area Planning

In 1969, an area planning approach, as advocated in the Arthur D. Little Report, was initiated by the Legislature to develop a State Master Plan for Vocational Education. The State was divided into 15 "vocational areas" whose boundaries were "along geographic labor market lines," or Standard Metropolitan Statistical Areas, SMSAs, which were being used by the Employment Department for reporting labor market needs information. The intent of this legislation, in addition to helping develop a state master plan, was to identify (1) program duplication across educational levels, including private schools, and (2) needs for vocational education that were going unfilled. Twelve planning areas were established and five were selected to pilot the process. Each was managed by a 21 member committee cross section of education, business, and community representatives. Funding for this effort came from federal vocational education funds. The expectation was that with all of the schools (high schools, community colleges, four-year colleges, regional occupational centers and programs, county schools, adult schools, and private schools) working together on area planning, duplication would be eliminated, gaps in training needs would be filled, and greater efficiency and economy would result. The effort fell far short of expectations due to (1) the committees were powerless with no jurisdictional authority, and (2) virtually no attention or support was given to them by the state's vocational education leadership.

State Funding for Vocational Education Eliminated. Augmented finding for the administration of vocational education had been provided in the Annual State Budget for many years. In 1969, the Legislature removed $800,000 from the State Budget earmarked for the administration of vocational education. Vocational education was not unique. Other state educational programs receiving federal funds were also stripped of state funding. Efforts to restore state matching funds for vocational education were unsuccessful. In 1973, CACVE noted this in their Fourth Annual Report that all but a few positions in the Department of Education were supported by federal funds. CACVE questioned "to whom *is the State's educational leadership accountable to-the federal government or the people of California*"(California Advisory Council on Vocational Education, 1973). It recommended $800,000 be added to the Department's budget for the administration of vocational education and that the amount be increased yearly until state revenues totally supported vocational education. No action was taken on CACVE's recommendations. Thus, federal funds continued to be the sole source of funding for several years to come.

State Policy Enacted. The mission and direction of vocational education took on a variety of challenges in the early 1970s. These were initiated by changes in federal policy, a major increase in federal funding, and statutory direction adopted by the California Legislature.

The most significant state statute was enacted in 1974. It added to the Education Code Section 7504 (amended, now Section 51004):

> The Legislature hereby recognizes that it is the policy of the people of California to provide an educational opportunity to every individual to the end that every student leaving school should be prepared to enter the world of work; that every student who graduates from any state-supported institution should have sufficient marketable Skills for legitimate remunerative employment; and that every qualified and eligible adult citizen should be afforded an educational opportunity to become suitably employed in some remunerative field of employment.

Although it did not mention or make any specific reference to vocational education or specific level of public education, it implied that state funded programs should strive to achieve this policy enacted by the Legislature. In and of its self, it was a landmark declaration. At the time of its adoption, it was unique in the nation.

In December, 1974 CACVE advised the State Board of Education on what needed to be done to implement this policy. They recommended the following amendments to Section 7504 that were needed to fully integrate vocational education in the public schools:

> By the completion of elementary school (kindergarten through grade six), students, in addition to having mastered basic educational and communication skills, should understand the concepts of careers, appreciate the value of productivity and roles of the employee and employer, and be familiar with a wide variety of occupations.

By the completion of junior high school (grades seven through nine), students should be familiar with the broad cluster and families of occupations, be aware of the prerequisites for employment in the various kinds an fields of work, and understand the ways of changing and/or progressing from one occupational level to another.

Also, they should develop an awareness of their own abilities, interests, and aptitudes in relation to various career options and opportunities

Before leaving high school (grades ten through twelve) students should be able to assess their own potential and participate in making informed decisions regarding their immediate educational and occupational goals. Their options should include access to occupational programs which prepare them for immediate employment upon graduation, for continued occupational education at the postsecondary level, or for exit to the labor market prior to graduation. Throughout the adult years, individuals should be able to plan and select from continuously accessible preparatory programs which provide education and training for employment and/or advancement in a job of their choosing.

No effort was undertaken by vocational education or the State Board of Education to act on CACVE's recommendations and capitalize on this powerful policy adopted by the Legislature. Implementing federal policy with its ever changing program requirements, coupled with increased fiscal resources remained the primary focus of vocational education.

Career Education

In 1971, the U.S. Commissioner of Education, Sidney P. Marland raised the question, *"For what are we educating our youth?"* He stated that it was his belief that education must be "useful" and that education should be "career-oriented." His idea was to enrich schooling by inking career concepts and the real world of work applications across the entire curriculum at all levels, K-12. Not only was a student to learn math, English, and science, but they would also know how and what they learned applied to everyday work and living. Students would explore careers, determine how and make career decisions, and initiate career paths to a career and an occupation.

Vocational education was only a single component of Career Education. Uniquely, vocational education served as resource to other curricular area to assist them in modifying their curriculum. To the detriment of vocational education, federal funding for Career Education was provided from Vocational Education Act finds. This brought some discomfort to vocational education's leadership. However, it also brought discomfort to other curricular areas which would have to make major reforms by infusing vocational education strands across all subjects, K- 12. AB 1331 and AB 1486 were enacted by the Legislature in 1969. The intent was to conduct a large scale comprehensive program of individualized instruction based on performance criteria that would integrate vocational education into the academic curriculum and provide students with information pertaining to careers, career options, and educational alternatives. The legislation contained the following requirements:

- To extend the use of individualized instruction on a large scale.
- To organize immediately a comprehensive program of individualized instruction based on performance criteria in a major urban school district.
- To address the range of socioeconomic educational problems of urban school districts
- To convert the K-12 curriculum to individualized instruction, and to articulate with the community colleges.
- To filly integrate vocational education with the regular curriculum in order to acquaint students with career alternatives and to enable them to acquire a combination of vocational and academic subjects.
- To accelerate large scale conversion of other schools in the state to programs of individualized instruction and integrated vocational education.
- To design and test criteria and tools for measuring educational performance.
- To evaluate: (1) the effectiveness of individualized instruction and (2) the problems of conversion.
- To provide precise information on the fiscal requirements for converting schools to programs of individualized instruction.

AB 1331 and AB 1486 provided for the use of Elementary and Secondary Education Act, ESEA, and Vocational Education Act funds to implement the requirements in the statutes. A question arose as to the authority of the Superintendent of Public Instruction to direct ESEA and VEA unit leaders in the California Department of Education (CDE) to apply, in some part, federal funds towards this effort without apparent regard to federal guidelines and/or state plans which dictate the use of these funds. The fiscal question halted the implementation of AB 1331 and AB 1486.

In September 1971 the CDE established a Task Force to develop and implement the career education concept in California by redirecting vocational education staff positions to provide leadership. Eight Career Education sites were funded from a $1.4 million vocational education grant provided by the U.S. Secretary of Education. Two other sites were funded for three years utilizing $1.2 million in federal vocational education funds allocated to California. Although the Task Force was not established in response to AB 1331 and AB 1486, the elements of the two bills were incorporated into their efforts. Considerable progress and success was achieved in California to develop the concepts of Career Education across grade levels and subject matter, but the reform effort fell short of its expectations as soon as federal funds were withdrawn.

Manpower Information System

The success of vocational education is measured on how well it prepares and assists individuals in finding employment. Reporting of this information is required in federal law in the form of student follow up. Vocational education is also measured on how well it supplies qualified program graduates to fill the current job demands of the state. Part of the equation for a Manpower Information System requires forecasting job needs to ensure vocational education is meeting current needs. In the late sixties, at least three research efforts were undertaking by vocational education to develop a Manpower Information System to project employment needs to serve as a basis for curriculum development and/or modification, and to assist in the guidance process.

In 1974, the Legislature directed the Superintendent of Public Instruction, Chancellor of the Community Colleges, and Director of Employment to develop a system to be housed in the CDE. However, since the Employment Department had a mandate to provide employment projections, they took on the primary responsibility to coordinate with the state educational agencies for its development. A Task Force was formed consisting of all agencies involved in vocational education and job training. It was chaired by Benjamin Hargrave from the Employment Department. The Task Force reviewed a number of research efforts to model projecting job needs. Three of these were funded by the CDE. All models were rejected and the system utilized by the Employment Department to project job needs was adopted. Ultimately, it would be utilized in the development of the State Occupational Information System which will be discussed in further detail in this review. The rationale for this decision was the Employment Service was mandated by law to make job projections. Therefore, there was no need for duplication of effort.

Summary

Vocational education through three quarters of the 20th century had a rich history and made a valuable contribution to economic well-being of California; from its beginnings in the early 1900s vocational education was considered an important and integral part of the public school program. Efforts to house vocational education in separate high schools did not persist nor were they successful. The educational community believed it was in the best interest of students to acquire their basic academic and vocational skills in the same institution. The introduction of vocational education into the public schools was essentially the first educational reform undertaken in California. It has been well documented that the introduction of vocational education to the school curriculum was influenced by practical needs Vocational education did not originate, nor persist by chance or accident. It began and progressed because of choice, not chance. Vocational education was established in the public schools because of economic and social necessity, and its existence depends on how well it can adapt and address these needs.

Primarily driven by federal policy, state level leadership and substantial state legislative policy support, vocational education flourished over the better part of the 20th century. However, it was the subject of continuous scrutiny and assessment. Although vocational education was given several opportunities to make major reforms, and take advantage of strong legislative support, it elected to stay the course. It was driven by increasing numbers of students in need of occupational skills, and the underpinning of a long history of federal policy direction and financial support. Its leadership did not have a clear vision of its own on what was best for vocational education in California. They elected to operate exclusively on federal law and funding. At times, this was not always easy and proved to be detrimental in the long run as will be shown further in this review.

The remaining sections of this history will overview how vocation education fared during the final quarter of the 20th century. It will show how vocational education had to (1) adapt programs to serve an expanding and diverse student population in need of skills to become gainfully employed, (2) adjust to changing state and federal vocational education and job training policies, (3) respond to changes in state fiscal and educational policy to achieve educational reforms, (4) respond to growing discontent among its constituency and the Legislature, and (5) attempt to redefine its role in meeting state and national goals for education. The review will also focus on what was accomplished along with some shortcomings and missed opportunities.

O'Lawrence, H. (2013)
The Historical Critique of Career and Technical Education in California from 1900 – 2000 and the
Status of California Community Colleges in the 21ˢᵗ Century
Santa Rosa, California: Informing Science Institute

Chapter Two

Recent Times:
The Volatile Years 1975-2000

Reform of Intermediate and Secondary Schools- The RISE Report

The final quarter of the 20th century finds vocational education facing many more challenges and scrutiny. Unhappy and unwilling to implement the recommendations contained in the Arthur D. Little Report, a $250,000 CDE study was initiated using vocational education funds in July 1974. It was completed by the middle of 1975. A broadly represented 37 member Commission was appointed by the Superintendent of Public Instruction, Dr. Wilson Riles, with the charge to *"draw a framework for overhauling education in California's 1.600 intermediate and secondary schools"*. The Commission was chaired by Leland B. Newcomer, President of Laverne College. The Superintendent asked the Commission to:

- Envision an educational system that could respond continually to changing needs in the next century;
- Identify the skills and competencies individuals will need to survive and function effectively in the next 25 years;
- Chart ways to make schools more effective, more enjoyable, and more conducive to a continual interest in learning;
- Identify the goals California's schools should be meeting now and through the year 2000;
- Recommend immediate and long-range changes to bring about the desired results.

The Commission sought the views of scores of individuals and organizations within education and outside the schools. The public was invited to speak at 21 public forums where it heard from a total of 315 speakers, representing either themselves or organizations. They presented oral and written testimony. In addition, the Commission reviewed research and previous reform studies, and they heard from nationally recognized authorities at their monthly meetings.

During its deliberations, the Commission recognized the diversity of student needs within California's schools. They set-out to build an educational framework for educational change that would serve all students much as did the Arthur Little study. The Commission developed a philosophy of what they felt were characteristics of an educated person. They were spelled-out in the form of ten characteristics much like the "ten cardinal principles" found in educational pedagogy. First, they said, the educated person should have a thirst for knowledge. This will motivate them to continue learning throughout their lifetime. Second, an educated person should have the skills to find work and succeed in it. Other principles dealt with self-esteem, valuing the environment, valuing all people equally, understanding the democratic process, being able to read, write, speak, and compute, understanding the economic system, having a basic understanding of human biology, and being sensitive and appreciative of the arts, literature, etc.

The Commission's recommendations primarily focused on the student, the learning environment, teachers, the instructional process, resource allocation, and the promotion of education. The recommendations were somewhat global focusing on educational goals or expectations. Among the numerous recommendations offered by the Commission, the following were pertinent to vocational education:

- Learners should be able to gain skills and knowledge in a variety of locations-both on and off the traditional school site.
- Learners should be offered increased opportunities to gain firsthand learning experiences by means of study, observation, service, participation, and work in the school and community.
- Learners should have extensive and continuing opportunities for career awareness, exploration, and preparation.
- Instructional programs should aid each learner in developing self-awareness and self- direction while expanding one's awareness of occupations, clusters or related occupations, and the changing employment market.
- Instructional programs should continually emphasize career planning and opportunities in relation to subject matter. Actual work situations and resource personnel from the com-

munity should be used to aid the learner in developing career objectives and alternatives.

- Each learner should be assisted in formulating appropriate attitudes about the personal and social significance of one's own work and the world of work.

- In familiarizing the learner with the world of work, the instructional program should provide the learner with an understanding of the economic, social, and political roles of trade unions, professional associations, corporations, other business and professional enterprises, government agencies, and consumers of goods and services.

- Each learner should have an opportunity to gain an entry-level, marketable job skill prior to leaving school.

- Instructional programs should acquaint each learner with the importance of continuing education as a means to satisfy the ever-changing requisites for stability and advancement in employment careens.

- Each learner should gain the knowledge, experience, and skills necessary to begin implementing career objectives and to become acquainted with various routes for career advancement.

- Learners should become familiar with successful techniques for seeking and obtaining employment.

- School systems, through cooperation with appropriate local and state agencies and organizations, should assist in the placement of learners who desire employment while they are enrolled or after they have graduated.

The vocational education community was generally comfortable with the RISE Report and its recommendations; the reforms cut across the entire curriculum and would have evolved over time. Looking for a quick fix, vocational education's leadership could not envision how the broad set of recommendations would benefit the subject matter orientation of vocational education. However, upon taking a closer look at the recommendations one could see that they were consistent with the existing mission and objectives of vocational education. The goals represented an ideal which vocational education was trying to achieve. Unfortunately, there was no model program or school district functioning with all of the components in place.

Vocational education's leadership exerted no organized statewide effort to support implementation of the recommendations. In the end, the RISE Report had even less impact on the direction of vocational education than did the Arthur D. Little Report. Essentially, none of the RISE Report recommendations were implemented. Thus, another opportunity to capitalize on an important, far reaching and supportive report was simply filed away.

It is not certain what Dr. Riles intended to do with the RISE recommendations, if anything. Dr. Riles was already heavily involved at the time advancing his own initiatives in Early Childhood Education. Following submission of the Report, Dr. Riles did announce the creation of a special task force to develop a strategy and necessary guidelines to implement the Commission's recommendations. However, nothing came of their efforts.

Program Enrollment Surge

With the passage of the 1963 and 1968 Vocational Education Acts enrollments grew rapidly. There appeared to be a direct correlation between increased funding and growth. Enrollments, for example, were reported to have doubled from approximately 500,000 in 1963 to 1,000,000 students in 1968. By 1975 enrollments reportedly had risen to approximately 1.7 million, of which approximately 1 million were enrolled in the K-12 system.

Enrollments continued to grow which became a major problem for vocational education.

The reporting of vocational education enrollment figures deserves a brief explanation. One of the federal requirements is to annually report enrollment figures to the U.S. Department of Education. For many years the state reported its figures by combining K- 12 and community college figures even after the community colleges separated from the jurisdiction of the State Board of Education in 1967. Further, the figures were not accurate for several reasons which even exist today.

Enrollment figures are based on school district reports submitted annually to state vocational education personnel in the CDE. Many of these reports were often late, sometimes as much as two years. So, as vocational education enrollment reports were submitted to the state the totals were adjusted. Thus, it was possible to find as many as three different figures for the same year in different CDE documents. Further, there was and continues to be a problem with duplicate counts. Students who are enrolled in more than one vocational education course are counted more than one time. In the 1960s, it was common practice, and in some cases required under the State Plan, to offer vocational education classes in two-hour blocks of time. This was a factor during this time period of rapid growth. Also, students had more freedom to select course offerings as electives. Some chose a vocational education route through high school rather than the college preparatory route. All of these contributed to the large enrollment growth and inflated figures.

Finally, it is impossible to accurately reconstruct the enrollment counts for this period of time because all of the records maintained by the CDE have been destroyed, and all the U.S. Department of Education's records prior to 1981 have been destroyed. The only figures, as accurate as they are, are found in Wesley P. Smith's *History of Vocational Education in California 1900-1975* written in 1979, and in CACVE Annual Reports. According to Smith, there was an increase of 600,000 students in vocational education between 1970 and1 975--from 1,134,357 to 1,761,424 students. These figures are shown in Table 1.

Table 1.
Enrollment in Vocational Education Programs in California
1970-71 through 1974-75

Year	Total Enrollment in the State
1970-71	1,134,457
1971-72	1,130,337
1972-73	1,289,458
1973-74	1,426,073
1974-75	1,761,42,

Smith reported that in 1970 roughly 40 percent of the 1,134,357 students, or 425,294 of them were enrolled in K-12 programs. He did not indicate what percentage were secondary students. Adult enrollments figures were not broken down by secondary and community college enrollment by Smith.

Table 2.
California Student Enrollments in Vocational Education
1968-78

Year	Secondary	Community College	Adult	Total
1968-69	347,411	303,605	290,873	941,889
1969-70	408,325	305,046	194,649	908,010
1970-71	533,912	338,564	325,555	1,198,031
1971-72	592,616	329,641	311,663	1,233,920
1972-73	587,615	329,641	311,663	1,233,920
1973-74*	643,566	533,191	463,771	1,640,528
1977-78**	679,227	589,678	486,960	1,755,865

*estimated enrollment
**projected enrollment

Source: California State Department of Education, Vocational Education Support Unit

Table 2 is taken from CACVE's Fourth Annual Report for fiscal year 1972-73 which was prepared from enrollment data supplied by the CDE in 1973. It illustrates that estimates could be off as much as 100,000 or more from year-to-year without considering inflated numbers due to counting some students more than once. To make things even worse each year, without any enrollment figures yet in hand, the CDE would project enrollment figures two year hence as shown below for fiscal year 1977-78.

Beginning in 1980, enrollment figures for vocational education were collected by the California Basic Educational Data System, CBEDS, maintained by the CDE. The enrollment numbers reported by CDE represent a "snap shot" of school enrollment in various classes on a particular day in the school year. A tally of class enrollments in every classroom in the state is taken and electronically reported, using a course coding system, to the CDE. Basically, it is a one-day census of student enrollment. These figures are used to report annual enrollments in vocational education. No adjustments are made for students attending more than one class in vocational education. Thus, annual enrollment figures reported by vocational education are somewhat inflated.

The 1988-89 Annual Performance Report indicates that there were 1,495,258 students enrolled in vocational education. Of these, the enrollment data indicated 937,007 were enrolled in high school vocational classes, and 368,490 in the ROCPs. In contrast, virtually every table analyzing enrollment data in the Report was showing where the numbers came from, in some cases multiple sources including CBEDS and various vocational education reports.

Accuracy did not improve over the next decade. The 1998-99 California Annual Performance Report for Vocational Education indicates there were 1,503,149 students enrolled in K- 12 vocational education programs in 1998-99. Of this count, 832,686 were secondary students and 246,200 were ROPC secondary students. This adds-up to 1,078,886 secondary students enrolled in vocational education. CBEDS data reports there were 1,659,030 high school students enrolled in 1998-99. Doing the math, it appears that 65 percent of all high school students were enrolled in vocational education that school year which is not true. It is something less, but there is no way to determine the exact number until some other reporting system is developed.

Five-Percent Budget Cap

The more serious enrollment problems occurred in the Legislature as the result of increased a.d.a. reporting by districts. Program growth did result in more state financial support for vocational education programs because the four hour limitation on generating a.d.a. had been removed by the Legislature in 1967. School districts were utilizing every possible means to generate an a.d.a. Some marginal practices were employed. There were questions in the Legislature about the legitimacy of some of the a.d.a. figures reported by districts, particularly some secondary adult schools and community colleges. In 1976, to curb growth and resolve the problem, the Legislature placed a five percent cap, a state funding limitation, on all adult and vocational education programs and services. This action did have a significant impact on vocational education programs offered in secondary, ROCP and secondary adult education programs.

In April of 1976, the CACVE conducted a sampling of 360 school districts and 69 ROCPs to ascertain the impact of the five percent cap on state finding. CACVE found that virtually half of the districts and two-thirds of the ROCPs had to reduce their vocational education programs and services. The most interesting and important finding was that approximately one-third to one-half of those districts responding to CACVE's survey that reported "no reductions occurred" qualified their response noting that:

> *"Although there was no reduction this year, there would be next year, and the "cap" had limited growth of this year's new programs. Further, as many as 80 percent anticipated the need to reduce vocational education programs or services next year."*

This was just one of several decisions by the Legislature that would have a negative impact on the future growth and role of vocational education in the K-12 system.

Commission on Vocational Education

The ink was hardly dry on the RISE Report when Dr. Riles appointed a 32 member Commission of Vocational Education in April 1978. The charge given to the Commission by Dr. Riles was to *"advise him on what vocational education services should be provided for the students within his responsibility."* Approximately $250,000 of vocational education funds was directed by Sam Barrett, State Director of Vocational Education, to support the work of the Commission. The objective of the Commission was to make recommendations defining the major components of vocational education in grades K-12. To accomplish this charge, the Commission was asked to consider a wide spectrum of quality, scope, and content questions regarding vocational education. The issues which were to be addressed included:

1. The vocational and career needs of students

2. The needs of industry, labor, and society

3. The capacity of the educational system to respond to the needs of industry, labor and society

4. Strategies and resources, both fiscal and human, needed to support quality vocational education programs at the local level

The Commission deliberated for ten months and issued its report on February 28, 1979, *"A Unified Approach to Occupational Education."* The Commission collected input from 907 persons in 50 public input sessions throughout the state. The Commission also held six hearings to get reaction to its draft report. Just as the same with previous reform studies, vocational education was not the exclusive topic of the report. The Commission determined that it had to address the whole of education to ensure its recommendations would meet the goal of quality vocational education for all students. The Report contained 122 rec-ommendations which were very specific and on task as what had to be done and by whom. No one was excluded, even the Legislature. The basic assumption of the Report was:

> *"that every person in California should be prepared for quality of life and work, and such preparation can best be achieved through a system of education that is unified at all levels, elementary through higher educa-tion. "*

It defined a unified system as one that develops basic skills, interper-sonal relationships, occupational skills, and citizen responsibilities leading to quality life and work through various components, one of which is occupational education. The Report further stated that:

> *"Although the major responsibility of the occupational education is work preparation, all other components, at all level, share in that respon-sibility. Conversely, occupational education must include the vital basic, interpersonal, and citizenship skills that are primarily the responsibility of the other components. Since vocational education specific responsibility is work preparation, a more descriptive term for this component is occu-pational education. "*

Even though the changing of the name to occupational education may seem insignificant, vocational education had long recognized that it had an image problem: sewing, cooking, and shop-the programs gen-erally found in the back of the school. The image grew out of a long history and assumption that vocational education was the place to serve those students "who were not going on to college." It was an elitist point of view imposed on vocational education by fellow educa-tors. It was not a valid assumption. The Commission felt it could ad-dress the image problem in this manner. There was no organized ef-fort to make a name change as recommended by the Commission at the K-12 system. (In 2000, all references to vocational education were changed to *"career technical education"* in state statutes. The bill, AB2907 (Mazzoni) was sponsored by the CDE.)

The Commission very carefully outlined what would comprise a uni-fied educational system. Several significant features included:

- Defining roles and responsibilities for each level and compo-nent
- Sharing information, curriculum ideas and criteria for student outcomes among all entities and individuals at all levels

- Establishing program standards at each level of instruction with achievement met by meeting performance competencies
- Standards adopted by the Legislature
- Awarding credit for skills learned inside and outside of the system
- Providing a new form of high school transcript and report card to certify a student has achieved competency
- Using clearly outlined assessment procedures

The Commission specified the establishment of a planning process which included a State Plan. The Plan would contain the objectives to be addressed by the Unified Educational System. Each school district would be required to prepare a plan that specified the outcomes expected from the educational activities within the district. Finally, each school site would have a plan on how it would conduct the best educational program for each student.

None of the Commission's recommendations were implemented by Dr. Riles. This further alienated the vocational education community towards the management of the CDE and contributed to less favorable support for vocational education in the Legislature. There are other factors which contributed and they will be discussed further in this review.

The Arthur D. Little Report, the RISE Report and Commission on Vocational Education's Report, had similar themes. It was that preparation for an occupation could only be achieved through the integration of vocational education into the entire educational process. Vocational education could no longer remain an island, separate but within the public schools system, and changes needed to be made to restructure all education to fully integrate vocational education into the curriculum. Preparation for work and a career is a shared responsibility across all curricular areas and subject matter. Similar themes are occurring in present day reforms efforts, but from a slightly different perspective which will be discussed in further detail.

Proposition 13 Impact

On June 6, 1978, voters in the State of California approved Proposition 13, which is known as the Jarvis-Gann Initiative. The main provision of this measure limited taxes on all property to one percent of the property's full market value, and "rolled back" assessed values of real property to 1975-76 levels.

According to a May, 1978, report by the Office of the Legislative Analyst, the passage of Proposition 13 was expected to have a significant fiscal impact on local school districts. Property tax revenues were projected to represent over half of 1978-79 school district income (53.5%). However, under Jarvis-Gann, funds available to school districts would decrease by 29.8% to the K-12 system. This projection was based on the assumption that property taxes were prorated in direct proportion to the previous year's taxes and no alternative revenue sources would be developed.

Late in June of 1978, a conference committee of the Legislature decided that 1978-79 property tax revenues would in fact be allocated in the same proportions as 1977-78 revenues. Approximately $2.27 billion was allocated from the state surplus and granted to school districts. The net result for the K-12 system was an average loss of ten percent with no district loosing more than 15 percent or less than 9 percent.

CACVE conducted a study of the impact of Proposition 13 on vocational education. The study was completed in March of 1979. The Council surveyed all school districts, adult schools, ROCPs, and community colleges. Approximately one-third responded to the survey. The study confirmed that budgets were decreased and enrollments were down in vocational education, with the greatest losses in the ROCPs and adult schools. About a fifth of the respondents reported they were anticipating returning or releasing their 1978-79 federal vocational education funds due to the unavailability of local matching finds. Further, at least 86% of those responding anticipated further cuts in 1979-80.

Overall, a quarter of the responding institutions reported that they had eliminated selected vocational education programs as a result of Proposition 13. Over half the K-12 districts, ROCPs and adult schools reported eliminating summer sessions. The elimination of total programs (as opposed to classes or sections within programs) was most frequently among ROCPs; over half did so. Respondents reported eliminating classes or sections as a result of Proposition 13 with considerable greater frequency than they eliminated programs. Across all levels, 42 percent of the responding institutions reported eliminating classes or sections. Secondary districts eliminated classes or sections less frequently (36 %), with adult programs and ROCPs falling in between 37% and 42% respectively.

In addition to cutting programs, districts cut support services such as counseling and career guidance services. Overall the respondents reported curtailing 279 and eliminating 34 special supportive programs or services, for a total of 313 programs cut back or eliminated. Of these 42% of these occurred at the secondary level.

There were also staffing changes resulting from Proposition 13. From the respondents, they reported a total of 284 personnel changes. The largest percentage of these was among instructional staff the least of which occurred at the secondary level. The second most frequent personnel change was the elimination of support staff, and, third, administrative staff. In addition, over two-thirds of the ROCPs reported they were dropping expansion plans, while only 29 percent of the secondary school districts did so.

The CACVE study did confirm that Proposition 13 did have a negative impact on vocational education. However, it was only the beginning of other negative forces that would take their toll on vocational education.

Change in Federal Policy

For nearly a half century, 46 years, federal policy and support for vocational education did not change dramatically. Some minor additions were made, but no substantive changes were made until 1963 when federal policy, which had been primarily directed to vocational education subject matter, state level leadership support, and teacher training, was changed. The emphasis changed to making vocational education programs more accessible to special populations – the handicapped and disadvantaged.

The Vocational Education Act of 1963 increased federal funding and for the first time had policy language which provided that funds could be used *to* serve *students who have academic, socioeconomic, or other handicaps that prevents them from achieving stability or advancement in employment.*

In 1968, the Act was amended and established the first special set-asides for programs and services to the disadvantaged and handicapped. Twenty-five percent of the finds in excess of fiscal year 1969 allocations to the state, but not less than 15 percent available to the state, were to be spent for the disadvantaged. Also, no less than 10 percent of the funds made available to the state were to be spent on the handicapped.

In 1976, the Act was amended again and funding increased as were the requirements spelled-out in law. Some of the significant additions were:

1. Each recipient of funds was required to establish a local advisory committee to advise them on labor market and program needs.

2. Each recipient was to coordinate with other providers including job training programs in the area.

3. No funds could be used to supplant state or local funds-the funds were to supplement existing resources.

4. The state had to continue allocating approximately the same proportion of finds at each level as it did the previous year.

5. At least 10 percent of all program funds were to be allocated to pay 50 percent of the cost of vocational education for the handicapped.

6. At least 20 percent of all program funds were to be allocated to pay 50 percent of the cost of vocational education for disadvantaged persons, for persons who have limited English-speaking ability, and for stipends based on proportion of limited-English speaking individuals to the total population age 15-24.

7. At least $50,000 had to be spent to administer statewide efforts to reduce sex stereotyping in vocational education.

8. Policies and support services developed to ensure equal access for women in nontraditional program, including day care.

9. Establishing programs and services for displaced homemakers.

10. Allowing private school students to participate in vocational education programs offered in the public schools.

11. Preparing a five-year plan as well as an annual program plan and accountability report.

12. Expending at least 20 percent of program improvement finds on vocational guidance and counseling.

13. Defining the role and responsibilities of consumer homemaking programs to better serve special needs population.

The issue of "maintenance of effort" and "supplementing versus supplanting" requires a brief explanation. First, federal law requires the state to expend an equal amount or greater each year for vocational education than it did the previous year. The philosophy is that federal funds are to act as stimulus to foster the growth of vocational education. This is what is meant by *"maintenance of effort."* Second, given the large increase in federal funding for vocational education, there was a tendency to replace local vocational education support with federal funds. This included teacher salaries. This practice is known as *"supplanting."*

The supplanting aspects of federal finding also served as a means for some districts to eliminate vocational programs that had been shifted to federal. When they were directed by the state to return to district support, it was easier for some to simply eliminate the program. Although no exact figures are available, this did happen to a number of vocational education offerings in local districts.

The Act was amended several times in the 1980s and 1990s. With each revision there were changes in policy accompanied with increases in funding. The most noticeable change was that vocational education and job training policy became increasingly interwoven. This will be illustrated in further detail in the review of several state initiatives undertaken in the 1990s. Greater emphasis was given to coordination and planning efforts to avoid duplication and maximize the use of federal and state resources. Also, vocational education policy moved further and further away from general program support to fostering educational reform and the integration of vocational and basic academic skills. In 1984, for example, the requirement for the Five Year State Plan was that an assessment was to be done of the quality of vocational education in terms of:

> *"the capacity of programs to facilitate entry into, and participation in, vocational education and to ease the school-to-work and secondary-to-postsecondary transition" "the capability of vocational education programs to meet the needs for general occupational skills and improvement of academic foundations in order to address the changing context of jobs."*

Other changes were support for counseling and guidance and the need for coordination and joint planning with other training providers. The 1984 Amendment more fully outlined the use of funds for "career" guidance and counseling. The emphasis was on student access and support rather than on process and vocational education subject matter as spelled out in the earlier Acts. Regarding coordination and joint planning, the State Plan had to:

> "*describe the methods proposed for joint planning and coordination of programs carried out under this Act with programs conducted under the Job Training Partnership Act, the Adult Education Act, title I of the Elementary and Secondary Education Act of 1965 as modified by chapter 1 of the Education Consolidation and Improvement Act, the Education of the Handicapped Act, and the Rehabilitation Act of 1973, and with apprentices hip training programs.*"

In addition to providing access to additional under-served target populations, the Act provided state assistance for vocational education support to Community-Based Organizations. Federal policy was being influenced by special interest groups attempting to make federal educational policy and funding serve their client base. It was the era of major social change, and vocational education was not exempt.

In 1990 even the Title of the Act gave a clue where federal policy was going, the "Carl D. Perkins Vocational and Applied Technology Act." The Act required the State to "develop and implement a statewide system of core standards and measures of performance for secondary and postsecondary education programs." These core standards were to address academic and vocational education competencies in the context of educational reform. The core measures will be discussed in detail in the review under "accountability."

The Carl D. Perkins Vocational and Technical Education Act of 1998 made some minor but significant changes. The first was the "sole state agency" requirement regarding the administration of federal funds in the state. It was changed to "eligible agency" which could possibly open up the issue of governance again. The issue of governance will be discussed in detail later in this review. Throughout the Act there are increased references to technology use in the classroom and distance learning. The lack of technologically and technically skilled workforce was a focal point of discussion in Congressional debate on the legislation. There were numerous references to coordination with job training programs. The Act allowed the state the option to submit a unified plan to enhance coordination between vocational education, job training, and adult education. Another change was funding for Tech Prep programs. These programs support work-base and work-site learning in conjunction with the private sector and uses of technology and distance learning.

The most important change is the flexibility it affords the state and local recipients. All categorical funding categories for special populations were eliminated but it placed accountability on the state to address the needs of these groups as well as the issues of gender equity. The State Gender Equity position was retained. However, increased accountability was the cornerstone of the Act which will be discussed further in this review.

Finally, it abolished the State Council on Vocational Education (CACVE) and its advisory role in providing citizen oversight in the planning, coordination, funding, and assessing the effectiveness of vocational education and job training efforts in the state that function under the State Plan for Vocational Education. However, the need for a State Council has not gone away and there are some indications it may resurface in the new millennium.

Serving Special Needs Populations

The Vocational Education Act of 1963 initiated a new era in vocational education. Not only did it provide increased funding, it also began national efforts to make vocational education more accessible to special populations, e.g., handicapped, disadvantaged, and limited English and non-English speaking students. Another target population was women which will be detailed in "gender equity" section of this review. Finally, one percent of the state's basic grant had to be allocated to programs that served the incarcerated in our state's penal system. This program is not discussed in this review.

Handicapped

In 1968, the Vocational Education Act provided the first set aside for the handicapped. This proviso in vocational education legislation came at time when there was a major national effort to provide protection, access, and programs/services to mainstream the disabled in the schools and society. At least 10 percent of the funds allocated to local school districts were to be used to provide:

> *"vocational education for handicapped persons who because of their handicapping condition cannot succeed in the regular vocational education program without special educational assistance or who require a modified vocational education program. "*

In 1976, the federal Act was modified requiring:

- The five-year and annual plans for vocational education to be consistent with the State Plan for Special Education under Section 61 3(a) of the Education for All Handicapped Children Act.

- Renovation and remodeling of facilities to comply with the Architectural Barriers Act of 1968 to make them physically accessible to the handicapped

- Handicapped students being able to participate, to the maximum degree possible, in all vocational education programs available to regular students or in the least restrictive environment.

- Ten percent be allocated to vocational education programs for the handicapped.

In 1977, CACVE prepared a comprehensive resource monograph on programs and support services available to serve the handicapped. It *was* titled *"Barriers* and *Bridges."* In addition to providing common definitions, describing barriers, and promising trends, it made specific recommendations to all levels of government and the community as to what needed to be done to assist the disabled to acquire skills and services in order to become self-sufficient.

During the development of the CACVE report, the Council enlisted the help of Assemblyman Frank Lanterman to call a meeting of all the state agencies involved in working with the disabled. This included several units within the CDE. The purpose of the meeting was twofold. First, it was to establish communication among and between agencies and units within agencies. It was interesting to note that communication between special education and vocational education in the CDE was lacking. Second, each of the agencies was involved in needs assessments and conducting a census of the people they should be serving. The Department of Rehabilitation Director, Ed Roberts, was in the process of conducting a special census with windfall money his agency had acquired. Mr. Lanterman and CACVE suggested that it would be in the best interest of all the agencies to combine their census efforts so they could coordinate serving individuals across the entire state program delivery system. For many of those attending the meeting, it was the first time the agency representatives had ever met. When the meeting ended, there was no consensus agreement, everyone went back to doing their thing at their respective agency and the Department of Rehabilitation did their own census survey.

The major rationale for preparing the handicapped for employment can be expressed in terms of an investment. For example, according to Sylvia Porter, a reporter for the Los Angles Herald Examiner:

> *"For every $1,000 our nation invests in rehabilitation of the disabled, our economy get back $9.000-an awesome 9 to 1 return, reflecting the taxes paid by that rehabilitated individual to the federal, state and local governments when he gets a job; the halt of social welfare payments when he is able to subsist without this aid; and the funds that flow with multiplying force from this worker as he spends his earned dollars."* (Porter, October 17, 1976)

In 1977-78, ten percent of the district basic grants and program improvement funds were allocated to school districts through a formula. Fifty percent was based on the number of economically disadvantaged enrolled in the district, which forced the majority of the handicapped finding to go to larger urban school districts. The minimum district grant was $100 per student. A substantial number of districts did not utilize the funds because they could not match their grant with state or local funds. Another problem encountered by districts was the requirement that the money could only be spent for those costs in excess of regular program costs. The issue of supplanting came into play. Federal policy became a barrier for years until 1987 when the Legislature put into statute Section 56456:

> *"It is the intent of the Legislature that districts, special education local plan area, and county offices may use any state or local special education funds for approved vocational programs, services, and activities to satisfy the excess cost matching requirements for receipt of federal vocational education fund& for individuals with exceptional needs. "*

Available program enrollment figures for 1978-80 did show an increase in handicapped students being served by vocational education, 14,877, up some12.9 percent. Unfortunately, no documentation with accurate enrollment or outcome data is available from state sources to give a true picture of what occurred in the 1980s in terms of (1) the percentage of handicapped served versus the number that were eligible to participate, and (2) how well they succeeded upon program completion. The 1991-1994 State Plan indicated that approximately 31,700 handicapped students were being served in the K-12 system.

No major changes took place in the 1984 Act, but in 1990 the set aside for handicapped was eliminated. Millions of federal vocational education funds were expended over the years to provide technical assistance to districts to better assess, counsel and serve the handicapped;

develop resource materials and curriculum; adapt programs to provide access; utilize technology and adaptive devices; provide facilitators and instructional support staff; in-service teachers, administrators and counselors; and develop transition programs for the handicapped. However, it is difficult to assess how effective the educational system through the efforts of regular vocational education improved the ability of the handicapped to succeed and sustain themselves in the workforce once they left the confines of the public schools. There is one program that did achieve success and based on results was written into state law. That program was "Project Workability" or, as it is now called, WorkAbility.

Project Workability was the creation of Gail Zittel, a Consultant in the CDE working in Special Education. Although Workability began with special education funding in 1982, the program was transferred to vocational education the following year since the CDE then believed that having federal funding from two programs for special education students would encourage local support for the program. Workability was a program to change the attitudes of the public about the employability of special or "disabled" students.

The program was based upon the consolidation of all funding sources to one end – to find employment for this population in any way unique to the community and the student's needs. The Department of Rehabilitation and Employment Development Department joined to support the program by signing an interagency agreement, and the program began by first designing an evaluation tool to see if it worked. Twenty-six districts, county offices, and ROCPs began the task of designing assessment tools, training students, locating curriculum, encouraging the inclusion of special education students in vocational and work experience programs, and then placing them in real work situations, not in a sheltered workshop environment. Private sector placement employment, both paid and unpaid, was offered to the thousands of students who might have never experienced real opportunities to sample something other than classroom training.

The project worked so well that in 1985, the Legislature provided over $1 million in state dollars to expand the program to new sites, and, with federal finds, the program grew. The Legislature passed legislation in 1987-88 making Workability I an official transition program for the handicapped. Soon Workability II and III began in adult and post-secondary programs, and federal Rehabilitation Act finding was added to its support.

The key to the success of the program was mainly due to the rigorous collection of data on work found for students and savings of Social Security income and other welfare related support for students who had left high school. The return to the state investment was apparent to employers who found reliable workers with low turnover rates and satisfied customers. Many private employers have joined in the program as sponsors over the years of its operation.

In 2000, there were approximately 50,000 students served out of 165,000 students eligible for the program. The employment success of students is well documented. In 1995, follow-up data showed that 68.2 percent of the students were still working two years after completing the program. Annually over 10,000 employers have found Workability students well-prepared for entry-level employment, reliable employees, and assets to business. Workability has received national and state recognition for its success in matching young adults with disabilities to employers.

Although the set aside for the handicapped was eliminated in 1990, the state is still accountable to ensure that this population is being served by vocational education. A system of core measures and standards were developed in 1992 by the CDE which were to be used to assess educational outcomes for all students. Other program criteria for programs and services to special populations were defined in the 1994-1996 State Plan.

Not much difference can be found in the core measures developed for non-handicapped students – they fall into the same general areas of program completion, high school graduation, placement, etc. However, they are couched in terms used for measuring the performance of handicapped students.

With the elimination of categorical funding, school districts tend to spend less and less attention to former program mandates and move on to other things. This is very apparent in the 2000- 2004 State Plan for Vocational and Technical Education. With possibly the exception of Tech-Prep, it does not specifically address any plans or objectives to serve special populations. The Act requires the state to describe its strategy on how it addresses the needs of special populations.

Such a strategy is not clearly defined in the Plan as was noted by the U.S. Office of Education in its review of the Plan. The accountability responsibility for special populations has been shifted to the school districts which are required to conduct an annual program evaluation which must address access, success, and progress of special needs students. This includes recruiting, enrolling and placing special needs students in jobs.

Disadvantaged and Limited English Speaking

The 1963 and 1968 Vocational Education Act contained language allowing the use of federal funds for support of persons who have academic, socio-economic, or other handicaps that prevent them from succeeding in the regular vocational education program. In 1976, a set-aside of 20 percent of the state allotment was to be used to pay for 50 percent of the cost of vocational education for disadvantaged persons (other than handicapped persons), for person who have limited English speaking ability, and for providing stipends in work study programs. Similar problems occurred in the allocation and expenditure of these funds as it did to the 10 percent set aside for the handicapped. At first, the matching requirement made it difficult for many school districts to justify the use of the finds with a local match. Attempts were made with the U.S. Office of Education Officials to allow various state appropriated funds for the disadvantaged in state initiated programs to be used to satisfy the matching requirement.

Matching remained a problem. In 1979, CACVE did an assessment of how successful the state was in addressing this new mandate. It tried to determine what effect federal funds were having in increasing the number of disadvantaged served by vocational education. Unfortunately, no such data were available to make that determination. Further, data that were being collected contained duplicate counts which made it even more difficult to ascertain the impact of these targeted federal funds.

Federal funds were allocated to the schools districts based on a number of factors which drove the money to large urban school districts with high concentrations of unemployed, large numbers of limited and non-English speaking, and the greatest number of low income families. This immediately changed entitlement allocations to a majority of the school districts. In spite of the increase in federal funding and targeting resources to the disadvantaged, many districts were unable to use the funds due to the matching requirement, or because of the small amount received. This plagued statewide program efforts to address this requirement in federal law.

In random visits to school districts, CACVE observed that there were innovative programs and solid support services available to "some" disadvantaged populations. However, to generalize CACVE's impression or to determine the results of those programs/services was difficult. Adequate data to permit meaningful evaluation of these programs was just not available. CACVE also reviewed the planned assessment tools that would be used to measure program effectiveness, PAR, DRA and PAVE, which are discussed in further detail in this review. It determined that the state was tracking the availability of programs and services, but nothing was being done to conduct substantive evaluations to assess program outcomes. CACVE concluded:

> *"the state cannot determine, on the basis of data currently collected, what are the most effective ways of spending money to serve the disadvantaged. Nor can it know the effect those services are having on the individuals receiving them, either in terms of their success in vocational education, or in the job market."*

According to CACVE, 1979 funding to support district efforts to address the vocational education needs of limited-English speaking students was put on hold. Due to a lack of resources and staff support, none of the objectives and activities outlined in the State Plan was realized. During the 1978-79, state planning staff suggested eliminating from the Five-Year State Plan all measurable objectives regarding limited-English speaking persons. This was supported by the CDE and State Board of Education.

In 1981, CACVE reviewed program enrollment data which were now available. It found that the number of disadvantaged and limited and non-English speaking student participation in vocational education varied between 1978-1980. Programs requiring non-federal matching funds for excess cost had decreased 13.5 percent. Special programs for the disadvantaged that required no match were up 289 percent. On the other hand, programs serving limited and non-English speaking students were down 36.7 percent.

In July of 1981, CACVE issued a comprehensive overview of programs and services for limited and non-English speaking in California tilted, "Horizon." It was a similar monograph to one done by CACVE on the handicapped. The purpose of CACVE's effort was to increase awareness of the educational needs of the limited-English proficient population and to promote increased priority for vocational education services to limited-English proficient persons by encouraging coordination of service delivery. The issues in this monograph were similar to those previously addressed by CACVE on meeting the education and training needs of the handicapped.

In 1991, the State Plan indicated vocational education was serving approximately 32,400 limited-English proficient students. In 1978, the number served was reported to be 8,794 students and this dropped to a low of 3,724 in 1978.

In the narrative of the1998-1999 California Annual Performance Report it states that at the secondary level, a total of 880,311 students were designated as "special populations" under the 1990 definitions in federal law. Of these, 622,867 were secondary students and 257,444 adults. However, Table 11 in the same document gives a summary of the special population's enrollment figures for 1998-1999. It is reproduced below as Table 3. Simple addition finds that the numbers found in the narrative of the report titled "Special Populations, Disabled, LEP and Disadvantaged" do not reconcile with the Table 11 in the 1998-99 Annual Performance Report. Again, it illustrates the problem with the accuracy of vocational education enrollment figures.

In the 2000 State Plan for Vocational and Technical Education, there is absence of directed services or state leadership to this special population as categorical funding was eliminated in federal law. However, the responsibility to serve the limited-English speaking population has been retained by school district's which are held accountable in their annual program assessments.

Gender Equity

As the Civil Rights and women's movements gained momentum in the 1960s, the Vocational Education Act Amendments of 1968 added language making gender equity activities an allowable expenditure of federal funds. It was not until the Title IX Educational Amendments of 1972 to the Civil Rights Acts of 1963 and 1964 that vocational education programs were advised that they could no longer steer men and women to different occupational activities. School districts were required to report annual course enrollment proportions by gender to the Office of Civil Rights.

Table 3.
Vocational Education Services to Special Needs Students
1998 - 1999

Handicapped Students Served	Where Served	Enrollment
Mainstreamed	High Schools	60,563
	Adult Schools	6,095
Special Classes	ROCPs	17,849
Disadvantaged Students Served		
Mainstreamed	High Schools	339,337
	Adult Schools	41,938
Special Classes	ROCPs	56,245
Limited English Speaking		
Mainstreamed	High Schools	129,243
	Adult Schools	32,192
Special Classes	ROCPs	17,256
	Total:	700,718

In 1974, the Women's Educational Equity Act was passed and provided funds to develop bias-free curricula as well as training and research about women's equity. The Vocational Education Amendments of 1976 was the next federal law to provide funding for gender equity. The Act required that as a condition to receive federal finding the state:

> *"Shall assign such full-time personnel as may be necessary to assist the state board in fulfilling the purposes of this Act by:*
>
> *(A) taking such action as may be necessary to create awareness of program and activities in vocational education that are designed to reduce sex stereotyping in vocational education;*
>
> *(B) gathering, analyzing and disseminating data on the status of men and women, students and employees in the vocational education programs of that state;*

> (C) *developing and supporting actions to correct any problems brought to the attention of such personnel through activities carried out under clause (B) of this sentence;*
>
> (D) *reviewing the distribution of grants by the state board to assure that the interests and needs of women are addressed in the projects assisted under this Act;*
>
> (E) *reviewing all vocational education programs in the state for sex bias;*
>
> (F) *monitoring the implementation of laws prohibiting sex discrimination in all hiring, firing, and promotion procedures within the state relating to vocational education;*
>
> (G) *reviewing and submitting recommendations with respect to the overcoming of sex stereotyping and sex bias in vocational education programs for the annual program plan and report;*
>
> (H) *assisting local educational agencies and other interested parties in the state in improving vocational education programs for women. "*

The Act also provided that the state had to reserve $50,000 to carry-out the equity provisions of the law. A Sex Equity Coordinator position was established in the CDE to manage the new vocational education requirements. In 1977, the position was filled by Connie Gipson.

The Act stipulated that program improvement, research, curriculum, and vocational guidance funds could be used to overcome sex bias in vocational education. Finally, it stated that priority should be given to funding exemplary and innovative projects designed to reduce sex stereotyping in vocational education.

The 1976 Vocational Education Amendments made a very powerful commitment to achieving gender equity provisions in federal law. However, there was general resistance to the new provisions and most school districts showed little awareness of the requirements. The National Institute of Education documented the persistence of sex segregation in vocational education in 1984 which led to more specific requirements in the passage of the 1984 Carl D. Perkins Vocational Education Act which took effect in 1985. The most significant of these was the targeting of 57 percent of the state grant to special needs groups to enhance their participation in vocational education, These were termed as *"national priority programs"* and funding was allocated accordingly:

- 10% was allocated for programs and services to handicapped students
- 22% for the disadvantaged, including limited English proficient individuals
- 12% for adults who were in need of training and retraining
- 8.5% for single parents and homemakers
- 3.5% for programs designed to eliminate sex bias and stereotyping in vocational education

Because of the priority given to eliminating sex bias and stereotyping in vocational education, the Sex Equity Administrator became very influential in state level decision making processes about the structure of vocational education. With mandates in hand, efforts got underway to implement federal requirements early in 1977. At first, emphasis was given to providing technical assistance to district and state staff, conducting professional development efforts, and reviewing all instructional materials to ensure they were free of sexual bias and stereotyping.

Vocational education personnel needed to become aware of the requirement in federal and state statutes. Both state and local personnel needed assistance in developing curricular strategies and instructional materials to assist students select career paths that would include non-traditional jobs and careers, i.e., jobs primarily filled by males or females. Therefore, considerable time was devoted to capacity building. Numerous conferences and meeting were held. Materials were developed and disseminated defining the problems along with strategies on how to address them.

School district personnel found these invaluable. They were used to assist them achieve the gender equity mandates in vocational education. In the early 1980s, the next thrust was a series of specialized projects and linkages with the private sector to assist in the development of non-traditional program strategies. It was apparent that barriers not only existed in the schools, but also in the community. Efforts were undertaken to develop materials to overcome some of these barriers across all segments of the community, especially in the minority community. A mentoring approach, pairing students with role models, was utilized and materials developed.

One program in particular worth mentioning was directed to the Latino fathers to overcome their influence over their daughters. To have a daughter consider pursuing a non-traditional career field was not accepted in the Latino culture. Fathers opposed it and were even reluctant to allow their daughters to go to school beyond the local area. Generally, anything beyond 50 miles or more was not acceptable. The mentoring program that was developed was so successful that grade point averages rose, dropout rates decreased, and more Latino girls went to college. An interesting side benefit was that the program brought female adults back into the schools from the success the younger girls were having in high school. The materials developed for the program have been used throughout the nation.

In the 1980s, sex equity linkages were established with the apprenticeship community. It involved the Education Committee of the State Apprenticeship Council, CACVE, CDE, and the Chancellor's Office of the California Community Colleges. Two issues brought them together. The first concerned state funding for apprenticeship classes offered in the public schools. State legislation resolved this issue with a new funding mechanism for apprenticeship classes. The other issue concerned bringing more girls and women into the apprenticeship system. With assistance of the Operating Engineers Local Number 3, a series of guidance videos were developed for use in the schools. One of the main audiences of these videos were vocational industrial education teachers who were reluctant to enrolling girls in their programs because they believed the unions would be a barrier to placing them into jobs where entry was dependent on serving an apprenticeship.

Other successes were achieved in the early 1990s. A joint effort was undertaken with the Society of Women Engineers, and a nontraditional program was developed in Environmental Technology. The program was offered for high school students at Tri-County ROCP and at Diablo Community College. An element agreed upon by the Society of Women Engineers was that the Environmental Technology program had to articulate between the secondary schools and community colleges.

Considerable effort was done with specialized projects to address the problem of teen pregnancy with equity funding. The focus of these programs was to provide instructional resources and strategies to girls participating in single parent programs. The focus of the resources developed was (1) avoiding second pregnancies which included the "Just Say No to Sex" program as well as prevention, (2) understanding options available, (3) developing life and career plans, and (4) committing to becoming self-sufficient. The success of these programs carried over into the 1990s with the funding of a number of Teen Parent projects. These programs provided pregnant teens and teen parents with information about vocational education and services that could enable them to further their education and become economically self-sufficient.

Project SOLO was another successful program. It was designed to encourage adult single parents, displaced homemakers, and single pregnant women to enroll and complete vocational programs that lead to gainful employment. Each participant was assessed and a personal vocational education plan developed. Participants received guidance and support services to help them reach their goals, heard presentations on non-traditional occupations, and received assistance in securing employment and additional training. Housing project and Section 8 residents were targeted; child care, transportation and clothing were provided to some participants. Each SOLO project was a collaborative effort between the secondary schools and community based organizations. Sixty-seven of these projects were funded in 1998-99.

The Connection Leadership Project was a successful and valuable resource to statewide gender equity efforts. The project was located in the Pierce Joint Unified School District in Arbuckle, California. The project developed numerous publications, curriculum materials, books, videos, annual data collection, and resource displays for equity network regional meetings and seminars. The project also operated the SERVE Lending Library. The Library served as a resource for research, data collection, and the coordination and dissemination unit for the state equity program. It served over 350 school districts and 600 equity programs throughout the state. The Library was functioning in 2000 but with its future in doubt.

The Carl D. Perkins Vocational and Technical Education Act of 1998 eliminated targeted funding for sex equity. The new Act no longer sets aside funding for Single Parent, Displaced Homemaker, and Single Pregnant Women programs and programs to eliminate sex bias and stereotyping. Instead, it imposes an accountability indicator requiring states to measure the progress students pursuing occupations nontraditional for their sex. Based on these changes, 1998-99 was the last year districts received direct grants for sex equity programs, services, and activities. The Act requires a competitive granting program which does limit the CDE's ability to impact local programs on a statewide basis.

Program Improvement and Leadership

From the beginning of federal support for vocational education, vocational education staff in the CDE had assumed a leadership role for stimulating and improving vocational education programs and services in California public schools. By its design, the 1917 Smith Hughes Act provided a relatively small amount of money, which was designed to assist the state develop vocational education in specific subject matter areas. Given that there was virtually no leadership for vocational education in the public schools at the time, it was not a difficult decision to make. In 1917, California's public school enrollment was only 125,000 students and 8,000 were enrolled in vocational education. California's share of federal funds was only $70,476 in 1919-20.

The State Plan standards adopted by the State Board of Education in 1917 to support local districts were so rigid that the districts complained to the Federal Board for Vocational Education. The Board responded in a way that it was to become a policy of the Board and its successor the U.S. Office of Education. The Board stated that California had adopted a State Plan that had been approve by the board; therefore, the state must be responsible for the conduct of the program unless it could be shown that the state was in violation of its own plan.

This philosophy prevailed and when federal funding increased in the 1960s and even more dramatically in 1976, the role of state leadership was enhanced. The 1976 Act provided specific funding for program improvement, curriculum development, teacher training, research, demonstration, and innovation. The CDE basically took control over millions of federal dollars and new staff positions were established to manage them. This will be shown in the review of governance below.

Program growth accelerated rapidly and leadership positions were quickly established in the school districts to manage the federal funds and satisfy the planning, project writing, and reporting required to secure vocational education funds from the CDE. These personnel were generally seasoned vocational education educators familiar with the inner workings of planning and delivering vocational education programs and services to students.

Vocational education administrative leadership grew in the districts to the point where they organized themselves into several professional associations. In this manner they could share ideas, provide for professional growth, and position themselves to influence decisions regarding the use of federal vocational education funds managed by the CDE as well as policy and fiscal decisions of the Legislature. The most prominent of these associations were the California Directors of Vocational Education and the California Association of Regional Occupational Centers and Programs. The California Directors of Vocational Education eventually became the California Association of Vocational Administrators in the 1980s. Then, in the early 1990s they changed their name to the California Association of Leaders for Career Preparation. Both of the organizations are still active in 2000.

School district leadership positions in vocational education began to be eliminated as program enrollment began to decline following passage of Proposition 13, school reforms in the 1980s and tighter restrictions on the amount of funds a school district could spend on the administration of vocational education. By the 1990s, leadership for vocational education in many school districts was assumed by other district administrators often without a background in vocational education.

The CDE also experienced a decline in vocational education staff positions. The most significant of these was the near loss of the State Director's position. In 1991-92, the State Director of Vocational Education position remained vacant for approximately one-year. The position could have been eliminated because State Personnel Rules state that if a position remains vacant for over a year it is abolished. During this time period, management direction for vocational education was being given to CDE staff by a non-managerial staff member, Allan Holmes, who was assigned this duty by the Associate Superintendent, Sally Mentor. She eventually assumed the Directors position in 1992.

These were difficult times for state staff. One the first actions taken by Sally Mentor was to announce that 60 percent of the vocational education staff were going to be terminated and the regional offices housing vocational education staff would be closed. The Los Angeles and Oakland offices were closed. Mentor explained that the reason for closing the offices was for cost saving purposes. However, both offices had long term leases which continued to be paid by the CDE. At the urging of the vocational educational community contact was made with State Senators Rose Ann Vuich and Bill Jones and Assemblywoman Doris Allen. They voiced a number of concerns including that federal vocational funds were being diverted to the California School Leadership Academy via sole source contracts through Alameda County. Sally Mentor was also the Director of the California School Leadership Academy. The legislative members contacted Congressman Calvin

Dooley who requested an Auditor General audit. The audit did not uncover any problems and no action was taken by the U.S. Auditor General. Veteran CDE professionals familiar with the issue believe that the audit wasn't very thorough. Sally Mentor left the CDE shortly thereafter.

Audits were not new to vocational education. Over the years, fiscal and program reviews were done by the U.S. Department of Education, the Auditor General's Office, and the General Accounting Office. Also, periodic state audits have been conducted by the State Auditor. These in turn are forwarded to the U.S. Department of Education for review and disposition. In May of 1999, for example, the State Auditor completed an audit of the CDE on how federal funds were being used to administer vocational education. The report concluded that the reorganization of the CDE, which redirected vocational staff to new responsibilities, had resulted in diminished services to school districts providing vocational education programs. State leadership funds were being used for other purposes. They further stated while federal guidelines do not appear to allow the use of Perkins finds to administer other programs, the CDE has not maximized the effectiveness or availability of Perkins vocational services at the local level. Although the audit found exceptions to the CDE's use of federal funds, no punitive action has been taken by the U.S. Department of Education.

With each CDE reorganization, starting 1974 through 1995, vocational education leadership positions were reduced in number, and in many instances the staff were assigned to perform other functions in the CDE. Then in 1998, the new Carl D. Perkins Vocational and Technical Education Act placed a limitation on the use of funds for state administration of vocational education of five percent, and ten percent for leadership activities. Eighty five percent of the federal funds had to be allocated to the schools. No more than five percent for administration which also reduced local leadership funding for vocational education. At the state level, CDE went from a high of 187 staff positions in 1975 to only 30 authorized positions in 2000. Thus, the basic question is will this leadership void at the state and local level make the challenges facing vocational education in the new millennium difficult to meet or will a new breed of leadership emerge?

Governance of Vocational Education

Governance of vocational education is one of the most complex and perplexing issues that still remains unresolved. It basically involves a power struggle over who has control of over approximately $125 million of federal vocational education funds with increases anticipated in future years.

Secondarily, but of significant importance, is the concern of vocational teachers, particularly those in rural and small school districts. They have been and continue to be concerned with the decline of program and staff development services provided to them through the leadership of state subject matter staff. In 1977, they began an effort to take matters into their own hands to establish a separate governing board for vocational education, assuming this would bring pressure to bear to on the CDE to resolve the problem. They took their case to the Legislature and legislation was introduced in the Senate, SB 1028 (Dills) and a companion bill the following year in the Assembly, AB 2242 (Collier). These bills would have established a separate Board for vocational education. They will be discussed further in this review.

Separation of the Community Colleges

In order to understand the turmoil and why governance is such a large issue in vocational education, one only needs to trace the problem back a few years to 1967 when the Legislature separated the community colleges from the jurisdiction of the State Board of Education. This was the point when the problem of governance became a concern. The State Board of Education's historical exclusive role of managing federal funds for vocational education was soon to be challenged.

The Arthur D. Little Report had reviewed the issue of governance and determined it was inadequate. It had recommended that:

> *"the current Joint Committee on Vocational Education continue a while to gain experience in joint management of vocational education, however, eventually an expanded Joint Board of Vocational Education should be formed. The Joint Board would draw equal members (at least two or possibly three to five) representing other important segments of the public interest in vocational education."*

Near the completion of the A. D. Little study in the spring of 1969, the vocational education staff in the CDE was asked to make a choice of working for the Chancellor's Office of the California Community Colleges or to remain in the Department. In July, 16 professional and nine clerical positions were transferred to the Chancellor's Office. Their responsibilities would be to provide support to 70 community colleges serving approximately 300,000 occupational students. The Department retained 135 staff positions, 81 professionals and 54 clerical. These staff were responsible to provide services to some 360 secondary and unified districts serving approximately 600,000 vocational students.

These figures are not all that significant, but must be noted as contributing to the governance issue. The reason is, the role of state staff had traditionally been to provide leadership in the vocational education subject matter fields of agriculture, business, home economics or homemaking, and trade and industrial education. State leadership positions can be traced back to 1912.

When it came time for state staff to choose between the CDE and Chancellor's Office, two major factors influenced their decisions. One was the sole State agency feature in federal legislation, and the other was allegiance to the maintenance of subject matter services in secondary schools. The State Board of Education had retained its control of federal funds. To some, support of Chancellor's Office staff was not assured. Other staff were deeply committed to subject matter activities and did not wish to sever ties with the CDE. Vocational education leadership in secondary districts was not strong during this era while community college leadership was very strong. A sense of competition and jealousy surfaced with the split.

Leadership Role of State Staff

The leadership role of state staff is of sufficient importance to describe in more detail. With the passage of the Smith Hughes Act in 1917, federal matching funds were provided to establish vocational education in the public schools. The Act provided support for agriculture, trades, industry, home economics, and teacher education. The state's role in teacher education is important and will be discussed in more detail below.

Aided by new federal legislation which supported leadership in distributive education, technical education, and vocational teacher training, the role of state staff was strengthened in the 1930s, 40s, and 50s. However, the major stimulus affecting state leadership came about with the passage of the Vocational Education Act of 1963, VEA 63, and its Amendments in 1968. The level of federal funding had a direct relationship to the role of state staff in vocational education. Prior to the passage of Vocational Education Act of 1963, $1 million of the $3 million of federal funds flowing into the State were retained at the state level. Those funds were added to approximately $700,000 of State General Funds to administer vocational education. A large portion of the $1.7 million was utilized for teacher training and direct services to school districts. District leadership was lacking, especially at the secondary level, and state staff was called upon to fill this void.

Over the years, state vocational education staff developed close working relationships with virtually all teacher training institutions in California. Many of these relationships exist today, especially in staff development and improvement efforts, curriculum development, and research. However, unlike most agriculture, home economics, and business education teachers who have a degree before beginning to teach, most trade and industrial education teachers, many health teachers, and ROCP teachers are not products of a four-year teacher training program. They come from business and industry with practical work experience but with not much more than a high school diploma. This required specialized teacher training programs to be developed for them on how to teach their craft or trade. The state's role in teacher training was enhanced due to the lack of a viable vocational education teacher training program in the State Colleges and University system. The client group did not fit the mold of higher education's philosophy, and even less, available offerings.

State industrial education staff in the CDE had to assume a major responsibility in teacher training efforts. Teacher training efforts were conducted by state staff at various sites throughout the state, including the University of California, Berkeley, Davis and UCLA, Cal Poly San Luis Obispo, Cal Poly Pomona, and Chico State College. State staff in the other subject matter areas took a lesser but active role in teacher training. The role of teacher trainers has diminished and virtually does not exist in 2000.

An analysis of state administration of vocational education is shown in Table 4. The analysis was taken from a review of annual Governor's Budgets. The data reflects support services and administrative costs of vocational education over a 15 year time period. Unfortunately, the various Budget documents did not provide comparable data, nor did they separate administrative costs from services to school districts, teacher training activities, etc. However, the data does illustrate the impact of federal funding on state level management of vocational education.

Table 4.
An Analysis of State Operational Costs and Staffing of Vocational Education
1963-64 through 1977-78*

Authorized Position							Support Level		
	State Department of Education			Chancellor's Office Community Colleges			State Funds	Federal	Total
Year	Profes-sional	Clerical	Total	Profes-sional	Clerical	Total			
63/64	59	50	109				707,159	1,002,212	1,709,371
64/65	57	50	107				741,069	1,161,129	1,902,198
65/66	56	50	107				759,900	1,139,905	1,897,805
66/67	n/a	n/a	130				852,513	2,184,784	3,037,297
67/68	n/a	n/a	148				837,946	2,112,695	2,950,631
68/69	n/a	n/a	132				727,063	2,056,077	2,783,140
69/70	81	54.8	136	16	9.4	25.4	764,274	2,694,276	3,458,550
70/71	85	57.4	142.4	18	8.9	26.9	0	4,173,733	4,173,733

Year	State Department of Education			Chancellor's Office Community Colleges			State Funds	Federal	Total
	Profes-sional	Clerical	Total	Profes-sional	Clerical	Total			
71/72	88	59.9	147.9	18	9.9	27.9	0	4,326,169	4,326,169
72/73	104	76.1	180.1	18	10.9	28.9	0	6,152,679	6,152,169
73/74	104	81.1	185.1	19	10.5	29.5	0	6,654,818	6,654,818
74/75	106	81.3	187.3	20	10.5	30.5	0	8,306,687	8,306,687
75/76	94	67.3	161.3	20	10.5	30.5	150,000	8,402,829	8,552,829
76/77	94	63.2	157.2	23	10.5	33.5	344,384	8,613,920	8,958304
77/78	90	58.7	148.7	25	10.5	33.5	463,556	9,420,377	9,883,933

*Source 1963 through 1978 Governor's Budget (1963-69 community colleges were under the direction of the state Department of Education)

Use of Special Set-aside Funds

The role of state staff was enhanced each year through the use of "special set-asides for staff initiated projects to serve statewide programmatic needs." These special set-asides were mainly taken off the top of Part B (funds for district programs) and Part F (Consumer Homemaking funds) of federal funds available to the state. Table 5 illustrates the magnitude of these resources. Records were not readily available to determine fiscal policies prior to 1968-69. Table 5, therefore, represents policy developed by the Joint Committee on Vocational Education from its establishment in 1968.

Table 5.
A Summary of Special Set-aside Fund*
1968-69 through 1976-77

Year	VEA Part B	VEA Part F	Other
1968-69	$784,00	-	$400,000
1969-70	$800,00	$117,910	$250,000
1970-71	$800,00	$61,203	$461,000
1971-72	$831,150	$208,150	-
1972-73	$1,981,874	$314,699	-
1973-74	$798,858	$200,000	-
1974-75	$797,300	$225,000	-
1975-76	$797,300	$225,000	-
1976-77	$709,300	$187,000	-

*Source: Joint Committee on Vocational Education Agenda and Minutes

Although the use of these special set-asides enhanced the impact of state staff services to school districts, some serious questions were being raised by the Joint Committee and the Legislature on their use. Upon analysis, it was determined that the set-asides were used to greatly expand established state level services. Many innovative programs were developed, teachers, counselors and administrators trained or in-serviced, curriculum materials produced, disseminated and implemented, teaching methods improved, promotional materials developed, vocational student organizations nurtured and expanded, teacher training programs improved, and quality of state-level services to districts improved. Simply stated, state vocational education leadership had an impact all the way down to the classroom. Finally, something that cannot be taken lightly, a constituency base supporting state staff activities was indirectly, not by design, established.

Although the positive outweigh the negative, the negative aspects represent the major dimensions of the governance issue taking place in 1977. Negative issues contributing to the problem included:

- The Joint Committee on Vocational Education virtually rubber stamped all staff recommendations. The relationship of staff initiated projects or needs to state priorities and criteria were never fully understood by the Committee.

- The CDE and Chancellor's Office staff became engaged in open competition for VEA funds which resulted in little concern for articulation of services, development of duplicate systems and services, and a lack of unity of purpose within state-level leadership for vocational education.

- The outcomes or resultant benefits of special set-aside projects were rarely shared with the Joint Committee unless they ask specifically for a report from staff.

- In some instances, special set-aside funds were poorly managed. This often resulted in duplication of effort, and inefficiency.

- The state expanded its role in program operation holding an edge over school districts and teacher training institutions in the allocation process of VEA funds.

- The Auditor General's audit had reported that VEA funds were being diverted from local assistance, thus diminishing the effectiveness at the local level.

Role of the Joint Committee on Vocational Education

The role of the Joint Committee on Vocational Education, (Joint Committee) became a major factor. The Joint Committee was conceived in September 1968 in order to foster and maintain an articulated and coordinated delivery system: K-14 and adult. It exemplified the philosophy that vocational education was a "part of" rather than "apart from" education. Further, it supported the belief that vocational education policy could not be formed in a vacuum. The Joint Committee was established through a signed agreement between the State Board of Education and Board of Governors of the California Community Colleges. The charge to the Joint Committee was to provide the State Board of Education, which maintained the sole state agency responsibility for federal funds, mutually agreed upon policy recommendations for approval. The Joint Committee included three members from each Board and the Superintendent and Chancellor or their designee.

For all practical purposes, the creation of the Joint Committee allowed the State Board of Education to focus its attention on other educational matters. So complete was their attention to other matters, the State Board all but abdicated its authority to the Joint. Committee and approved with little debate or discussion all of their recommendations.

The role of the Joint Committee was quickly determined to be an allocation and project approving/recommending body. The 1969-70 administrative budget for vocational education was discussed and recommended for approval at their June 1969 meeting. It was the only time the vocational education administrative budget was filly reviewed and recommended for approval to the State Board of Education by the Joint Committee.

Membership on the Joint Committee varied year-to- year. Continuity and interest were difficult to maintain. Action taken by the Joint Committee, by and large, was done without full understanding of needs, priorities, criteria, and clearly defined Joint Committee policy. Very simply stated, the Joint Committee operated from a very narrow, piecemeal, crisis management perspective rather than from policy-control position. This manner of operation allowed state staff to control the direction of vocational education rather than the policy makers.

The failings of the Joint Committee cannot be attributed to a single item. The responsibility must be shared by members of the respective Boards, the Superintendent and Chancellor, the vocational education leadership in both agencies, and to a lesser degree, the Legislature. Members of the Boards, for example, failed to fulfill their obligation to serve as educational policy makers. The philosophy underlying the establishment of the Joint Committee that vocational education was an integral and important part of education was only given lip service. Vocational education appeared not to be a priority, yet the vehicle to make it so existed.

The Superintendent and Chancellor failed to provide leadership and direction to the Joint Committee. The appropriate role of these educational leaders was to give guidance and assist policy Boards to make informed decisions. Both abdicated their responsibilities. State vocational education leadership failed in this regard too, possibly by design.

Separation of the community colleges from the purview of the State Board of Education is attributed to the Legislature. The political aspects far outweighed the effects on educational policy during the legislative process and debate. The results were detrimental to both adult and vocational education. The stage was being set for competition, duplication and increased state costs, etc.

Several costly but ineffective mechanisms were put in place by the Legislature to address the problem of duplication and delineating program responsibilities on deciding who would serve whom. These were funded with federal vocational education funds. None of these efforts were very successful for a number of reasons, including a lack of attention by state vocational education leadership to provide direction and support.

The Legislature approves the vocational education administrative budget when it takes action on the CDE's budget in the annual State Budget process. Vocational education's budget received very little scrutiny by the Legislature as it was primarily funded with federal funds. The only exception was when the Legislature redirected some of vocational education's funds for some specific purpose such as finding regional planning. In general, the number, purpose, and role of state staff were not a big issue. The needs and specific outcomes of vocational education were only discussed when policy legislation was introduced. The Legislature did not provide adequate oversight and responded only to individual legislative members and constituent concerns such as were mounted in the governance of vocational education. In time, this would change.

GAO Report

There were other contributing factors. In 1974, the General Accounting Office Report to the Congress *"What is the Role of Federal Assistance for Vocational Education"* had *a* major impact on the Vocational Education Act Amendments of 1976. The Report found:

- The use of federal funds had not been adequately evaluated;
- Federal funds had often been used to maintain existing or traditional programs rather than for the expansion of vocational education;

- A large portion of finds were retained at the state level for the administration of vocational education.

California was one of six states audited by the GAO. The report made reference to the California Advisory Council's Fourth Annual Report citing the recommendation that the state should start paying the cost of administering vocational education. Neither the State Board of Education or Legislature implemented this recommendation, but the U.S. Congress did. In the middle of the governance debate, a budget augmentation was submitted by the CDE and Chancellor's Office to retain 35.5 staff positions to administer the new federal act. Assemblyman Perino introduced legislation to fund the positions out of the General Fund. No state funds were committed and a significant number of positions were eliminated.

Entitlement System Adopted

In 1968, the State Board of Education adopted a staff recommendation to replace the costly "project" method for allocating federal funds with an "entitlement" system through a complex formula calculation. Coupled with the staff recommendation was a proviso that no district allocation would be reduced more than 10% from the previous year. The major benefactors of this policy were the community colleges who did well in securing funds for their projects. They had strong leadership and support to develop project applications. Although the community colleges had approximately half as many students enrolled in vocational education, they captured nearly 50% of the funds. At least one large community college district, San Francisco, experienced a 10% reduction annually for eight years to get to its actual formula entitlement allocation. It was ironic that one of the arguments advanced by the Board of Governors of the California Community Colleges for a stronger role in the governance of vocational education was to ensure an equitable share of federal funds for community colleges. The entitlement system, designed to provide administrative convenience, later proved to be an administrative nightmare when funding formulas required modification to assure an equitable distribution of funds. Equitable was generally defined as not dramatically changing the amount K-12 and community college districts received year to year.

Department of Education Reorganization

Another factor which continues to plague vocational education is the ever changing administrative structure of the CDE. Since 1974, vocational education personnel have gone through a number of organizational and leadership changes in the Department. These will be discussed at different interludes in this review.

In 1974 they were reorganized into a Matrix Management System used by business. Approximately 26, or one-fourth, of the vocational education staff were redirected to other service units in order to effect a comprehensive approach to school district services, and to provide varied inputs into the administration of education within the CDE.

The reorganization failed, but the wounds had yet to heal. As vocational education instructional services to school districts began to diminish, pressure was brought to bear on the CDE by the Legislature relative to the redirection of staff. The Matrix became a topic of discussion in the Legislature during the governance debate.

Audits and Reviews

The U.S. Office of Education entered the scene next. An audit exception became apparent and with the threat of having to return a large sum of federal funds, most the staff were returned to their original duties. However, some staff were retained in other service units for a while longer. The Department negotiated with U.S. Office to increase indirect costs the Department charged vocational education. These funds were used by the CDE to help fund newly established positions. The end result, school districts got less money as state administration costs rose.

In November 1976, the Auditor General reported that:

- VEA funds designated for local assistance had been diverted to improperly fund state operations;
- $384,456 of VEA funds had been forfeited due to poor fiscal management;
- There was a large surplus of VEA funds unexpended over a five-year period of time;
- There were some unauthorized bank accounts being maintained by State staff.

In April 1 977, the Legislative Analyst issued a report on vocational education. In addition to examining the Legislature's role in establishing vocational education policy, the report dealt with nine other issues. The major issues included:

- Changes necessary to provide an efficient system of state level administration of vocational education;
- Steps necessary to provide for effective coordination of vocational education at the regional level;
- Procedures for maximizing the productivity of funds for vocational education research, exemplary, and innovative programs, and curriculum development;
- Requirements for adequate accountability and evaluation in vocational education.

The Report provided a basis for both the Legislature and Department of Finance to recommend a 50 percent reduction in state vocational education staff over a two year period of time. The Report was the most extensive report done by Legislative Analyst on vocational education. The final 1977-78 Budget Act language stipulated an immediate reduction as of June 30, 1977, of four professional and 16 clerical positions in the CDE and two professional positions from the community colleges staff. It also required a reduction of 26.5 professional and 9 clerical positions from the combined CDE and community colleges staffs as of June 30, 1978. Although a fervent and bitter debate ensued, the Department of Finance recommendations prevailed. Vocational education lost 32.5 professional and 25 clerical positions in one year. The largest number of these were from the CDE.

Role of Board Members

Probably one the more significant factors was the addition of Dr. Michael Kirst from the State Board of Education and Dr. Steve Weiner from Board of Governors to the Joint Committee in January, 1977. Both men were recognized as important figures in relationship to their advisory role to Governor Brown on educational policy. Bill Honig was also a member of the Joint Committee for a period of time which may have been a factor in his perception of vocational education when he became Superintendent.

During Dr. Kirst's and Dr. Weiners's tenure on the Joint Committee, a new perspective or role was established. The Committee began to question staff recommendations in terms of needs, priorities, criteria, impact of previously funded projects, evaluation results, and they often requested additional information, etc. State staff became very uneasy. Some observers felt the Joint Committee was finally beginning to assume a true policy role. Others argued the Committee had become too involved in the operation and administration of vocational education.

In addition to Kirst's and Weiner's membership of the Joint Committee, a new assertive role was assumed by the Board of Governors of the California Community Colleges. The role can best be described as one of advocacy for community college interests with objective of an equal share in the governance of vocational education.

1976 Vocational Education Act Amendments

The largest factor to impact the governance issue was passage of the Vocational Education Amendments of 1976. In its original form, the Act would have provided only approximately $1.25 million to California for state administration. The state would have to match this amount within three years. Further, the Act did not provide for the support of local administrators of vocational education. State-level operations and local leadership would have been drastically cut under these provisions. During the development of technical amendments to clean-up problems identified after its passage, the CDE was successful in advocating changes which would allow the expenditure of Subpart 2 (local program support) and Subpart 3 funds (program improvement) for state and local administration. The matching requirement was not changed. However, there were few dollars available for administrative activities. It was possible they would need to use a large portion of Subpart 3 finds to retain the staff positions that the Legislature planned to abolish.

To complicate matters further, the new Act required greater administrative detail. The state, as well as local school districts, was spending an inordinate amount of time attending to paper work detail. School district complaints about this had been voiced both to the Joint Committee and CACVE. A number districts concerned about the new requirements said they were giving serious consideration to not making applications for federal vocational education funds. The Act placed special emphasis on providing access and special services to special needs populations, the disadvantaged and handicapped. The matching requirements were such that many districts would possibly have to return their allocation to the state. Further, the criteria for distributing the funds virtually drove the bulk of the funds into larger urban centers and left rural and small school districts with token support. Coupled with certain curtailment of state-level subject matter support, these districts were the most vocal for a change in the governance of vocational education.

SB 1028 Introduced

SB 1028 was introduced by Senator Ralph Dills along with 23 co-authors. They represented over half of the State Senate. They were from both sides of the aisle which assured passage. This proposal was generated out sheer frustration by a number of state vocational staff, vocational leadership in professional teacher associations, and members of the Legislature. It focused attention on vocational education, its needs, administration, organization and management. The message was loud and clear, something had to be done.

CACVE took a very active role in opposing the legislation. CACVE conducted a massive investigation of how other states where organized to administer vocational education. They surveyed school districts, vocational leaders, teachers and school personnel to gain their opinions on this matter. CACVE presented its findings to the Senate Education Committee in June 6, 1977 along with others who were there to support and oppose the legislation.

The California Postsecondary Commission also entered into the governance debate. In 1976, the Commission had proposed in its Five-Year Plan that a staff-level planning council be established to bring together public and private secondary and postsecondary education segments in a comprehensive planning effort. Action by the Commission's recommendation was deferred when the Vocational Education Act was amended to require a similar advisory panel at the state level. Also, the Legislature had passed AB 1 82 1 (Montoya) in 1975 creating Regional Adult and Vocational Education Councils, RAVECs, to carry out a similar process at the local level.

In 1977 the Commission advised the State Board and Legislature that (1) RAVEC membership should be broadened to include private education, and (2) the authority of RAVECs should be expanded to include the planning and coordination at the state level. Neither of the Commission's recommendations were considered. In December of 1977, the Commission adopted a resolution supporting a separate Board for Vocational Education. The Commission noted that the U.S. Office of Education had rejected a new Cooperative Agreement between the two Boards where there would have been some shared policy authority through the actions of the Joint Committee. The Cooperative Agreement was revised and the Joint Committee retained its advisory role to the State Board of Education. In acting on its resolution, the Commission provided a set of principles from which it made its recommendations. The Commission proposed that any new governance mechanism for vocational education should:

> 1. be broadly representative of the general public, the world of work and the education system;
>
> 2. not impose addition levels of bureaucracy;
>
> 3. not isolate vocational education from the mainstream of general education;
>
> 4. not significantly disrupt present administrative functions;
>
> 5. enhance planning, coordination, and participation of all levels and segments of statewide and regional organizations in planning and coordination; and,
>
> 6. plan and coordinate the entire vocational sector, not just federally-funded programs.

In a private meeting between Senator Dills and Superintendent Riles, there was an agreement to delay the legislation with the intent that Dr. Riles would initiate efforts to reform vocational education and resolve the problems of effectively administering vocational education programs in the CDE. Dr. Riles appointed the Commission of Vocational Education in April of 1978. Unfortunately, due to the lack of follow through by Dr. Riles on the RISE and Commission recommendations, the issue of governance didn't get resolved.

Vocational Agriculture Takes Action

Concerned with their ability to continue to provide direct services and leadership to agriculture programs in the state, Don Wilson Manager of the Agriculture Unit in the CDE and the agriculture community went to the Legislature in 1981. Agriculture, being the number one industry in the state, had a large constituency, many of whom were members of the Legislature. The Legislature enacted SB 187 (Nielsen) which establish vocational agriculture as a mandated state program, Section 52450 of the Education Code. It directed the CDE to adopt rules and regulations to enforce the program. It noted that the law did not create any new mandates on school districts. In other words, retain what was there and if there is growth, so be it. This was a successful strategy for agriculture as would be proved in later years. The legislation established a permanent vocational agriculture Unit staffed and funded with redirected CDE funds. To this date, the number of staff positions which were in place in 1981 has remained constant and program enrollment has increased while most other vocational education programs have shrunk.

In 1983, the Legislature enacted an Agriculture Vocational Education Incentive Program as part of SB 813 the educational reform bill adding Section 52460 of the education Code. Money derived from horse racing revenues collected by the state was utilized to fund the incentive grant program. Annually, funds are placed in the Governor's Budget. They are made available to school districts through an application process to the State Superintendent of Public Instruction. The funds can be used for purchasing or leasing of agricultural equipment or any non-salary items. The law also provides that the district match the grant allocation. However, the Superintendent of Public Instruction could waive this requirement if it were determined that it was a financial hardship for the districts to come-up with the matching funds. Many districts have requested the waiver.

By 2000, an excess of $48 million in incentive grant finds had been distributed to school districts. In 1983-84 over 60 percent of the grant money was used by districts to purchase new or replace old equipment. In 1988-99 only a little over 23 percent of the funds were spent on capital items. The bulk went for such items as computers and peripherals, equipment and tools, text books, laboratory manuals and science equipment, and farm facility construction and repairs. With these added resources, vocational agriculture in California was being conducted in state-of-art facilities and technology, with adequate instructional materials, tools and equipment. Vocational agriculture students were the primary benefactors of the incentive grant program.

Vocational Education Division Abolished

In 1995 the Vocational Education Division was folded into a new organizational structure in the CDE. This was one of many organizational changes faced over the years. An internal review of the administration of vocational education was conducted by the CDE in 1986. It noted that over a ten year period of time, 1976-1986, the Vocational Education Division had experienced at least seven substantial reorganizations. During this time period, there had been three different State Directors of Vocational Education. The reported noted that the gaps in leadership as a result of the vacancy of the State Director position ranged from six month to over a year. A review of the various reorganizations revealed attempts to adapt to inherent personnel constraints and position limitations, rather than a vision of an organization supporting a specific goal and mission. The review offered a number of substantive recommendations to strengthen the role of the State Director of Vocational Education and the Divisions role in educational reform. The review had little impact.

The Vocational Education Division had grown out of an organizational structure in the CDE beginning with Commissioner of Vocational Education in 1913. Subject matter supervisors were added, ultimately organized in subject matter bureaus, then into a Division of Vocational Education. The Division which evolved and flourished for the better part of a century, no longer exists. With the exception of vocational agriculture personnel, vocational education staff were redirected to new assignments, and for some new responsibilities. Any potential for mounting a unified effort to forge a direction or vision for career-vocational education became even more difficult. If it were to happen, it would have to be done through the leadership of a Superintendent of Public Instruction who is committed to seeing that vision implemented.

Home Economics Takes Action

Concerned with their ability to receive statewide subject matter support services and support for FHA-HERO, the parents of former state and national FHA-HERO Officers and home economics teachers took their concerns to the Legislature in 1996. SB 1454 was introduced by Assemblyman Dave Kelly. The statute defined consumer home economics education and home economics related occupations programs as essential to the economic growth of California. The Legislature established a permanent Home Economics Careers and Technology Vocational Education Unit appropriately staffed with qualified home economics education trained staff to assist school districts. The bill created the establishment of a broad based advisory committee to assist in the development of recommendations for curriculum and strategies to implement the program throughout the public schools system.

The Committee was appointed by Superintendent of Public Instruction, Delaine Eastin. It held a series of meetings between August 1999 and January 2000. Foremost in the deliberations of the committee members was to develop a series of business-oriented strategies that addressed instruction about and in all aspects of Home Economics

Careers and Technology Education (HECT). The committee presented its recommendations in July 2000.

In its Report, the committee pointed out the significant contributions HECT programs make to the State's economy. It noted that 29.6 percent of California's jobs, 14,684,200, were in the eight career pathways provided for in the HCET program. Further, that the eight pathways represented by HCET are integral to California's largest and rapidly growing industries. These industries include:

- Hospitality, Tourism and Recreation employ 685,000 workers-estimated growth 18% by 2006;

- Food Service and Restaurant Industry one of the largest retail employers in the state-24% growth by 2006;

- Child Development and Education projects as many as 200,000 new pre-school, elementary and secondary teacher needed in the next decade-6% growth

- Fashion Design, Manufacturing and Merchandising includes the second largest manufacturer in California with two major fashion centers-an increase of 18% by 2006;

- Consumer Services-to meet the needs of 3 1 million California residents---28% increase by 2006;

- Food Science, Dietetics and Nutrition is a growing career field--projects an increase of 19% by 2006;

- Family and Human Services-an increase of 19% by 2006;

- Interior Design, Furnishings and Maintenance increase of 7% by 2006.

In support of their recommendations that on-going support from the State Budget for HCET programs should be provided, the committee pointed-out the fiscal impact of these industries on California's economy. Collectively, the industries served by just four HCET programs generate more than $108 billion in revenue and $10 billion in sales taxes for the state. Further, they recommend doubling the scale, scope and magnitude of HCET programs over the next three years.

In 1998, SB 1832 (Kelly) was passed, which added Section 53495 to the Education Code creating an incentive grant program for home economics. The grant program is to remain in effect until January 1, 2003, unless extended by the Legislature. The purpose of the grants was to improve, expand, and establish instructional programs in home economics careers and technology vocational education to improve the academic achievement and career preparation of students. This includes the mission of home economics careers and technology vocational education to link science, technology, career-technical and life management skills to prepare students for entry into technical careers and postsecondary education, as well as managing work and family roles.

$200,000 was appropriated in the Budget Act in 1998. A total of 27 incentive grants were made available to school districts in June 2000. The grants impacted 18,369 students at the 27 incentive grant sites. The schools improved or expanded 27 Consumer and Family Studies programs and 24 Home Economics Related Occupations Programs including preparation for high demand careers in Food Service and Restaurants; Hospitality, Tourism, and Recreation; Fashion Design, Manufacturing and Merchandising; and Child Development and Education. With a modest investment, the sites were able to redirect programs to focus on knowledge, skills, and attitudes needed to succeed in these career paths as well as contribute to academic achievement.

The State Budget has not provided additional funding since 1998, or funding to implement the Advisory Committee's recommendations; and the incentive grant provision sunset in 2003.

Community College Encroachment

Another potential governance issue came to the forefront in the late 1990s. In some areas of the state, community college districts had been aggressively competing for secondary vocational education programs offered by ROCPs. In Santa Barbara County, for example, the community college offered financial incentives to school districts to provide their students vocational education classes. In some instances, the incentives represented cash payments to the district from a.d.a. generated by the community college for programs offered to high school students under the concurrent enrollment provisions in state law.

State law, which was established in 1976, provides that high school students may enroll concurrently for advanced academic or vocational work "at the community college." This may be found in Education Code Sections 48800 through 48802. When the law was passed, both the community colleges and school districts received a.d.a. funding for the students who were attending the community colleges. This incentive was removed by the Legislature in 1985. Now only one, either the school district or community college district, can receive a.d.a. funding for the student's attendance at the community college.

In Santa Barbara County, school districts received from the community college a $500 incentive per a.d.a. from the income generated by community college classes offered to high school students on the high school campus, not at the community college. A number of the classes were not even of college grade, and some of the students were only 9th graders. In some instances, the program was taught by the high school teacher who received a $500 stipend. These practices are contrary to the statute that allows the student to attend the "community college" for "advanced academic and vocational work."

There are other examples which could be cited in Santa Monica and in San Mateo, El Dorado, and Contra Costa Counties. In Contra Costa County, the issue was solved by another review of existing articulation agreements between the colleges, school districts, and the ROCP. In some areas of the state, districts have been offered up to $1,100 in return for offering community college classes to their students. This practice has been exploited throughout the state with encouragement of staff in the Chancellors Office of the California Community. Basically, it is being used by the community colleges to help them generate more a.d.a. It is also generating more a.d.a. for the secondary schools. A similar practice in the 1970 led to the five-percent cap.

Community college personnel cite SB 292 (Costa) as the vehicle that supports community colleges to offer such programs to the high schools. The intent of the bill was to correct the limitation on state a.d.a. funding to school districts for students enrolled in part-time community college classes. It was sponsored by a coalition involved with the Butte County Office of Education which also maintains a ROCP program. The bill passed in 1996 added Sections 46146 and 76002 to the Education Code. Under state statute, the community colleges are able to:

> *"admit a special part-time student who is eligible to attend a community college under the concurrent attendance provision ...for purposes of receiving state apportionments, a community college district may include high school pupils who attend a community college within the district pursuant to Section 48800 and 76001."*

Existing statute 76001 states that the *community college* may *admit a student* as *a special part-time student who is eligible to attend the community college.* It is apparent that there are still some legal questions on how the statute is being interpreted and utilized by the community colleges.

This issue has the potential of being very detrimental to vocational education programs offered by the ROCP. The ROCP is limited by law. They cannot accept a secondary student until they have met the minimum day requirement of high school attendance - 240 minutes. The end result is the ROCP will have few high school students as enrollees if more and more students participate in community college concurrent enrollment classes. Thus, the ROCP will rely more and more on serving adults rather than high school students which were its primary responsibility when the ROCP was initiated in state law.

The Decline of Vocational Education

A national pattern was fully underway in the early 1980s that showed a decline in vocational education enrollments due to increasing academic standards. Already impacted by Proposition 13, California was no exception, enrollments and course offering were in a step decline. Several sources verified this was happening.

In 1984, for example, a study was conducted by the CDE on the effects of Senate Bill 813 graduation requirements on vocational education. They found there had been consistent declines in vocational education enrollments, full-time teachers and average daily attendance beginning in 1981. Enrollments were declining at the rate of about eight percent per year, compared to total high school enrollments of about one percent per year. In a separate report to Superintendent Honig in December of 1984, Barbara Price reported that she had found a decline in enrollments and vocational course offerings in 60 of 68 districts she had interviewed. The decline in vocational education was confirmed again in1989. The Department conducted an analysis of enrollment and course offering in vocational education and found the number of vocational education classes had declined 33 percent from 1981-1988, course enrollment down 44 percent, and the number of full time equivalent vocation education teachers down 50 percent.

To understand the decline in vocational education in the 1980s, one needs to look at all of the contributing factors and vocational education's response to the negative influences on its program.

Impact of Educational Reforms

California reform efforts got underway in 1983 shortly after the election of Bill Honig as Superintendent of Public Instruction with the passage of the Hughes-Hart Reform Act of 1983, SB 8 1 3. The Act increased high school graduation requirements to include:

- three years of English
- two years of mathematics
- three years of social studies
- two years of science
- one year visual or performing arts
- two years of P.E.

In addition to these requirements, it included an alternative means provision for students to meet graduation requirements. This provision was Section 51 225.3 (b) which states:

> *"The governing board, with the active involvement of parents, administrators, teachers, pupils, shall adopt alternative means for pupils to complete the prescribed course of study which may include practical demonstration of skills and competencies, supervised work experience or other outside school experience, vocational education classes offered in high schools, courses offered by regional occupational centers or programs, interdisciplinary study, independent study and credit earned at a postsecondary institution. Requirements for graduation and specified alternative modes for completing the prescribed course of study, hall be made available to pupils, parents, and the public."*

Efforts to provide leadership and support to implement this provision in law failed from the lack of support by the Superintendent. This was very disheartening to the vocational education community. Many had attended a 1986 statewide vocation education conference to hear the Superintendent speak where he spoke favorably about vocational education. In his speech, Bill Honig stated:

> *"Vocational education is a partner in the reform of high school education, that vocational education courses should receive academic graduation credit, and that the "applied" instructional methodology used in vocational education is an "excellent way" to learn academics."*

In addition, he emphasized the importance of vocational programs and student standards, rigor, course sequences, performance testing, and a "program approach" to vocational curriculum. This is what everyone in vocational education wanted to hear. However, actions in the CDE did not reflect Mr. Honig's words regarding the value and role that vocational education would play in the reform of education in California.

In 1986, the Association of California School Administrators, ACSA, issued three position statements on the impact of vocational education resulting from the passage and implementation of SB 813. The position statements were backed up with a rationale and appropriate citations from state statutes. The positions statement adopted were:

- Schools must offer sufficient courses in a variety of programs to allow parents and students the latitude to select a course of study that meets the individual student's long term educational goals.
- It is the unique function of education to prepare students with life and employment skills as well as other components of an educational program which address the needs of the vast majority of K-12 and adult students. Secondary and adult students in vocational education learn problem-solving, analytical, communication, and interpersonal skills in a practical application mode.
- Schools are responsible for providing a balanced curriculum and alternative methods of meeting graduation requirements. The appropriate school curriculum and graduation requirements must be determined by each local school board.

The California Business Roundtable, a supporter of the need for educational reforms was also a critic of how reform efforts were being managed. In a lengthy and detailed report prepared for the Business Roundtable by Berman, Weiler Associates in 1988, they let it be known the reforms were not necessarily going in the right direction. Here are a couple excerpts that are examples of their critique of the reforms initiated in SB 813:

> *California education has reached an historic turning point. The public school system is not on the verge of collapse. On the contrary in has shown some improvement. But will the current approaches to improving the system enable public education to keep pace with future needs at a price that society can effort?*

> *The improvement strategy depends heavily on putting more money into the existing system. The financial implications or relying on this approach is staggering. At best, then, an improvement strategy might increase student performance to a level at or slightly above the national average, or the average of comparable Eastern industrial states. However, this level is simply too low to the meet the challenges of the future.*

> *California may no longer have an educational system in constant crisis, but it will have a mediocre system in which students will perform far below their potential and increasing below levels attained in other countries.*

And there will continue to be a large, permanently underemployed, large-ly illiterate underclass dependent on welfare, and crime, along with many entry-level employees in need of costly remedial training. The financial and social burden to society and business of continuing this ineffectual approach to education has never been fully calculated.

In December of 1987, prior to public distribution of their report, Paul Berman spoke to CACVE. He noted the business community was very concerned about future labor shortages that would be fueled by ill prepared graduates and fewer young workers entering the labor market. He stated that it would easier for students to get a job if they had specific job skills, computer competence, as well as basic skills. He suggested there was a need to restructure education where by all students would have mastered basic academic skills by the tenth grade. At this point, students would be given a choice of the schooling they would receive for the remaining two years. Some could choose to attend schools that specialize in vocational education, college preparation, art, or even attend the community college or university. Within the school structure, various instructional methods and techniques should be utilized to address the different ways by which students learn their basic academic core subjects. Some students learn by doing and others in intellectual settings. He also suggested that some form of competency testing including practical demonstration of skill should be utilized at the completion of the tenth grade. Testing would help assess where the students was academically and should not be used for educational placement. Additionally, greater flexibility was needed. In many ways, he said, vocational education had a better model for instruction than did the academic programs.

Vocational Education's Role in Educational Reforms Impeded

Very quickly it appeared to vocational educators that every means to discourage implementation of the alternative means provision in law were underway internally in the CDE. Staff in the Curriculum and Instructional Leadership Branch of the CDE were directed by Deputy Superintendent, Dr. Jim Smith, that vocational education courses could not serve as alternatives for academic subject requirements. Dr. Smith was second in command in the CDE. Pressure was immediately brought to bear from the educational community throughout the state. It caused the CDE to modify their policy. The CDE conceded that, in "some cases," vocational education courses/subjects "could" provide partial credit for academic requirements. In no case, however, would they allow "one-for-one" credit.

On January 29, 1990, Deputy Superintendent Smith informed the vocational education staff that no vocational education course could receive academic credit in the Investment in High School Initiative underway in the CDE. This directive placed an insurmountable barrier in the way of vocational education's participation as a full partner in the CDE's high school reform and restructuring initiatives. To ensure this directive would not be circumvented, the Commission On Teacher Credentialing staff was lobbied by the CDE staff to institute policies which would prevent vocational education teachers from teaching subjects for which academic credit was received by students. The CDE's efforts were not all that successful. Some vocational education teachers opted to return to the private sector when their programs were eliminated. However, many vocational teachers already had credentials which allowed them to teach other subjects in the high school. They were reassigned by school districts to teach math, science, etc. and performed successfully. There is no evidence to show they were not successful.

In addition, State University and University of California system officials were also urged by the CDE to resist accepting any vocational education courses satisfying A-F college entrance requirements - even though many vocational education courses contain more rigor and meaningful content than some of the academic courses that were accepted by the University. The agriculture interests immediately mobilized and secured support from the faculty at the State University system and the University of California to support the acceptance of vocational agriculture classes for science credit. However, over time other vocational education subject area classes were accepted once vocational education became familiar with the criteria used for course approval used by the University of California and State University systems.

The University of California and State University systems were most helpful in this regard. The University of California, for example, recognizes:

> *"that many schools are guided by the reform initiatives that encourage the integration of academic and career-related content for courses that are both rigorous and relevant. These rigorous applied academic courses may be approved by UC if teachers focus on the academic content, using the career-related content as an application and extension of the core*

> *knowledge taught in the academic area."* (California Advisory Council on Vocational Education 15th Annual Report, 1983)

Vocational classes which emphasize applied science and math applications have generally found it easy to satisfy the course approval requirements.

The University of California has taken an interest in how well students taking courses which emphasized an applied approach to teaching basic academic skills compared to the traditional academic classes. Several studies have been undertaken by the University and to no surprise to vocational education, students who were products of an integrated applied curriculum in high school did better than students in a the traditional academic program. In a controlled research setting involving two groups of students, academic performance was measured. The results found:

> *"While the academic performance of the two groups of students did not differ significantly, their attitudes, motivations and confidence in their ability did. There was not a statistically significant mean difference between the integrated and traditional samples on the percentage of change between the pre-and post-test scores. However, the student expectations survey did reveal some affective differences between the students in the two samples. Mean differences favored the integrated teaching style, with t-test significant at the .05 level for students 'perceived ability factor and for the item of students being, excited about the lesson. Overall interest in the subject was significantly higher for the students in the integrated course. When students asked if they felt the lesson was more interesting and relevant to their future, those taught in the more integrated way had significantly higher mean scores."* (California Advisory Council on Vocational Education 15th Annual Report, 1983)

Early indications in the other University studies are finding the same results. Students were more motivated and excited about their lessons taught in an applied setting. Also, they could see the applications had a relationship to their future.

Model Curriculum Standards Development

A glimmer of hope that the CDE would implement curriculum standards was noted early in the reform efforts in 1984. The CDE initiated a process to define the role of vocational education within the context of SB 8 13. A planning document was developed to aid in the discussion. The focus of the document was on:

- Comprehensive career guidance services beginning in the early grades ending with placement and follow-up;
- Competency-based vocational education curriculum including a core curriculum which could be utilized to deliver basic academic skills;
- Work experience.

In support of this effort, Senator Gary Hart included $10 million in SB 786 for vocational education curriculum development. The bill passed but was vetoed by the Governor. In 1984, Assemblywoman Marion Bergeson introduced ACR 93 which requested the CDE to develop curriculum standards for vocational education consistent with graduation requirements and to determine (a) if the vocational education needs of students were being met, and (b) the effects of graduation requirements on vocational education. A report was to be prepared by January 1, 1986, by the CDE and submitted to the Legislature. After searching the State Archives, contacting the History Clerk of the Assembly and reviewing CDE records, nothing could be found indicating such a report was submitted. An ACR has no power of law. If an agency decides it doesn't want to respond, it is not obligated to do so.

In 1991, the Legislature modified Section 5 1226 of the Education Code regarding the development of Model Curriculum Standards:

> *The Superintendent of Public Instruction shall coordinate the development, on a cyclical basis, of model curriculum standards for the course of study required in Section 51225.3 and for a vocational education course of study necessary to assist school districts with complying with subdivision (b) of Section 51228 ...*
>
> *The superintendent shall, to the extent applicable, incorporate the integration of vocational and academic education into the development of curriculum standards for vocational education courses. The standards for vocational education course of study shall be adopted by May 1, 1991.*

Section 51228 is of equal importance. It was adopted in 1983 and amended in 1986. It pertains to the demonstration of competencies. The most pertinent sections of this provision are:

> *(b) Any school district which adopts a required curriculum that meets or exceeds the model standards adopted by the State Board of Education pursuant to Section 51226 shall be deemed to have fulfilled its responsibilities pursuant to this section. (c) Any school district which adopts a required curriculum pursuant to subdivision (c) that meets or exceeds the*

> *model standards development the State Board of Education pursuant to Section 51226, or which adopts alternative means for pupils to complete the prescribed course of study pursuant to subdivision (b) of Section 51 225.3, may substitute pupil demonstration of competence in the prescribed subjects through a practical demonstration of these skills in a regional occupational center or program, work experience, interdisciplinary study, independent study, credit earned at a postsecondary institution, or other outside school experience, as prescribed in Section 51225.*

Although the development of Model Curriculum Standards for vocational education was assigned a low priority in the CDE's Publications Unit, the vocational education staff had initiated development of standards in 1985. They were the first Division in the CDE to develop model curriculum standards for each of the vocational subject matter areas.

The standards were submitted for review, editing, and publication in 1986-87. The process of preparing them for publication proceeded into 1991 at which time they were withdrawn by the State Director of Vocational Education, Jim Allison. In excess of $300,000 had been expended at this point in time. The documents were withdrawn at a time when legislation was being considered to modify Section 51226 to require publishing the vocational education curriculum standards. The CDE had testified to the Legislature that it was in the process of printing and publishing the Vocational Education Model Curriculum Standards and Frameworks and there was no need for the legislation. The Legislature found this not to be true, so the statute passed and was signed by the Governor.

Although the Model Curriculum Standards for vocational education have yet to be adopted by the State Board of Education all have been published. These include:

- Home Economics Education Career Path Guide and Model Curriculum Standards, 1994.
- Business Education Career Path and Model Curriculum Standards, 1995.
- Industrial and Technology Education Career Path Guide and Model Curriculum Standards, 1996.
- Health Career Education 2000: A Program Guide, 1998.

Agriculture elected to publish and disseminate their model curriculum standards through a contract with University of California at Davis. All agriculture teachers have been in-serviced on the use of the model curriculum standards. Agriculture was one of the first vocational education subject matter areas to get their standards into the schools and used. This was very beneficial as agriculture has been very successful in getting its courses approved to meet A-F requirements. The CDE presented model curriculum standards for vocational education to the State Board of Education for adoption in 2002.

Vocational-Technical Management Advisory Committee

In order to alleviate growing concerns that vocational education was being excluded in the educational reforms, Superintendent Honig appointed an advisory committee. Representation on the committee included superintendents, vocational education directors, and business and industry representatives. The Committee was chaired by Dr. Norm Eisen, Superintendent of Whittier Union High School District. As a former work experience coordinator, Dr. Eisen was respected by the vocational community.

At their February 27, 1985, meeting the topic of "academics and vocational education" was discussed. Superintendent Honig outlined five areas he considered important to the committees discussion:

1. Academics are vocational education, at least in part. It is necessary to talk about a strong academic program even when you are referring to the non-college bound; most vocational educators agreed with this statement.

2. Vocational education courses should be available and supplemental to skill development. Typically, what happens at the high school site is that the vocational educator does not coordinate plans and activities with other faculty.

3. Vocational education courses need standards comparable to the model curriculum standards just developed.

4. Educators need to focus on the stronger components of vocational education such as ROCP, office skills, clusters, vocational agriculture, rather than the industrial arts and homemaking. Where should we put our resources?

5. Magnet schools, i.e., "fame schools," are an important solution to the problem of vocational education. There needs to be a shift from specific technical training to generic skills training with strong academics hooked into the program.

The committee met the better part of a year and made a number of recommendations to Superintendent Honig. Early in February of 1986, they offered 15 recommendations in response to the charge given to them by Honig. The recommendations provided detailed suggestions on how to approach the issues identified by the committee that needed attention by the Superintendent. Some of the recommendations included in the committee's report included:

1. Elimination of Unnecessary Duplication. Steps should be taken to eliminate unnecessary duplication that currently exists in the various components of vocational education. In many areas of the state, there are several providers, proximately located, with costly facilities duplication effort, competing for students, while providing identical vocational education functions. Area articulation and coordination committees should be formed to identify primary and secondary responsibilities for the components of a comprehensive vocational education delivery system. The CDE should adopt a State Model for delivery of vocational education. Area articulation and coordination committees should review, revise as appropriate, and implement the model in order to make efficient use of the dollars available for vocational education. The committee should use local educational agencies' vocational education plans as a basis for making delineation of function decisions.

2. Vocational Courses Reinforcing Basic Academics. Local school districts and ROCPs are encouraged to review the curriculum in their vocational education offerings, and determine what courses provide an opportunity for students to acquire and reinforce their basic academics, meet graduation requirements, and obtain necessary employability skills...vocational education and basic academics should not be viewed as competitive or alternative learning, but rather as complementary learning. There are many opportunities, particularly for the non-college bound youngster, to obtain basic academic skills in an applied manner through vocational education. Basic academic education requirements have been written as competencies and published in the state model curriculum standards, Vocational education courses have also been devised in terms of competencies. Provisions should be made for students who successfully complete these courses to

be awarded the appropriate academic credit toward meeting graduation requirements.

3. Employability Skills. All educational agencies are urged to emphasize employability skills throughout the curriculum and the co-curriculum. Employability skills considered very important for entry-level positions include attitudes, abilities, and behaviors associated with a sense of responsibility, self-discipline, pride, team work, and enthusiasm. Employers also put a high value upon ability to learn, ability to change, and problem-solving skills.

4. Criteria for Standards. The CDE should recommend standards and criteria for vocational education as models for implementation by local school districts. Vocational education standards and criteria have been a major issue among vocational educators in California. A variety of standards and criteria have been developed; however, none have been accepted by all facets of the vocational education community.

5. Statewide Performance Indicators. The following indicators of performance should be considered for adoption as an integral part of the "statewide report card program." (a) The number of vocational education courses approved by the local school board to meet state graduation requirements. State graduation requirements are those specified in SB 813. (b) The number of students who have completed a vocational education program. A vocational education program is a planned sequence of academic and vocational courses that prepare students for graduation, entry into identified occupations, and/or advanced training. (c) The number of students who have completed a community-based vocational education course. Community-based courses are those which allow students to experience real job situations in the community and strengthen partnerships between business/industry and education.

6. Teacher Training. The CDE is urged to work closely with California University system and other institutions of higher education to train new vocational education teachers and in-service present ones.

7. Articulation with Community Colleges. In an effort to maintain appropriate roles, eliminate duplication of services, and operate in a cost effective manner, every effort should be

made to articulate vocational education programs with the community colleges. For instance, institutions serving vocational students are urged to plan and implement such cooperative programs as the 2 + 2.

Following the submission of the committee's recommendations, Dr. Eisen met privately with Superintendent Honig and urged him to implement the committee's recommendations. The committee was disbanded shortly thereafter and minimal action was taken on the recommendations.

Model High School Report Card

Vocational education hasn't fared well in other CDE's reform efforts. Several examples can be cited. Vocational education was all but excluded in the Model High School Report Card. The Model Report Card was developed by Superintendent Honig to give to school districts a vehicle to inform the public on the success of their educational efforts. There were no meaningful criteria included for vocational education outcomes in the model report card guide provided to school districts.

In addition, the CDE created a school assessment procedure that favored programs that conformed to the State Model Graduation Requirements adopted by the State Board of Education, as opposed to those found in state law. These involved the use of "Quality Indicators." This included measurements such as California Assessment Program scores, the number of students taking college preparation courses, attendance rates, etc. These were all combined in a Performance Report. Each school then received a percentile rank of its performance-and thus an indication of its "educational quality" in relation to other schools in the state. The quality indicators generally reflected college preparation and did not give weight to vocational education courses. This had a direct impact on what programs were selected at the local level by school districts to meet state graduation requirements.

Vocational education was also excluded from participating in the utilization of Educational Technology funds to develop state-level initiatives to strengthen the use of technology in the classroom. Vocational business education courses had already made strides in the use of technology in their curriculum, and would have benefited from the additional financial support.

About the same time as Senate Bill 813 was passed the State Board of Education unanimously approved new State graduation requirements guidelines in their publication "Raising Expectations: Model Graduation Requirements." The intent of the model requirements was to improve the quality of education in California. It added more to the requirements for graduation than SB 813. Table 6 shows the difference between SB 813 and the suggested requirements in the Model approved by the State Board of Education.

A majority of school districts changed their graduation requirements to meet the mandates of the law. A few elected to incorporate the objectives and course content in the Board Model. Some Districts even added their own requirements. This had a direct impact on the retention and availability of vocational education classes in the high school.

Table 6.
A Comparison of State Board of Education Model Graduation Requirements and SB 8 13 Graduation Requirements

State Board of Education Model			Senate Bill 813	
Subject Area		Required	Subject Area	Required
Computer Studies		1 Semester		
English		4 Years	English	3 Years
Foreign Language		2 years in the same language	Fine Arts/Foreign Language Visual or Performing Arts/or Foreign Language	1 Years
Mathematics Algebra 1 Geometry District option	1st year at least	3 years	Mathematics	3 Years
Natural Sciences Science I (Physical-Earth Science I (Life)	1 Year	3 Years	Science Biological Physical	2 Years

Social Sciences World Civilizations: History, Geography and Culture U.S.: Ideals, Institutions and Traditions, Individual Rights and Civic Responsibilities; I Political, legal, and ethical perspectives II Economics	1 Years 1 Year 1 Semester 1 Semester	3 Years	Social Studies U.S. History, Geography, World History, Culture Geography and American Government, Civics, Economics	3 Years
Visual and Performing Arts		1 Years		
Physical Education		2 Years	Physical Education	2 Years

*Amended by Chapter 1753, Statutes of 1984 (Assembly Bill 3212)

Computer Studies

In 1983, the State Board of Education adopted a computer studies curriculum course which could be utilized to satisfy the one semester course requirement in the Model Graduation Requirements adopted the Board. The course was developed by a Consultant at the University of California at Davis under the direction of Dr. Jim Smith and the Curriculum and Instruction Leadership Branch. A draft of the model curriculum standards were circulated for public comment. The draft suggested that computers belonged in all academic and vocational areas of the school. Yet, there was a total lack of specific reference to occupational goals in the draft document. The document also stated that the ultimate application of the computer was to program them and that all students should learn the fundamentals of computer programming.

Within the Vocational Education and Adult Education Divisions in the CDE, business education had developed, with the assistance of the private sector, a computer education curriculum guide which identified various competencies associated with computer use. These competencies ranged from the very basic understanding of the computer or computer literacy level, to direct applications as they related to employment. The guide did not address computer programming because it was a very low job demand area.

It was very apparent that there was very little interface between the CDE Divisions. This was brought to the attention of the State Board of Education prior to their adoption of the computer education standards. Board member Angie Papadakis forcefully raised the issue before the Board and the draft was circulated to the Business Education Unit for review. Following the review by Business Education, which offered a number of specific additions to the draft standards, no substantive changes were made and it was adopted by the State Board of Education.

Proficiency Tests

In 1980, the Legislature had added another requirement which possibly had a greater impact when coupled with the new graduation requirements. It pertains to the passing of basic skills. This is contained in Section 5 141 2 of the Education Code. The Code states:

> *"No diploma, certificate or other documents, except transcripts and letters of recommendation, shall be conferred on a pupil as evidence of completion of a prescribed course of study or training, or of satisfactory attendance, unless such pupil has the standards of proficiency in basic skills prescribed by the governing board of the high school district, or equivalent thereof pursuant to Article 2.5 (commencing with Section 5121 5) of Chapter 2. "*

Students who do not pass basic skills tests must receive remediation, which usually means taking the course again during the next school year or going to summer school in order to pass the proficiency test. In 1984, it was reported the number of students failing proficiency tests varied from twenty-four to as high as sixty-one percent, depending on grade level.

For some students, repeated failure in passing proficiency tests led them to dropping out of school. U.S. Department of Education data indicated that 31.3% of California students who entered the ninth-graders failed to graduate by their senior year in 1982. A California report, Conditions of Education in California 1984 found:

> *"California's high school dropout rate increasingly exceeds the national average. This is not simply because the state's proportion of dropout-prone, e.g., limited English speaking students, is higher than the nation-*

> *al average. It is also the case in California that above average percentages of white, middle class, suburban, and female students do not complete high school. ...the most common reason California students give for dropping out include poor grades, a felling that 'school was not for me, 'pregnancy, and choosing to work. "*

There was a sense of urgency among vocational educators in the early 1980s as they saw a steady decline in vocational education enrollments. It was evident to them that the "quest for excellence" as exemplified in California's reform movement was causing students to be disenchanted with school. Vocational education had long served to attract students who would otherwise drop out. Research supported their assumption. A 1983 study entitled *"Vocational Education and the High School Dropout"* using survey data from a nationally representative sample found that:

> *"participation in vocation in vocational education clearly is one of several elements that can help retain students who otherwise would leave school. "*

In 1985, the National Commission on Secondary Vocational Education published a report: *"The Unfinished Agenda-The Role of Vocational Education in the High School."* It analyzed the mission of secondary schools and, in particular, the role and function of vocational education. The Commission raised a very serious concern that reforms to increase academic achievement did not take into account individual differences and needs of students. The Report said:

> *"Recent criticisms of our secondary schools have documented growing deficiencies in the academic preparation of students. Many states have responded to these criticisms by increasing the number of academic courses required for high school graduation. The assumption is that more academics, which may be the best preparation for college, is also the best preparation for life. This assumption is wrong. The response by the states... ignores differences in student interests and abilities, and it ignores the needs of those high school students who do not plan to go to college and who purposefully chose a vocational program. "*

The report further notes that there is the tendency of secondary schools to over-value college preparation despite the fact that roughly eighty percent of all American jobs to not require a college degree, and most students will not obtain one. The statistics on high school completion have not changed dramatically over the years. In the 1960s, approximately 70 % of the students entering high school were graduating. Four of the seven (57%) went to college but only two received a four year degree. By 1993, the number of students graduating from high school had increased to roughly 75 %. Forty-two percent went on to higher education. Of these, 17% graduated in 4 years, another 4% took longer, 21 % received a certificate or AA/AS degree, but 58% never finished college. In California and the nation, approximately 13% of the population are graduates of a four-year institution.

By the mid 1990's, educational reforms changed direction with greater emphasis given to accountability and testing student outcomes in basic skills. However, there was a glimmer of hope that vocational education would be considered as federal policy began to focus on strategies to transition students from school-to-work. These will be discussed further on the review.

Credentials and Teacher Training

As previously noted, many vocational teachers do not enter the teaching profession through the academic route with a degree from a four-year institution of higher education. They come from business and industry and require specialized instruction on how organize themselves to be able to teach a vocational education course or program. These teachers are primarily trade and technical education, health, and ROCP teachers.

With the passage of Proposition 13 in 1978, nearly half of the secondary vocational teachers left the profession or took other assignments in the school districts. Consequently, many of the teacher training institutions that were preparing teachers saw their enrollments begin to decline. In 1988, AB 1725 (Vasconcellos) eliminated credentials for community college teachers. The Board of Governors of the California Community Colleges was given the authority to issue credentials based on regulations adopted by the Board. No longer were vocational teachers in the community colleges required to meet the same requirements as their counterparts in the K-12 system. This had a major impact on vocational education teacher preparation programs. Over time, many of the vocational education teacher training programs were eliminated from the colleges.

There remains a demand for teacher preparation primarily for part-time adult teachers and for ROCP teachers who begin teaching with a single subjects teaching credential. Under state law, any local educational agency, LEA, may offer a program for these teachers. A LEA may be a school district, county office, or a four-year institution of higher education. The teachers receive a preliminary credential to begin teaching but are required to complete a minimum of 12 units of instruction in teaching methods and one unit in health over a two to three year period of time. The number of units taken depends on an evaluation of their professional and work experience. Under state law, educational credits can be granted for work experience. Upon completion of these requirements, they are granted a clear credential and are only required to participate in continuing education classes as are all other teachers-150 clock hours every five years. Some of these vocational teachers continue their education and eventually earn a college degree.

Legislative Support Sought. In 1990, Assemblywoman Doris Allen, introduced AB 847. The bill was introduced at the request of a coalition of vocational education teacher associations and the Vocational Education Alliance (VOCAL). The Act added Sections 52910 through 52913 to the Education Code which declared:

> *"That it is in the best interest of the state to provide all students with a cohesive and well articulated system of career-vocational preparation and occupational training which prepares students for roles as family members and community members, leaders and productive workers. The Legislature finds that Education Code 51225.3(b) is currently being under utilized by school districts."*

> *"That students in California's public schools face inadequate access to quality career and vocational preparation and occupational training programs, and declares that providing high quality curriculum and instruction in this area is a high priority of the state. The Legislature believes that all students should be prepared with basic job entry skills at the completion of his or her schooling. The Legislature declares that a student's pursuit of career-vocational preparation programs in secondary school and his or her satisfaction of the admission required necessary for baccalaureate postsecondary education should not be mutually exclusive."*

The bill defined applied academics and funding to provide grants to school districts who wish to develop and implement the provisions of the statute. Initially, $1.5 million was included in the bill for implementation. The bill signed by Governor stated that funding, to the extent made possible, would come from the Budget Act. No funds were appropriated.

In 1988, 1989, and 1990, VOCAL involved Senator Seymour who introduced legislation that would have provided $25 million for school districts to implement the alternative means provisions of SB 8 13. Two bills were introduced and both failed passage.

In 1990, VOCAL got Assemblywoman Allen to introduce AB 1953, titled: *Pilot Projects in Applied Academic Areas and Programs.* The statute, found in Sections 52980 through 52983, mandated the CDE to select six school districts to pilot test the development of alternative means whereby students could meet academic graduation requirements through their participation in applied academic areas and programs as specified in the alternative means provisions of state law. The districts were to be given a one-time grant, not to exceed $30,000, to administer the pilot projects. AB 1953 directed the CDE to award two grants of $30,000 to large school districts, two grants of $25,000 to medium school districts, and two grants of $20,000 to small school districts. The districts were to report to the CDE by November 30, 1993 on the efforts to implement the provisions of AB 1953.

The statute followed the procedures already outlined in law on how to implement the alternative means provision. In addition, it defined what applied academic programs were; it specifically named them as:

> *"the vocational education subject areas of agriculture, business and office education, marketing, consumer an homemaking education, health careers, home economics related occupations, industrial arts, technical trade, and industrial education and methodologies, including but not limited to, work experience, cooperative vocational education, and community classroom. "*

Concerned that the Superintendent and State Board of Education had not adopted model curriculum standards for vocational education, AB 1953 also added this language to Section 51226:

> *"The Superintendent shall, to the extent applicable, incorporate the integration of vocational and academic education into the development of curriculum standards for vocational education courses. The standards for vocational education course of study shall be adopted no later than May 1, 1991."*

A search was done in the CDE to ascertain how successful the provisions of AB 1953 were implemented. There were no records that show that $150,000 was granted to six school districts to test the alternative means provision of SB 813. Also, as previously noted, it was determined that the model curriculum standards for vocational education had not been adopted by the May 1, 1991 deadline given by the Legislature.

Integration of Academic and Vocational Education. What goes around comes around. In the 1970s, efforts were made to implement the Career Education Model proposed by the Commissioner of Education, Sidney P. Marland. The model utilized a curricular strategy for infusing vocational skills and applications throughout the entire school curriculum, K-12, and continuing through the adult years. The U.S. Office of Education designed the career education program around fifteen occupational clusters into which all occupations could be conceptually subsumed. A comparison of the 2000-2004 State Plan for Career-Technical Education clusters strategy to the Career Education clusters is shown in Table 7.

In the 1970s, the U.S. Office of Education proposed that elementary school children be exposed to all fifteen clusters when they were developing an awareness to the world of work, that they choose a narrower, more circumscribed focus on fewer clusters for deeper exploration in junior high school, and that they select and train in an occupation at the senior high school level or beyond.

Career education was described as a continuing process of making work possible, meaningful, and satisfying to the individual, gave special attention to assisting persons as they move toward vocational education maturity, and the choice (and likely re-choosing) of a primary work role.

Table 7.
A Comparison of Career Education and State Plan Clusters

Career Education Clusters*	State Plan Clusters**
Agriculture and natural resources	Agriculture and natural resources
Business and office	Business and finance
Construction	Building trades and construction
Communications and media	Arts, media, and entertainment technology
Consumer and homemaking education	
Environmental control	Energy and utilities
Fine arts and humanities	

Career Education Clusters*	State Plan Clusters**
Health	Health services
Hospitality and recreation	Hospitality, tourism, and recreation
Manufacturing	Manufacturing and product development
Marine Science	
Marketing and distribution	Retail and wholesale trade
Personal services	
Transportation	Transportation
	Fashion and interior design
Public services	Public services
	Engineering
	Public and private education services
	Information technology

* Source: Ken Hoyt, (1972) Career Education: What It is and How to Do It

** Source: 2000-2004 State Plan for Vocational Education

Vocational maturation was pictured as occurring in growth stages. In sequential order they were:

1. Awareness of primary work roles played by persons in society;

2. Exploration of work roles that an individual might consider as important, possible and probable for himself or herself;

3. Vocational decision making (which may go from a highly tentative to a very specific form);

4. Establishment (including preparing for and actually assuming a primary work role);

5. Maintenance (all of the ways in which one gains-or fails to gain-personal meaningfulness and satisfaction from the primary work role he or she has assumed).

The most recent State effort to implement educational reforms focus around the interrelationships found in the existing career-vocational education model curriculum standards, Tech Prep programs, and other initiatives underway by the CDE. These initiatives include efforts to implement the CDE initiative, Second-to-None, the Partnership Academies, and the U.S. Department of Education sponsored New American High School initiative. The underlying supposition is that vocational and technical education, if it is to be successful, must be an integral part of state and local reform efforts.

The integration of academic and vocational education model proposed in the 2000-2004 State Plan for Vocational and Technical Education is a composite of successful models reviewed by the CDE. The CDE model includes the following features:

- An integrated program of learning that combines basic academic and career related content;
- Interdisciplinary course work that connects basic academics to a career-related or work-related context;
- Articulated course work that spans the educational segments and is sequentially more challenging;
- Substantial support from partners (especially business and higher education) beyond the school setting

Accordingly, these approaches are to help students not only to understand the importance of mastering academic content in order to prepare for career selection and entry, but also to prepare for postsecondary education opportunities throughout the student's working life. The CDE has configured such an approach into a continuum format which is shown in Table 8.

Table 8.
Integrated Academic and Career-Related Education Continuum

Career Awareness	Career Exploration	Career Orientation	Career Preparation
Interdisciplinary activities based on 10 common elements	Interdisciplinary activities based on 10 common elements, plus work-based explorations (guided study tours, service learning, community service).	Interdisciplinary activities based on 10 common elements, plus work-based experience (job shadowing, mentoring, service learning	Career-specific content including 10 common elements, plus work-based learning (internships, cooperative education).
Industry sector context	Industry sector context	Industry sector/ Cluster context	Career-specific content
	CTAP* portfolio assessment	CTAP portfolio and ACE** Core assessment	CTA/ACE Career-specific assessment

*CTAP –Career Technical Assessment Program (locally administered)
**ACE-Assessment in Career Education (available statewide, scored by the State)

In a comprehensive approach, students are first introduced to career awareness activities in early school years. Then, they are more directly engaged in interdisciplinary work-related career exploration activities in the middle school and early high school. The next step involves more direct involvement with interdisciplinary career orientation activities that might include mentoring and job shadowing before the final step of the sequence-actual enrollment in specific career preparation, cooperative education, and internships. Actual job preparation does not occur until the 11th and 12th grade. This approach assumes no one drops out of school. For those students who drop out of school, they have no choice by to seek other routes to employment and a career.

The ten common elements referenced on the continuum are industry skills and knowledge elements necessary for success within any career or occupation. These include:

1. Leadership and teamwork

2. Ethical and legal practices

3. Employability skills

4. Career development

5. Technology literacy

6. Safety and health issues

7. Critical thinking and problem solving

8. Interpersonal skills

9. Communications

10. Systems

Every student, regardless of his or her goals, would benefit from attaining this set of basic skills and knowledge. According the 2000-2004 State Plan for Vocational and Technical Education, these elements are embedded into academic content through integrated activities and projects offered in collaboration with vocational and technical education programs, business and industry partners, and career-specific education segment partners.

The fifteen industry clusters identified by the CDE were selected based on the following criteria. Each industry sector:

- Has an identifiable industry connection within the sector
- Offers at least 100 individual job titles
- Has a core content of at least 7 standards
- Offers high employment opportunity
- Has a high growth potential
- Provides for work-based learning opportunities

The U.S. Department of Education has identified 16 career clusters that have been crosswalked with those selected by California, which is essential for reporting annual results to federal authorities. Finally, the industry clusters have been matched to the traditional five-subject matter areas generally identified with vocational education. The cluster approach expands the career options for students. The clusters have been grouped in six broad categories that clearly match the five existing vocational and technical education programs. The addition of the sixth subject matter area, "art, media and entertainment technology," incorporates career preparation for one of the state's highest growth industries. The six industry sector groupings are shown on Table 9.

Table 9.
Vocational and Technical Programs and Industry Sectors

Agriculture Education	Business & Marketing Education	Health & Human Services
Agriculture & Natural Resources	Business and finance	Health Services
	Information Technology	Public and Private Education Services
	Retail and Wholesale Trade	Public Services
Home Economics & Careers in Technology	**Industrial & Technology Education**	**Arts, Media & Entertainment Technology**
Hospitality, Tourism, & Recreation	Engineering and Design	
Public and Private Education Services	Manufacturing & Product Development	
	Transportation	

California Occupational Information System

As previously noted, vocational education and job training efforts are required to utilize employment projections so training efforts match needs. California had initiated an effort to develop a Manpower Information System in the early 1970s. Federal law addressed this need very specifically in 1976. Section 161 (b) of Title II of the Vocational Educational Amendments of 1976 states:

> *"By September 30, 1977, each State receiving assistance under this Act and under the Comprehensive Employment and Training Act of 1973 shall establish a State occupational information coordinating committee composed of representatives of the State board, the State Employment Security Agency, the State Manpower Services Council, and the agency administering the vocational rehabilitation program. This committee shall. with funds available to it from the National Occupational Infor-*

mation Coordinating Committee established pursuant to paragraph (I), implement an occupational information system in the State which will meet the common needs for the planning for, and the operation of programs of the State board assisted under this act and the administering agencies under the Comprehensive Employment and Training Act of 1973."

The California Occupational Information Coordinating Committee (COICC) was established through an interagency agreement pursuant to the California Five-Year Plan for Vocational Education. In the agreement, the CDE, Chancellor's Office of the California Community College, Employment Development Department, California Employment and Training Council, and Department of Rehabilitation agreed that the COICC would include a representative from each of the organizations. The agreement also specified that COICC would assume responsibility for directing the design, development, and implementation of the California Manpower Information System (CMMIS), which would serve as the occupational information system required in federal law. CMMIS was an outgrowth of research activities beginning in 1971 previously discussed. Other provisions of the agreement included that the system:

    a. would develop occupational demand and supply data based on uniform definitions and procedures established by the National Occupational Information Coordinating Committee (NOICC);

    b. would conform to the regulations and procedures established by NOICC; and,

    c. would be designed to meet the common needs for occupational information data at the participating agencies.

It began meeting in July, 1977. It officially became the State Occupational Information Coordinating Committee required under federal law on November 1, 1977, when a NOICC/COICC agreement was signed.

In September, 1978, AB 2020 was signed into law and became effective January 1, 1979. It added a new section entitled California Occupational Information System to the Education Code. Section 8122 states that:

"The California Occupational Information System is hereby designed as the official state program for the production of occupational planning,

administration and guidance information for use by vocational educators, education and training planners, students, and counselors. "

Section 8123 named the agencies previously represented on the COICC and added the Council for Private Postsecondary Educational Institutions. It went on to say that the representatives of the six agencies:

" .. .*shall cooperate jointly as the State Occupational Information Committee (thereafter referred to as the* SOICC) *to develop and implement the California Information System. The SOICC shall consult with other potential users of the system to maximize the collection of data and the development of a uniform system that can be used to the greatest extent feasible.* "

The COICC had a very rocky start. The Director of Occupational Education in the Ventura County Superintendent of Schools Office, John Van Zant, was named COICC Executive Director. He had previously served as Project Director for earlier CMMIS efforts. CMMIS staff became COICC staff. Funds were provided to the Ventura County Superintendent of Schools Office through grants and contracts from the CDE which served as the fiscal agent for COICC. In June of 1979 the Chief of the Employment Data and Research (ED&R) Division, EDD, Robert Hotchkiss, was elected COICC Chairperson. In September the Ventura County Superintendent of Schools, Dr. Jim Cowan, was sent a Standard Contract Agreement to provide COICC/COIS services covering the NOICC grant for October 1, 1979 to September 30, 1980. He returned the agreement to the CDE unsigned, noting that his office was no longer interested in serving as the COICC/COIS contractor. He further noted that there had been a continuing deterioration of working relationships between the people employed by his office to serve as COICC staff and the ED&R staff Also, since cooperation between ED&R and the COICC staff did not exist and the project director (COICC Executive Director) was leaving to accept another position, it was necessary to discontinue serving as contractor on the project.

There were a number of other projects or portions of projects completed by COICC staff at Ventura. Some of these activities were supported by NOICC for specific NOICC work, not COICC work. Other activities were funded by the National Center for Education Statistics (a project related to the Vocational Education Data System), and by the CDE from federal Vocational Education Act funds. At the time the work was assumed to be COICC work since it was related, one way or another, to COIS. Subsequently, however, COICC did not accept the resulting projects as COICC work, considering them instead as education products.

In November of 1979 CACVE undertook a study of the COIS and found many technical and organization problems and barriers existed which made progress on a state system difficult. The study was conducted under contract with Educational Evaluation and Research. The study was completed in April, 1 980. The study findings included:

- Considerable research efforts have been made by the Employment Development Department, Department of Education, and Chancellor's Office of the California Community Colleges necessary for the development of a state occupational information system. However, COIS has yet to disseminate any occupational planning, administration, and guidance information; and there is no written agreement that specifies each agency's role in disseminating COIS products.

- Although some efforts have been made to consult with other potential users of the system to maximize the collection of data and development of a uniform system, no systematic needs assessment has been conducted. Little contact has been made with the private sector or the California Postsecondary Education Commission.

- The reliability of supply data provided by the State Department of Education and Chancellor's Office is questionable. So far, no supply data are available from the Department of Rehabilitation. The state CETA Office has no authority over local prime sponsors so supply data are difficult to obtain.

It also found that there was a general confusion over what COICC and COIS staff should be doing and the role of the participating agencies. Even among agency and policy board representatives there were many different expectations in terms of the COICC purpose or function. The participating agencies attributed the confusion to the lack of clarity in the Education Code. The statutes did not specify who was responsible for assembling, compiling, and analyzing the information from the various agencies and delivering it to users. Further, there was confusion over what COIS should be, how it should operate, what the system should be producing and what it could produce. The study concluded that COIS was not yet a system, but rather a number of disjointed or separate computer programs that operate on a number of data bases.

The state statutes governing the COICC were repealed in 1983 and moved from the Education Code to the Unemployment Insurance Code (UI Code). The statutes were amended again. In 1990, SB1033 added the Department of Social Services to the COICC. The inclusion of Social Services into the process was due to their role in the placement of welfare recipients.

At its inception in 1976, the COICC functioned under the State Plan for Vocational Education, varying state laws and funding from NOICC--half coming from the U.S. Department of Education and half from the Department of Labor. This arrangement was troublesome for several reasons. First, there was the paperwork associated with two different funding sources. It was not an easy task. Second, the state was not always certain of federal funding of NOICC which was the source of funds for COICC. With the passage of the Carl D. Perkins Vocational and Technical Education Act of 1998, the requirements for a State Occupation Information Coordinating Committee were changed. Section 118 required the Governor and the agency administering the State Plan for Vocational Education to establish an entity in the state:

1. to provide support for career guidance and academic counseling programs designed to promote improved career and education decision making by individuals (especially in areas of career information delivery and use);
2. to make available to students, parents, teachers, administrators, and counselors, and to improve accessibility with respect to, information and planning resources that relate educational preparation to career goals and expectations;
3. to equip teachers, administrators, and counselors with knowledge and skills needed to assist students and parents with career exploration, educational opportunities, and educational financing;
4. to assist appropriate state entities in tailoring career-related educational resources and training for use by such entities;
5. to improve coordination and communication among administrators and planners of programs authorized by this Act and by section 15 of the Wagner-Pyser Act at the federal, state, and local levels to ensure non-duplication of efforts and appropriate use of shared information and data; and
6. to provide ongoing means for customers, such as students and parents, to provide comments and feedback on products

and services and to update resources, as appropriate, to better meet customer requirements.

In addition to changing the thrust of the statewide efforts to coordinate the use of information used in the planning and delivery of vocational education and job training programs, it placed both the authority and funding under the jurisdiction of one federal agency - the U.S. Department of Education. California was one of six states which elected to name the existing COICC as the entity to perform this function specified in Section 118 of the 1998 Carl D. Perkins Vocational and Technical Education Act.

This change in federal law was significant. It preserved the career development focus of NOICC and eliminated their charge to facilitate the development of an information system to match occupational supply with job demand in the states. For California, this solved the problem it was having in designing and implementing a comprehensive labor market and occupational supply and demand information system. The problem primarily centered on the inability of education and employment training programs to develop compatible systems to count the number of individuals enrolled and completing a specific occupation to match job needs for any given occupation. The reporting system for the K-12, for example, was different than the system used by the community colleges, which are in the higher education data collection system. Second, the demand side or the development of labor market information had improved significantly so that the information produced was fairly reliable for program planning purposes. However, the most important change was the emphasis given in statute on providing support for career guidance and academic counseling programs to improve career decision making by individuals.

At the same time Governor Pete Wilson had initiated an effort in June of 1994 to develop a School-to-Career Opportunities system through leadership of the State Job Training Coordinating Council. The Governor had given the Council his charge in Executive Order W-94-94 to implement a new federal act, the School-to-Work Opportunity Act. In the Executive Order, the Governor asked for recommendations on:

> *"policies, priorities) and a framework to establish a new school-to-career opportunities system that includes school-based learning, work-based learning, and support or connection activities that assist all students in meeting their career goals ... "*

The state had also initiated two very important provisions in law. The first is the State local Cooperative Labor Market Information System as specified in Section 10530 through 10533 of the Unemployment Insurance Code. The objective of the program is to:

> *"Produce, through extensive local participation and distribution in effective formats to all local users, reliable occupational information, and to achieve cost efficient production by avoiding duplication of efforts. The program shall be the primary source for local and statewide occupational information and shall be available in all labor market areas in the State. "*

The COICC sits in an advisory role to the State-local Cooperative. It is also responsible for providing definitions for the development of local occupational information surveys prepared by local education and training providers. Thirty seven of these have been published and collectively they provide an extensive employment outlook for the entire state. Each survey varies in the number of jobs it profiles, but each reflects the major jobs that are needed in the area that the survey is done. Uniformity of definitions and content on how each job is profiled is the responsibility of COICC. Job profiles include wage and fringe benefits; training, experience and other requirements noted; supply/demand assessment information; size of the occupation; employment trends-local and national; and other information which is important to know. This last piece of information provided to the user is very significant from a guidance point of view. It tells the reader:

- Where the job are;
- Methods used to fill job openings;
- Career paths-upward mobility clues;
- Important knowledge, skills and abilities needed for the job which can be acquired in school. Each knowledge, skill and ability is rated on a five point in terms of importance to the job.

In addition, each directory has a complete listing of all education and training providers in the region. Information is provided on what is offered, what services are provided, location, phone number, cost of program if applicable, etc.

The second new provision in law was a Performance Based Accountability System which became law with the passage of SB 645 in 1995, 'The Job Training Report Card Act." The Act requires federally and state funded education and training programs to participate in a California report card system by January 1, 2001. Primarily, it is an accountability system which requires program providers to report outcomes of their programs. All entities preparing individuals for occupations are required to justify their program by reporting job placement data. Program approval for the operation of vocational and job training programs is initially given when there is a demonstrated demand. If the program continues to successfully place individuals, then there is no question on whether it should continue.

These changes gave the COICC an opportunity to contribute significantly to the development of a school-to-career opportunity system which will be discussed in further detail in this review. Through the leadership of John Corcoran, who became Executive Director of COICC in 1995, the COICC took on a new focus on career development and career guidance information for use by students and adults. The new focus was due in part to the change in federal law as noted above. One of the first products COICC developed under the 1998 Carl D. Perkins Vocational and Technical Education Act was a Career Planning Guide for students and for individuals participating in job training programs. The Guides shows students how to:

- initiate a self-assessment process;
- match their skills and abilities to jobs and careers;
- learn more about the jobs, the careers and the industries that use the jobs;
- educate themselves to meet the needs of the jobs in the career of their choice;
- find their first (or next) job in the career;
- how to develop a career plan;
- find job opportunities;
- develop a resume;
- prepare a job application;
- conduct themselves in an interview;
- keep a job.

In addition, the COICC developed a CD ROM aided career guidance resource tool to assist students and adults in career decision making and job selection. The CDs are given to all school districts and job training providers at no charge without restrictions on duplicating them. The CD is called the "*Golden State Career Videos*." The CD provides career guidance information on nearly 193 occupations in various industries. An additional 100 occupations will be added in 2001. The information is formatted in English and Spanish. The system is so successful it is being considered to become a national model by the U.S. Department of Education. Interest in the Golden State Career Videos has been expressed by Canadian and European governments.

Regional Adult and Vocational Education Councils

The Legislature established Regional Adult and Vocational Education Councils (RAVECs) in 1975 to replace existing Area Vocational Planning Committees and Adult Continuing Education Coordinating Councils. The Legislature, reacting to rapidly expanding enrollments and escalating costs in adult education programs maintained by the K-12 and community college systems, intended to encourage a more coordinated delivery of educational services to adults. Generally, the mandates of the RAVECs were to eliminate unnecessary duplication of efforts and promote optimum coordination and articulation of programs among the various adult and vocational education providers at the local level.

The minimum geographical limits of each RAVEC were established to correspond to the boundary of each community college district in the state. Of the possible 72 RAVECs, 71 were formed (two community college districts combined to form one RAVEC). Each RAVEC consisted of eleven members, four from K-12 districts, four community college members, one CETA Prime Sponsor representative, one County Office of Education and a private school representative. The primary task of the RAVEC was to:

- Foster a delineation of function agreement for adult education programs among the governing boards of the educational entities with the RAVEC district. The agreement would designate which entities were responsible for the various adult and vocational education program offerings.

- Help develop an articulation agreement among the education entities with the RAVEC district. The agreement would emphasize the relationship of courses taught at various levels by different educational agencies so students could move through and avoid duplicating courses previously taken.

- Establish a broadly representative advisory committee of business, industry and community groups/interests to provide input.

- Develop a short term plan for the improvement of vocational and adult education within the region.

- Review and recommend for apportionment all courses under the purview of the RAVEC.

RAVECs operated for a short period of time, 1976 through 1978. In 1978, the Legislature eliminated funding for RAVECs. When the CDE and Chancellor's Office of the California Community Colleges appeared before the Legislative Budget Committee to justify continued funding they were asked about the value of RAVECs and what had they accomplished. Neither agency was able to present any evidence of what had been accomplished by RAVECs.

In the absence of an effective state planning process, CACVE conducted a study of RAVECs in 1980. During the time frame of their operation, CACVE found that 70 of the 71 RAVECs adopted delineation of function agreements and 67 articulation agreements. The range of articulation activities was diverse. Several RAVECs went beyond the mandated articulation function. The Cerritos RAVEC in Los Angeles County, for example, developed a computerized articulation matrix based on the U.S. Department of Labor Dictionary of Occupational Titles, (DOT) taxonomy. The matrix listed all courses offered in the region, indicated the DOT-classification job to which they lead, and at which level of instruction they were taught. There were RAVECs in the state that didn't even achieve a simple statement of agreement or articulation among the local delivery agencies.

Sixty-nine RAVECs prepared a short-term plan which, in widely varying degrees of comprehensiveness, analyzed needs and resources of the respective regions. The Cerritos RAVEC developed a comprehensive regional short term plan based on a complete inventory of credit and non-credit vocational and adult courses. The North Santa Clara RAVEC utilized not only the supply data generated by an inventory comparable to that of Cerritos, but also used region-specific job market demand data collected by Santa Clara County Office of Education. Other RAVECs did nothing more that outline a series of steps they would take the following year to address this mandate.

As a prelude to the short term plans, RAVECs established an inventory of adult and vocational education courses. These inventories also provided information needed for course and program review activities. Again, the range of inventories varied from very complete to not even a narrowly defined listing that was complete.

Course review activities occupied a significant portion of the RAVECs time and effort, since the enabling legislation emphasized the elimination of unnecessary duplication. Accordingly, many RAVECs concentrated their efforts on this review process and expended less effort on more vocational education-oriented planning activities such as job market survey and advisory committee deliberations. The San Mateo RAVEC created a detailed review process, using a preview subcommittee system and established criteria to examine all new course offerings. Several RAVECs, on the other hand, never even agreed on the scope or process of review.

Given that the CDE and Chancellor's Office of the California Community Colleges had not collected any data on RAVECs, the CACVE attempted to ascertain any quantitative data on the effects of the RAVEC review process. Only 16 courses of over 51,000 reviewed by all RAVECs in 1976-77 were designated unnecessary duplication, eight of which were eliminated and eight were transferred due to the adoption of delineation of function agreements. RAVECs also reported that 60 courses were eliminated before, during, or as a result of the review process besides the 16 designated as unnecessary duplication.

Perhaps the most significant CACVE findings were some of the less tangible effects of local planning efforts. RAVECs reported that the process prevented numerous course and program duplication from ever being proposed. The RAVEC activities also helped local agencies realize which courses were needed but not offered.

There were other problems and limitations which prevented RAVECs from being successful that identified by CACVE. These included:

- Mission of RAVECs - the state's mandate was-perceived as an attempt to eliminate courses at the local level. Many local educators were unhappy about state intervention within locally-controlled education. They felt RAVECs were nothing more than vehicles for wresting away one agency's territory to benefit another. Membership inequities and the mixing of vocational education and adult courses were difficult to reconcile. ROCPs, for example, were not routinely members of RAVECs.

- Definition of RAVEC functions - vagueness at the legislative and state administrative levels hampered regional efforts to implement their mandated responsibilities. Inadequate guidance and support from the CDE and Chancellor's Office of the California Community Colleges was provided to ensure

RAVECs would uniformly address their mandates. Each functioned independently in an ad hoc fashion interpreting their mandates from varying perspectives.

- Isolation of planning activities - RAVECs were not organized into a statewide network. They had no formal relationship to one another or to a statewide planning process. Although local districts were exposed to the information and plans developed with the region, no local agency was obligated to adhere to the plan developed by RAVECs.

- Operational barriers-limited funding of $35,000 was the most significant shortcoming. This was insufficient to provide staffing necessary to accomplish all tasks. Over half the costs were absorbed by local agencies. Interpretation of policy between the CDE and Chancellor's Office of the California Community Colleges was not always parallel. This contributed to discord and sometimes aggravated local conflicts.

With the elimination of state funding, another effort to promote regional planning fell by the wayside. Although some RAVECs took their mission seriously, the majority considered the mandate an imposition on local control. Also, some of the things that the more successful RAVECs accomplished have found there way into the system, one way or another. The need to implement an articulated and coordinated state delivery system for vocational education and job training would see another day in the 1990s.

Unifying Vocational Education. Several efforts were made to unify vocational education efforts from a planning, policy and organizational perspectives.

California Associations of Vocational Education

Due to its subject matter orientation, vocational education had as many as 53 specialized associations or groups with an interest in occupational, vocational or career education in the early 1970s. California was one of four states that did not have a statewide vocational education association.

A project was written by Tom Bogetich to explore the creation of a state vocational education association. It was funded by the CDE. A task force was assembled at Bass Lake July 22-23, 1971, to discuss the concept of such an association. The California Associations of Vocational Education, CAVE, was formed in June of 1973. It was active a number of years until it was disbanded due to the lack of interest and participation.

The proposed purpose of the Association was to develop a unity of purpose to advocate the need to improve and strengthen vocational education in California. However, it was formed as a loosely knit confederation-an association of associations because of the participating organizations wanted to maintain their own identity and activities. To reach agreement on any issue would require approval from each of the respective associations. It was another missed opportunity for vocational education to have a single voice and organizational structure to advocate a direction for vocational education.

O'Lawrence, H. (2013)
The Historical Critique of Career and Technical Education in California from 1900 – 2000 and the Status of California Community Colleges in the 21st Century
Santa Rosa, California: Informing Science Institute

Chapter Three

Supporters for the Advancement of Vocational Education

In mid-1977, the vocational education leadership in agriculture, home economics, and trade and industrial education recognized the need to speak politically about issues of common concern. An organization was formed and was designated as the *Supporters for the Advancement of Vocational Education (SAVE)*. Professional organizations in existence at that time were effectively providing input into the development of the State Plan for Vocational Education, drafting criteria for vocational teacher certification and licensing, and promoting the image of vocational education. Subject matter leaders and teachers perceived a need for a unified voice in the state legislature to advocate the need for improved funding, especially state funds for subject matter programs and vocational student organizations, and to speak out for alternatives to the governance structure for vocational education.

SAVE worked during the 1977 legislative session advocating the establishment of a separate board for vocational education. Their efforts were advanced in SB 1028 and AB 2242 which have been previously discussed. SB 1028 passed the education committees of the Senate and Assembly, but stalled in the finance committees due to fiscal concerns. SAVE'S efforts were responsible for the appointment of the Commission on Vocational Education by Dr. Riles detailed earlier is this review.

California Position Statement

In 1981, CACVE engaged representatives of 14 statewide vocational teacher and administrator associations in an effort to develop a position statement regarding the reauthorization of the federal Vocational Education Act. It was the first time that any of these organizations had meet collectively to address a common issue. The meeting was directed by Tom Bogetich, CACVE Executive Director with the assistance of former Council member Me1 Barlow. The first task at hand was to determine areas of common agreement. This was not an easy task. After two days of extensive discussion, a position statement was drafted that was acceptable to everyone. It was sent to members of the California Congressional delegation in Washington D.C. and to the Education Committees of the House and Senate prior to the passage of the Carl D. Perkins Vocational Education Act of 1984.

Comprehensive State Policy Development

Another unifying effort was undertaken by CACVE in 1982. It involved the development of a comprehensive state policy for vocational education. The need for state policy had been expressed in the Arthur D. Little Report and at various times by the Legislature. In response to AB 576, a report was prepared entitled *"Vocational Education and Youth Employment Training Programs in California. A Report to the California Legislature from the Assembly Bill 576 Task Group, December, 1980."* The Task Group concluded:

> *"With the expenditure of over $2 billion annually associated with these and related programs, there is a need for a clear and consistent state policy establishing their (vocational education and youth training programs) objectives in preparing youth for employment. There is currently limited state policy direction over a substantial portion of these funds, which are fragmented in a complex array of financing sources and delivery systems.*
> "

The Task Group developed a number of recommendations to more effectively link the private sector to vocational education and training programs. They recommended that all providers should:

- Define strengthened roles for employers in the design and evaluation of vocational education and employment training program, both through encouragement of their direct involvement in employment training programs and through definition of significant roles for them in local advisory bodies. Such roles should relate to promoting occupational training which (a) is responsive to the skill needs of employers, (b) provides students with the occupational competencies necessary to obtain and retain employment, and (c)includes assistance to students in entering the job market.

- Promote involvement of employers at the state and local levels in decisions regarding program offerings, with the aim of ensuring that vocational education and youth employment programs are responsive to both current needs of employers at the local level and changing labor market requirements ...

- Require local level planning. emphasizing partnerships between vocational education programs, the basic educational curriculum, youth employment training program, employers and the community, in order that these programs may draw upon the many resources available in schools and communities for effectively meeting the widely varying needs of the youth population.

- Increase funding of occupational training program which link vocational education with employment-based preparation in diverse sites throughout the community.

- Eliminate barriers to youth participation in productive work experiences through the removal of restrictions on the types of business operations and learning-related work experiences in which they can participate.

- Provide incentives for private employers to train at the worksite, to lend or donate updated equipment (for classroom and skills center instruction), and to participate in employee exchange program involving interchanges between skilled workers and vocational instructors.

The Task Group recommendations were consistent with the goals of vocational education. However, as previously noted these were ideals which at some point in time did work their way into federal vocational education and job training policies.

The Task Group was not the first to come to the conclusion that there was an absence of state policy for vocational education. In 1977, the Legislative Analyst had concluded that:

> *"California does not have comprehensive vocational education legislation. Statutes pertaining to vocational education are scattered throughout the Education Code. A clear statement of program goals and objectives applying to all levels of vocational education (i.e. secondary schools, ROCPs, community colleges, and adult schools) does not exist. Program priorities and functions (e.g., the relationship between vocational and general education, guidance and counseling functions) are not well-defined. The lack of comprehensive statutory definitions of policies and institutional relationships and responsibilities in vocational education has led to an absence of clear state policy beyond that required in federal law. We believe that state priorities and institutional relationships and responsibilities in vocational education must be clearly defined by the Legislature*

inasmuch as well over $450 million of state and local funds are spent annually in this area."

The CACVE Task Force developed specific legislative recommendations which addressed the need for educational reform to improve the quality and accountability of vocational education programs. In February 1983, legislation, SB 610, was introduced under the sponsorship of CACVE. The proposal was so complex that the CACVE found it difficult to gain a full understanding and support throughout the vocational education community. In its draft form, prior to it being placed into a legislative bill, CACVE took all pertinent sections of the Education Code governing vocational education and made changes and additions to create a policy foundation for vocational education. Pertinent features included (1) a coordinated and articulated planning process, (2) program accountability including student certification involving program advisory committees, (3) development of state program standards and local performance standards, (4) provisions for program improvement, (5) a proactive role for the private sector in planning efforts, (6) defining vocational education's mission and function as an integral part of the K-14 public school system, and (7) a new governance mechanism. The only missing component was the establishment of a state funding base for vocational education other than a.d.a.

CACVE's failure to secure support and passage of the comprehensive policy package for vocational education was due, in part, to the following:

- Lack of experience in legislative advocacy;
- Not using a seasoned Legislator with a history of support of vocational education to carry their bill;
- Introducing the bill in mid-session, which did not allow enough time to advocate the legislation;
- Moving too quickly and failure to take more time to develop the constituency base to understand the content and benefits of the proposed legislation;
- Understanding that legislative reform often moves incrementally rather than in an all inclusive manner – the bill was too complex for but a few to understand;
- Not developing a advocacy strategy with the various groups involved in the process to advance the legislative proposal;
- Not recognizing that certain factions of vocational education already had an agenda that they were pursuing which was self-

serving rather being for the good of all – the adoption of comprehensive policy for vocational education was not their priority;

As previously noted, the issue of an articulated and coordinated state system for vocational education and job training would come to the forefront again in the mid 1990s. This will be discussed in further detail.

Vocational Education Alliance

The Vocational Education Alliance, VOCAL, was initiated by the California Business Education Association on October 26, 1983. It brought together representatives from all the vocational education teacher's associations, namely the:

- California Business Education Association
- California Home Economics Association
- California Industrial and Technology Education Association
- California Agriculture Teachers Association
- California Association of Health Career Education
- Home Economics Teachers Association of California

VOCAL had as its purpose to advocate legislation that would promote vocational education and the vocational subject matter areas represented on VOCAL. Specifically, VOCAL listed its purposes as:

1. Networking with professional associations within vocational education to increase understanding and cooperation between these areas.

2. Drafting and supporting legislation that affects vocational education.

3. Reacting to current legislation that affects vocational education.

4. Selecting and supporting legislative advocacy to achieve the goals of VOCAL.

Over the years, VOCAL had been successful and continues working with legislators to introduce and advocate legislation which supports vocational education. Some bills advanced by VOCAL have been previously been noted.

Legislative Forum

In 1984, CACVE and the California Associations of Vocational Education, CAVE, invited all of the vocational education associations to join together in a Legislative Forum. The purpose of the Forum was to bring together all the vocational education community to exchange points of view on pending legislation before the California Legislature which would have an affect on vocational education. The anticipated outcome of the Forum, which functioned for a number of years, was to air out differences and developed a unified position on legislation.

The Unity Forum

The organizational meeting of the Unity Forum took place in July of 1985 in San Francisco. This meeting took place early on in the educational reforms which were impacting vocational education. Representatives of all the vocational education associations in California met to improve communications among and between the varied segments of vocational education. According to an account of that meeting, it was apparent to all that there was no unity of purpose. Teachers were promoting state mandated standards, compliance criteria, and restricted funding, while vocational administrators were calling for greater flexibility and local control. Conversely, some vocational education teachers and administrator were getting misinformation regarding directives coming from the State Director of Vocational Education. Two-way communication was a serious problem. The Unity Forum was established to provide a symposium for the improvement of two-way communication and provided a forum to express differing points of view in a positive constructive way without airing dirty linen in Sacramento.

The Unity Forum was convened on regular basis thereafter by the President of the California Association of Vocational Education, Evelyn Bachelor. The Unity Forum adopted a mission statement on career-vocational education and adopted a number of position statements. The Unity Forum met for a number of years and served as a sounding board to the State Director of Vocational Education. This process worked well; two-way communication was improved while the Unity Forum functioned. However, when Jim Allison was removed from his position in 1991 the Unity Forum was abandoned shortly thereafter.

California Action Team

In 1985, Jim Allison, State Director of Vocational Education, brought together a broadly representative group of approximately 70 individuals to form the California Action Team. They included representation from vocational teachers, administrators, local and state agencies, county offices, professional associations, and business and industry. The California Action Team was formed to advise, inform, and make recommendations to the State Director on all matters pertaining to the needs, priorities, and direction needed for California to maintain and expand quality programs of vocational education. A regional structure was established to carry forward information gained at meeting with the California Action Team and to serve as a communication link to ensure local input.

The first task undertaken by the California Action Team was to write a California Plan for Career-Vocational Education which was not driven by federal law. Such a plan had been advocated by the California Legislature and CACVE. The plan took over two years to write before it was ready for publication and distribution to local school districts.

The California Plan for Career-Vocational Education was developed in two parts. *"Part One: Policy Directions"* was finally published in January 1989. *"Part Two: Implementation Strategies"* was published in March 1990. Within the documents were issues, goals, priorities, and strategies to guide career-vocational programs at the local and state level. In general, the Plan was intended to serve as a resource to state and local policy makers, students, parents, employers, and the public at large.

Part I of the Plan states that its fundamental purpose is to establish a unifying mission for career-vocational education in California. The Plan states:

> *"The mission of career-vocational education in California is to enhance the personal and economic well-being of individuals and to develop human resources which contribute to the economic development of the state."*

Part II of the Plan represented a vision for career-vocational education describing an ideal to which it aspires. To achieve its vision, it notes that career-vocational education must:

- begin at an early age and provide students with the knowledge to make rational and informed choices about careers;
- be staffed with talented and committed teachers and administrators who are given the opportunity for personal growth

and development who are accorded recognition for their accomplishments;

- be a catalyst that motivates students to stay in school and to
succeed in work, the home, and the community;

- provide equal opportunities for all students, including un-
derrepresented and underserved students, in an atmosphere
free of bias, discrimination, and stereotyping;

- teach occupational skills and positive work habits while teach-
ing/reinforcing core academic, problem solving, and critical
thinking skills through the collaboration and joint planning of
vocational and academic faculty;

- be coordinated and articulated through all educational levels,
with close working relationships established among elementary, middle, and secondary schools; regional occupational
centers and programs (ROCPs); adult schools; and community colleges and other postsecondary institutions;

- operate in partnership with business, industry, labor, and
government to meet the emerging, changing, and expanding
need for well-educated and well-trained technical workers;

- provide quality programs and educational excellence for every
student;

- contribute directly to the economic well-being of individuals
and the state, in addition to providing person satisfaction to
individuals and their families;

- be relevant and accountable based on standards of quality
that are established, implemented, and measured in collaboration with business and industry;

- prepare a well-trained, literate, and flexible work force ready
to meet the current and future demands of a world marketplace.

Upon completion of the Plan, it was submitted to the State Board of
Education for approval. It was also submitted to the U.S. Department
of Education for information purposes to keep them apprised of California's efforts to forge a direction for vocational education outside
the dictates of federal law. The Plan was widely disseminated and a
series of workshops conducted to review the content and merits of the
documents. These workshops were offered by management involved
in the state administration of vocational education. The California Action Team which helped develop the document was not utilized in the
process. Local school district leadership did not take the effort very

seriously because there were no resources available, other than federal funds, to implement the Plan. Again, this was another missed opportunity by vocational education.

The Federation of Conferences

In 1995, a joint effort was undertaken by the State Council on Vocational Education, SCOVE (formerly CACVE) with the Long Beach Industry Education Council, to organize a state conference for all vocational education, job training organizations, and vocational teacher educators in the state. A planning committee was established which was co-chaired by Sandy Beck, Executive Director of SCOVE, and Cal Farmer of the Long Beach Industry Education Council. The purpose was to have all vocational education associations, the CDE, Chancellors' Office of the California Community Colleges, the California State University System vocational education teacher training personnel, and state and local job training organizations/agencies to hold their annual conferences together at one site. In this way they would be able to bring together the entire vocational education and training community to share and exchange ideas, improve communications and benefit from a variety of professional development sessions which would contribute to improving California's workforce system.

The Federation of Conferences was ultimately held in Long Beach October 21-26, 1996, with the support and active participation of numerous organizations in Long Beach. This included the Mayor's Office, City of Long Beach, Chamber of Commerce, Restaurants Association, Harbor Commission, Economic Development Department, and Greater Long Beach/Los Angeles World Trade Center to name a few. It was anticipated that 10,000 would attend. However, the best laid plans resulted in only 3,500 attending the conference. Thirty four organizations participated in the conference. Those who attended were very positive about the program offered to them.

One of the highlights and exciting features of the Conference was the "Emerging Technology Showcase." The showcase was organized by Larry Rathbun who was responsible for inviting major California employers to showcase their emerging products, services, and technologies for the purpose of interacting with vocational education and job training practitioners to discuss current and future job skills needed by business and industry. Attendees were able to meet and communicate with industry representatives knowledgeable about the products, services and technologies displayed and become aware of the specific competitive skills needed to utilize them in the work place.

The keynote speakers at that Conference were Philip Quigley, Chairman and CEO of Pacific Telesis and Harry Stonecipher, President and CEO of McDonnell Douglas. Their presentations were rebroadcast via Cable TV in the evening so participants who could not attend their presentation could view it in the comfort of their hotel rooms.

Approximately 22 breakout sessions were offered over the five day period to the participants. In addition, each of the organizations conducted their own meetings for three of the five day conference period. No effort has been undertaken to conduct another conference of this magnitude again. Another missed opportunity.

The Partnership Academy. In 1980 Hattie Harlow, director of the Mid-Peninsula Urban Coalition, a local community-based organization involved with improving minority employment, brought the academy concept to the attention of the Superintendent of the Sequoia Union High School District, Harry Reynolds. In 1981 the academy idea, which originated in Philadelphia in 1969, was initiated by the district. The electronics industry was engaged by Marilyn Raby to partner with the district and the community to develop an academy program to improve student performance. A computer academy was established at Menlo-Atherton High School and an electronics academy at Sequoia High School. This was the start of California's successful Partnership Academy program.

Due to its proximity to Silicon Valley and San Francisco, the program initially was referred to as the "Peninsula Academy." The academy program got off to a rocky start. Teaching staff was recruited from district staff and from over three hundred teachers in the district only three volunteered. The other teachers needed for the program were hired specifically for the program. The electronics and computer courses were taught by personnel on loan to the district from two participating companies, Lockheed Missiles and Space Corporation and Hewlett-Packard.

The reluctance of district staff to participate has been attributed to their perception that the academies were just another vocational education/work experience program. Even the Teacher Union members did not want any extra funds spent on the academies for fear of cutting into their programs and salary increases. Also, the academies had smaller class size, provided planning time for teachers, and served primarily at-risk youth. Students in the program entered with a broad range of abilities, skills and attitudes. This was troubling to them as they understood such students were more difficult to teach than regular classes. In spite of not having complete and unified support of district teachers, the academy programs were established.

During its rocky start in the Sequoia Union High School District, Superintendent Reynolds left the district and became superintendent the nearby East Side Union High School District in San Jose. With the benefit of Sequoia's experience in developing academies, Superintendent Reynolds immediately went to work to establish academy programs in the East Side Union High School District which over time proved to be some of the more successful academies in the state. By the third year of the Peninsula Academies there was positive evidence that they were becoming successful. Students were remaining in school and showed enthusiasm for the program. Evaluation data showed clear differences between academy students and their matched comparison counterparts on measures such as retention, credits earned, and pass rates on the district's proficiency tests.

The Peninsula Academies won a number of awards. At the end of the third year of operation, Sequoia won the California School Boards Association's "Golden Bell" award. The National Academy for Vocational Education named them as an exemplary program. They received a Private Sector Initiatives commendation from the President of the United States in 1986, and a Distinguished Performance Award from the National Alliance of Business in 1987. Other recognition was given to the program by the New *York Times* and *Phi Delta Kappan* as well as a PB S documentary on successful dropout prevention programs.

The Peninsula Academies caught the attention of the California Legislature. In 1984 Assemblyman Byron Sher introduced AB3 104 at the urging of Charles Dayton and Marilyn Raby. Sher successfully carried the bill in the Assembly and Senator Robert Naylor in the Senate. It was signed by Governor Deukmejian on September 29, 1984. The legislation provided ten planning grants of $25,000 each to ten school districts from January 1985 to June 1985. Each site that was successful would then receive $50,000 to implement its academy each year. The only requirement was that the districts had to match the amount with an equal amount of *"direct and in-kind support by the district"* and *"direct and in-kind support from the participating companies and a business related community organization."* The intent was to develop three-way partnerships among the state, school district, and supporting local companies. AB 3 104 called for an evaluation of the academies by the CDE after two years but no finds were appropriated for this work.

In the fall of 1985 ten new academies began operation. The success varied depending how well the districts utilized the strengths of the model developed in the Sequoia Union High School District. Some failed. Some of the more successful Academies were the two electronic academies in the East Side Union High School District in San Jose, the health academy at Oakland Technical High School in Oakland, and a computer academy begun at Hiram Johnson High School in Sacramento. Over the next several years, the Peninsula Academies began to show promise and efforts to expand the experimental program.

AB 3104 had a life span of only three-years. Senator Rebecca Morgan introduced SB 605 in 1987 to make the academies permanent in state law. It was signed by Governor Deukmejian in September 1987. SB 605 changed some provisions of the Sher bill. First, it provided for up to fifteen new planning grant applications for the next four years. However, the grants were smaller, $15,000 each. The maximum implementation grant was raised to $67,500. Funding of the academies was performance based. Each academy would have to submit data on how well their students had performed on measures of attendance (80 percent required) and credits earned (90 percent of those necessary for "normal progress toward graduation" required) in order to be reimbursed through the state grant. Districts were allocated funds based on a formula that required thirty students to qualify the first year, sixty the second and ninety the third year and thereafter.

The academy was thoroughly spelled out in law and each site was required to follow the model. Finally, the name was changed from "Peninsula Academy" to "Partnership Academy." No funding was provided in the legislation for evaluation. The William and Flora Hewlett Foundation took the lead to find support. Along with the Luke B. Hancock Foundation, they provided finds to the Stanford Urban Coalition to provide such technical assistance and support.

Forty new academies were established as a result of SB 605 and evaluation results were very encouraging. The legislation was renewed again in 1993 and 1999, which continued expansion to a total of 290 academies in 2000. In 1999, there were 240 state funded academies. One hundred and forty-eight were fully implemented with all components of the academy model. Thirty were in the second year of implementation; 42 in there first year of implementation; and 20 operating in a planning phase. Academies have been established in some 25 different career fields. Many others have been established without state funding, and in many districts there are now several non-funded academies for every one receiving a state grant. There are an estimated 500 non-funded academies functioning in California.

Academies provide students with three academic courses, along with one career-related course, in grades 10- 12. The intent is to prepare students for college and careers at the same time.

Academy components were spelled out in state law. In addition to the matching requirements previously noted, the district must assure that their *Partnership Academy will be established as a "school within a school."* Each academy student must be provided the following components which were spelled out in statute:

> 1 .   Instruction in at least three academic subjects each regular school term that prepares the student for regular high school diploma. When possible, these subjects should relate to the occupational field of the academy.

> 2.   A "laboratory class" related to the academy's occupational field.

> 3.   A class schedule which limits the attendance to the classes required in (1) and (2) to pupils of the academy

> 4.   A mentor from the business community during the pupil's 11th

> grade year.

> 5.   A job related to the academy's occupational field or work experience to improve employment skills, during the summer following the 11th grade. A student that must attend summer school for purposes of completing graduation requirements is exempt.

> 6.   Additional motivational activities with private sector involvement to encourage academic and occupational preparation.

With each revision of SB 605, the model has been fine tuned. One of the more significant elements of the program is the inclusion of the work experience requirement. The model calls for paid or non-work experience or internships to occur during the summer following the 11th grade. Some students gain additional work experience opportunities during their senior year, but it is not required under state law.

A four-year report was prepared on the effectiveness of the Partnership Academy, 1992-93 through 1995-96. It was conducted by Dr. Eileen Warren of the California Institute on Human Services, Sonoma State University in December 1998. The report was written in response to SB 44 (Morgan) in 1993 which made statutory changes governing Partnership Academies. The findings focus on the six areas identified in the legislation, namely:

- An analysis of the extent and degree of success of business and industry involvement, including in-kind contributions, mentor services, summer jobs, and assistance in job placement.
- The number of students obtaining employment, entering advanced training programs, and enrolling in postsecondary institutions after graduation.
- Attendance rates and credits achieved.
- The number of students who completed their high school education and graduated.
- An analysis of the extent to which components of the partnership program have been incorporated into the regular school program.
- Other information that may be of interest to the Legislature such as ethnicity and grade point averages.

The report indicates that the academies were effective across all six components analyzed. Two factors were impressive in the findings. The first was the leveraging of state resources to support and institutionalize the academies. Business and industry contributions represent almost 40% of academy funding compared to 24% of state funding. The use of state dollars to leverage this magnitude of private support for an educational program is unprecedented and represents efficient use of state resources.

Second, the clear and consistent effects on academy participants in the areas of attendance, credits earned, and grade point average. Student performance improved all three years students were enrolled in the program. Approximately 80% of students entering the academy in 1992-93 remained in the academy. At the same time, approximately 92% of students who left the academy program chose to remain in school but in a more traditional academic environment. The dropout rate for academy enrollees in 1995-96 was 3.1 % compared to 3.9% dropout rate for all high school students statewide in the same year.

This impressive considering over two-thirds of academy enrollees are considered to be "at risk" of dropping out.

Tech-Prep

By 1990, California and the nation were involved in major reform efforts in the public schools. In addition, the nation was facing major shortages in technically skilled workers to fill jobs critical to maintaining a competitive edge in the world economy. In California, a survey done by the Council on California Competitiveness released in April 1992 reported:

> *"In a 1990 survey, 77percent of California business leaders stated that the education level of job applicants is a major problem. Among the largest firms in California, 63 percent report new applicants for entry-level positions lack a satisfactory education. Overall, only an estimated 46 percent of new job applicants demonstrate adequate basic math and verbal skills on written examinations. "*

The Report went on to say that one company alone, Pacific Bell, estimates it has a cost of up to $14 million per year to provide remedial education for their employees. The Council concluded that:

> *"California must provide a public education system that will offer to all students equally the opportunity to fulfill their highest potential to get good grades, high-skill jobs, and become taxpayers. We do not necessarily need more money per child, but we do need more: strategic planning; accountability for results; career choices; intelligent use of resources; total schooling and career training directed toward high-skilled jobs. "*

In 1990 the Carl D. Perkins Vocational and Applied Technology Education Act revised the Federal Act and created a section titled the "Tech-Prep Education Act." In the Congressional findings it was noted that:

- rapid technological advances and global economic competition demand increased levels of skilled technical education preparation and readiness on the part of youths entering the workforce;

- a combination of nontraditional school-to-work technical education programs, using state-of-the-art equipment and appropriate technologies, will reduce the dropout rate for high school students in the United States and will produce youths who are mature, responsible, and motivated to build good lives for themselves;

- the establishment of systematic technical education articulation agreements between secondary schools and postsecondary institutions is necessary for providing youths with skills in the liberal and practical arts and in basic academics, including literacy instruction in the English language, and with the intense technical preparation necessary for finding a position in a changing workplace;

- more than 50 percent of jobs that are developing will require skills greater than those provided by existing educational programs;

- by the year 2000 an estimated 15,000,000 manufacturing jobs will require more advanced technical skills, and an equal number of service jobs will become obsolete;

- more than 50 percent of jobs that are developing will require skills greater than those provided by existing educational programs.

The concept for Tech-Prep was the idea of Dr. Dale Parnell, President of the American Association of Community and Junior Colleges. Dr. Parnell's idea was to:

- offer a first rate alternative to the traditional college-prep program for students who are unlikely to achieve a baccalaureate degree;

- offer students a solid-academic foundation based on concrete, real-life applications;

- coordinate the efforts of secondary and postsecondary schools to achieve maximum results in minimum time;

- effectively address some of the key differences in student needs, backgrounds, and learning styles; and

- provide students with the lifelong learning competencies they need and the flexibility they will need in the future-while providing employers with the kind of workers they need to remain competitive.

The revisions to the Perkins Act coupled with private sector concerns about the preparation of the workforce set the stage for the Tech-Prep program to make some major strides. The 1990 Perkins Act defines the parameters of a Tech-Prep program. However, rather than targeting the program to primarily at-risk students, it opened up participation to all students who could benefit from the program. The federal Act provides that any such program should:

- be carried-out under an articulation agreement between the participants in a consortium
- consist of 2 years of secondary school preceding graduation and 2 years of higher education, or an apprenticeship program of at least 2 years following secondary instruction, with a common core of required proficiency in mathematics, science, communications, and technologies designed to lead to an associate degree or certificate in a specific career field
- include the development of tech-prep education program curricula appropriate to the needs of the consortium participants.

The Act also provided for the training of teachers and counselors to ensure quality programs including student placement, and developing equal access services to special populations so they could participate and benefit from the Tech-Prep Programs.

By the end of the 1990s, nearly ninety Tech-Prep consortia were in operation at the secondary and community college level, some more successful than others. At the secondary level, six Tech-Prep Resource Consortia were established to serve as statewide resource centers to schools to assist them implement Tech-Prep. The Resource Consortia were establish in each of the six vocational subject matter areas with each specializing in a particular career pathway which evolved later on into industry sectors. Industry sectors will be discussed further in this review. Unlike other states, California chose to utilize the Resource Consortia or process approach at the secondary level rather that the "program" approach used in most other states and by the California community colleges. Available federal funding for Tech-Prep is basically split between the K-12 and community college systems. Both agencies administered the funds independent of one another even though the main purpose of Tech-Prep was to develop an articulated program between the two levels. Neither had an overall leadership plan, standards, or assessment criteria to measure how well the purposes of the federal Act would be implemented but the CDE had a strategy-Resource Consortia.

The Consortia approach was an attempt to maximize the use of limited resources available for Tech- Prep by providing leadership and technical assistance to the schools on a statewide basis in order to better serve the career and vocational needs of students. In this manner Tech-Prep resources would impact more students.

A Tech Prep student (not identified as one because they are not in a program) takes a sequential number of courses that are horizontally and vertically articulated beginning in high school, or even junior high school, through the community college which lead to a career. In some instances, the program could even articulate to the university level for some students. Horizontal articulation involves the integration of a common core of academic and vocational instruction which requires a planned team approach in the schools. Vocational and academic teachers work together to assist the student in acquiring a common core of basic academic competencies, and meet state academic and vocational program standards. The private sector is also involved in the process. This may include their involvement in program planning, student mentoring, and providing opportunities for internships, paid and unpaid work experience, as well as job placement. Work-based learning is an element of the Tech-Prep strategy. Tech-Prep is very similar to the Partnership Academy program but it is not limited to primarily serving at-risk students; it's for every student that can benefit.

The Consortia basically acted as change agents by providing technical assistance to help the schools develop 2+2 career pathways in each of the vocational subject matter areas. Each Consortia was allowed the freedom to determine how it would provide leadership and technical support to the schools. Technical assistance or leadership could be given to curriculum development, recruitment strategies, integrating vocational and academic curricula, student assessment, career guidance and planning, marketing strategies, building industry partnerships, etc. In addition, Consortia conducted a variety of regional workshops and organized an annual Tech-Prep Conference. The Conference has been well attended by academic and vocational education personnel, and business and industry representatives.

Each of Consortia plotted its own course of action and support efforts. However, after a period of time they saw the need to form a California Career Pathways Consortia to maximize their resources and eliminate duplication of effort. The collaboration would be able to facilitate the development of products (printed materials, videos, etc.) and provide better services (workshops, institutes, and technical assistance) which would result in continued progress toward a coordinated Tech-Prep strategy. They would also focus their efforts on 15 career elements, including:

1. Integration of curriculum

2. Career pathway sequences/articulation

3. Standards based curriculum

4. Workplace learning activities

5. Education-employer partnerships

6. Career awareness and guidance

7. Authentic student performance assessment

8. Career pathway assessment

9. Assessment of local career preparation system

10. Marketing and outreach strategies

11. System for local student follow-up

12. Secondary-postsecondary linkages

13. Students with special needs

14. Making changes associated with educational reform

15. Leadership activities for all students

An attempt was made early on in 1992 to assess the progress of the Tech-Prep efforts in the state. A five-year evaluation study was undertaken but proved to be of little value. The five year assessment only produced two reports, neither of which could be used to assess the overall effectiveness of statewide efforts to implement Tech-Prep. At best, Tech-Prep has been marginally successful, but now faces new challenges. The 1998 Carl D. Perkins Vocational Education and Technical Training Act places an emphasis on the "program" approach to Tech Prep. Thus, the Consortia approach which had been developing an evolving game plan may have run its course. The end result may be that fewer students will benefit from Tech-Prep utilizing a program approach which is limited to the number of programs that can be funded annually while the Consortia approach has the potential of impacting all schools. Thus, federal policy could become an inhibitor rather than a stimulator and another opportunity may be lost with this change in policy.

Accountability Systems

Following the passage of the 1976 Vocational Education Act vocational education staff in the CDE undertook the development of a number program assessment tools for program accountability and compliance. The assessment system was designed and managed by state vocational education staff. Technical assistance was provided through the use outside contractors.

At first, the assessment tools primarily focused on the process of planning, delivering, and administering vocational education in high schools, ROCPs and adult schools and not on program outcomes. Development of a program effectiveness tool would be undertaken in 1979-80. It would focus on student placement and employer feedback.

The Program *Administrative* Review (PAR) was designed to monitor, at the district or administrative level, compliance with federal and state regulations. The PAR was administered by state staff utilizing a check-list. Districts received a written feedback from a state staff specialist who administered the PAR. The state analysis would provide feedback and support where the districts were out of compliance. A fair number of districts were administered PAR. In 1978-79, for example, 88 secondary districts and 14 ROCPs were reviewed. The *Program Assessment-Vocational Education (PA YE) was* designed to assess program improvement by examining the effectiveness of educational process and the integration of collected data in the decision making process. The instrument used was a criterion based questionnaire that was self-administered by schools and ROCPs. The questionnaire was completed for each program by school staff. One-fourth of the districts and ROCPs were assessed annually. A sample of the PAVE assessments included a visiting team which validated the assessment and offered recommendations in areas where improvement was needed.

The *Desk Review and Field Audit (DM)* was primarily a fiscal audit of district records and procedures. The audits were designed to be done by CDE personnel. However, they generally were done under contract by a CPA firm. The audits were conducted on selected fiscal records sent to the state by school districts and ROCPs where fiscal concerns were identified. One-fourth of the districts and ROCPs were scheduled for possible reviews.annually. When the audit exceptions were found, the district or ROCP would be invoiced within 90 days to reconcile the audit.

The final assessment tool to be developed was the *Follow-up of Students and Employers (FUSE)*. It was designed to measure the effectiveness of programs and contribute to program improvement. Student questionnaires and employer surveys were to be administered by districts and

ROCPs. Feedback gained from students and employers would be tabulated and extrapolated to the effectiveness of programs statewide.

In 1979, CACVE conducted a review of the use and effect of evaluation results on planning and program improvement in 1978-79. CACVE found the assessment system to be lacking. Available evaluation data on planning and program improvement at the local level was difficult to assess. The dissemination of statewide summary data, aggregated from the 1978-79 data submitted to the state by local agencies, had yet to occur. It was expected to be available in early 1980. Local districts and ROCPs which had received PAR and PAVE reviews had received feedback from state staff. Although self-assessment information was immediately available from checklists assessment and formats to those who were reviewed, the Council concluded:

> *"No formal mechanism currently exists to monitor whether or not these data are used in planning and program improvement process and to what effect."*

> *"The effect of evaluation data on state level planning and program improvement is equally difficult to assess. Vocational education supply and follow-up data are made available to each state educational agency and to joint planning efforts through the current reporting mechanisms, though validity of those data is questionable. While 1978-79 data have not yet totally been collected, it is assumed that supply and follow-up data will be used by planners. There is no comprehensive planning model established however that formally links evaluation data to plan development, nor any mechanism that has monitored and measured to any degree the effect of evaluation data on the planning process."*

These systems were maintained for a number of years, but the actual number of districts and ROCPs participating annually fell off due to fiscal constraints, changes in federal policy, CDE data collection policy, and several other factors. The CDE for example, initiated a new data collection system in 1980, the California Basic Education Data System (CBEDS). The system was designed to collect information on all school enrollments, including vocational education. However, enrollment data collected by CBEDS was not comparable to data previously collected in the vocational education data collection system. Another example was the ROCPs. They went to the Western Association of School and Colleges (WASC), and worked their way into the Accreditation process to avoid some of the accountability processes imposed on them under the State Plan for Vocational Education. ROCPs were already required by state statutes to provide information on the placement of their students. With FUSE, they would have had a second required process to address. They wanted to reduce the paper work burden created by the state and control their own destiny. ROCPs received state a.d.a. and were not dependent on federal vocational education funds. However, they did come under the purview of the federal State Plan for Vocational Education.

The 2000-2004 State Plan for Vocational Education, approved June 29, 2000, did not show that any of these early accountability tools were still being used. It did, however, note that the Carl D. Perkins Vocational and Technical Education Act of 1998 required California to:

> *"report on the progress of students completing vocational education sequences designed to provide them with the academic knowledge and technical skills needed for further education and career success."*

To achieve this, California had to measure student outcomes in four core areas:

- Academic and occupational skills attainment;
- School completion;
- Placement in postsecondary education, employment or the military;
- Participation and completion of nontraditional programs.

Basically, this required new tools to be developed to satisfy changes in federal requirements. To address the new requirements, performance measures had to be developed to measure each of the core areas. This involved the establishment of performance goals, measures to judge them by, core indicators or targets to achieve, and levels of performance-a percentage to achieve or exceed.

A brief review of how the state addressed federal accountability requirements will be described below. When compared to the assessment tools used in the 1970-80's, it illustrates that costly changes do occur with each revision of federal law. New accountability tools, for example, often may not be completely operational/reliable within the five-year time period of the state Plan. Thus, it is often difficult to obtain consistent and comparable results over time to measure program results. To complicate matters further, the 2000-2004 State Plan indicated the level of performance to help measure the core indicators could be adjusted as more reliable/complete data became available in December 2000.

The State Plan outlines accountability and evaluation measures in each of the core areas. The performance goal for academic skill proficiencies is *"to increase the number of vocational completers who attain academic proficiencies."* The measure for this goal is *"the cumulative grade point average of 12th grade vocational program completers as of June 30 of their senior year."* This measure will be temporary until data from the new high school graduation exit exam and/or augmented STAR exam become available. The core indicator which was to be used states:

> *"The state will increase the percentage of 12th grade vocational program completers who earn a cumulative grade point of 2.5 or higher."*

The level of performance indicated is that 60 percent of vocational education program completers will earn a cumulative grade point average of 2.5 or higher by the 2003-04 academic year. However, it was noted that the state did not have a cumulative grade point average data on vocational education program completers and would have to adjust the level of performance when data become available.

The goal for occupational skill proficiencies was "to increase the number of vocational program completers who attain the vocational skills they need to pursue further education or work." This was to be measured by "vocational program completion." The core indicators which would be included:

> *"The state will increase the percentage of 12th grade secondary students who complete a vocational program sequence after completing a vocational course in any vocational area, as of June 30 of their senior year." "The state will increase the percentage of adult ROCP and adult education students who earn a Certificate of completion."*

The level of performance measure for secondary school completion was *"to increase the percentage of students who complete their education."* The state had identified that 14% of the students taking vocational education complete a vocational program, i.e., a series of courses. The 14% figure was set as a transition measure and would be adjusted when data on 12th grade student performance were available. The state planned to adopt new measures once these data became available.

For adults in the K-12 system, the level of performance measure was to raise the percentage of adults who receive a Certificate of Completion from 43.8% to 55% over the five-year period of the federal law. Further, that 73.9% of all adults that take initial course work in a ROCP or adult school would complete a vocational education program. Again, the measure would be adjusted when baseline data become available. (An author's note, this measure may need further clarification as the ROCPs do not offer programs per se, i.e., a sequence of courses as it is not allowed by law.)

The performance goal for secondary school completion was *to increase the percentage of students who complete their education.* The proposed measure was *the award of a diploma or its equivalent to secondary students.* The core indicator which would be used states:

> *"The state will increase the percentage of 12th grade vocational program completers who receive a secondary school diploma or its equivalent by June 30 of their senior year."*

The level of performance goal was to raise the number who complete a vocational program from 84.9% or greater in 1999-2000 to 92% by 2003-2004. Again, the level would be revised when data on student performance became available.

The performance goal for placement was *to increase the percentage of vocational program completers who are placed in postsecondary education or training, military or employment.* The assessment of this goal was planned to be done 6 months following completion of the program. The proposed measure to be used were *local follow-up of secondary and adult students completing vocational program, reported by placement in postsecondary education, military, or employment.* The core indicators to be used include:

> *"The state will increase the percentage of secondary vocational program completers who are placed in further education, employment, or military within 6 months following program completion."*

> *"The state will increase the percentage of adult ROCP and adult education vocational program completers who are placed in the further education, employment, or the military within 6 months following receipt of a Certificate of Completion."*

The level of performance would be determined by placement rate. The target was to reach or exceed 69.1% in 1999-2000 and increase it to 75% by 2003-2004. Again, the rate could be revised when data on student performance became available. The level of performance for adult vocational education completer was to meet or exceed 57.2% in 1999-2000 and increase to 63% by 2003-2004. The target would be revised when data becomes available.

Finally, the performance goal for nontraditional programs was *to increase the rates of participation and completion of males and females in industry clusters preparing students for occupations in which one gender constitutes less than*

25% of those employed. The proposed measure was the number of non-traditional student enrollments in, and completion of, vocational programs within industry clusters. The core indicators that would be used include:

> "*The state will increase the percentage of females at the secondary level participating in male dominated industry clusters and males at the secondary level participating in female dominated industry clusters associated with nontraditional employment.*"

> "*The state will increase the percentage of females at the secondary level completing male dominated industry clusters and males at the secondary level completing female dominated industry clusters associated with nontraditional employment.*"

> "*The state will increase the percentage of adult females enrolled in ROCPs participating in male dominated industry clusters and adult males enrolled in ROCPs participating in female dominated industry clusters associated with nontraditional employment.*"

> "*The state will increase the percentage of adult females enrolled in ROCPs completing male dominated industry clusters and adult males enrolled in ROCPs completing female dominated industry clusters associated with nontraditional employment.*"

The level of performance targeted at the secondary level was to raise the percentage of males and females participating in industry clusters from 16.1 % in 1999-2000 to 20.0% in 2003-2004. Also, performance expectations were to raise the percentage of females and males in ROCPs from 23.1% in 1999-2000 to 25.0% in 2003-2004. Again, the level of performance would be revised when student performance data became available.

Over the years, uniform and reliable data collection on student enrollment has been a problem for vocational education as previously noted in the discussion of COICC and COIS. Although, discussion have been held to solve this problem by utilizing a student driven data collection system using social security numbers, there is one barrier which may not be able to overcome. Federal law restricts collecting information on youth using social security numbers.

Finally, the 1998 Carl D. Perkins Vocational and Technical Education Act provides sanctions if the state does not measure up to its performance standards. It must then develop and implement a program improvement plan in the first year it doesn't measure up to the standards of performance. The state then has one year to make the improvements or funding may be withheld. If the state fails to make the adjustments two consecutive years the Secretary can withhold all or any portion of the grant to the state. However, the Secretary of Education can waive the sanctions if it is determined that exceptional or uncontrollable circumstances prevented the state from making the needed improvements. How this provision will be implemented has yet to be seen.

School to Career Opportunity System

Upon receipt of a planning grant of $750,000, collaborative efforts got underway in February 1994 to respond to the new federal School-to-Work Opportunities Act. The purpose of this initiative was to bring together employers, educators, students, and others to build a quality system that prepares youth for careers in high skill, high wage jobs. An interagency partnership was formed among the CDE, Chancellor's Office of the California Community Colleges and the Employment Development Department.

In June of 1994, Governor Wilson issued Executive Order W-94-94 to establish a new *"school-to-career opportunities system"* that included school-based learning, work-based learning, and support or connection activities that assist all students in meeting their career goals. A state initiative immediately got underway to address the Governor's Executive Order under the direction of the Governor's School-to-career Task Force. The Task Force was asked to submit to the Governor by October 3 1, 1994 a plan that contained all elements required by federal law.

This included such items as:

- a comprehensive vision for a school-to-career system;
- components necessary to implement the system consistent with the federal Act and other related federal laws including the Vocational Education Act;
- voluntary industry skill standards;
- utilization and improvement of labor market survey information;
- student assessment and certification system based on academic and industry skill standards;
- curriculum and school reforms that address school-to-career needs of students;
- statewide learning objectives;

- integration of work-based and school-based learning;
- integration of occupational and academic learning;
- professional development for teachers, counselors, administrators and industry mentors;
- a financial plan to ensure statewide implementation.

On November 18, 1994 a preliminary plan was sent to the Governor and the public for comments. Public hearings were held and the plan was modified accordingly. In August of 1996 California submitted a grant proposal to the U.S. Department of Education to implement a statewide school-to-career system. In November 1996, California received initial finding and over a five-year period anticipated receiving approximately $131.4 million to implement the system. At the end of five-years, the state would have to assume full responsibility for maintaining the system.

Funding of local school-to-work partnerships was provided through a competitive grant process that encouraged strategic activities that:

1. Integrate school-to-work principles throughout the educational system (K-18);

2. Connect school-based and work-based learning;

3. Promote community support for continued school-to-work development after state funding ceases;

4. Link school-to-work across workforce development, Welfare-to-Work, and the One-Stop Career Center System.

Some of the grant money was used for statewide activities such as technical assistance, marketing, regional coordination, and teacher preparation.

In 1995, the Legislature determined that development of a workforce "System" would require the simultaneous development of a single reporting system and passed SB 645, the Job Training Report Card Act. The Act requires many federally and state funded education and training programs to participate in California's report card system. This was a major undertaking that had numerous hurdles to overcome. The Act charged the State Job Training Council to be responsible for "*developing an education and job training report card program to assess the accomplishment of California workforce preparation system.*" By January 2001, there was to be a comprehensive Performance Based Accountability system (PBA) operating that would match social security numbers of former participants in vocational and workforce training programs with state and federal files that maintain employment records.

Any workforce and education provider receiving federal job training or vocational education funding was to, within the extent permitted by law, obtain social security numbers from participants 18 years and older for the purpose of tracking their academic achievement and employment history. However, in order for secondary level program administrators to comply with the federal Privacy Act of 1974, they would have to issue privacy notices to students informing them that their participation is voluntary. The system was to obtain information on such factors as program completion rates, employment and wage information for one and three years after completion of training, the relationship of training to employment, academic achievement for one and three years after completion of training, achievement of industry skill standards certifications, rate of change in status from tax receiver to tax payer, earnings before and after participation in the training program, and rate of advancement to higher education. After five years of development it was determined that the system still had some technical problems and was in need of some modification and fine tuning in order to achieve the desired purposes of a comprehensive PBA system.

California's Workforce Development System

Another collaborative effort impacting K-12 vocational education and job training efforts was initiated by the Legislature in 1996 as part of the Welfare to Work Act. They passed the Regional Workforce Preparation and Economic Development Act (RWPEDA). Senate Bill 1744 reauthorized the Act in 1998. The intent of the Act was:

> *"to move California toward a comprehensive workforce development system that would assure the State a world-class workforce capable of competing in the global economy of the 21st century."*

RWPEDA created a partnership which included the Secretary of Health and Human Services, the Secretary of Trade and Commerce, the State Superintendent of Public Instruction, and the Chancellor of the California Community Colleges. The Act required linkages with local government, economic development agencies and private sector employers to implement a comprehensive PBA system.

Each agency had a defined role in the collaboration. The educational system (pre-K through postsecondary) was "the foundation of the workforce development system." It was to provide the curricula, including credit and noncredit courses, certificates, and degrees, with subjects ranging from basic skills and entry-level employment training to advanced technical programs. Education was also to provide support services, including counseling, assessment, tutoring, child care, and where appropriate, one-stop delivery of services and training.

The economic development agencies role was to expand employment opportunities through the attraction, retention, and expansion of private sector business and industry. The private sector's role would be to provide employment opportunities, information regarding their training needs and requirements, work experience opportunities that help students develop relevant job skills and knowledge, and professional development opportunities that help educators keep programs current.

In April 1998, the three agencies entered into a Memorandum of Understanding (MOU) to carryout the provisions of RWPEDA to develop an integrated state workforce development plan utilizing a regional collaboration strategy. Their efforts resulted in the development of the California Workforce Development: *A Policy Framework for Economic Growth*. The document outlines a policy framework necessary to set the direction for an integrated, comprehensive workforce development system. The framework contained two kinds of policies: public policies that support the social and economic benefits to be achieved through the workforce development system, and system policies which were the foundations for the strategies and actions needed to create and maintain the system itself.

Workforce Investment Act

As part of the State Plan for Vocational Education, efforts are being directed to pursue implementation of RWPEDA Framework policies and recommendations that are most directly related to the requirements of the Workforce Investment Act (WIA) and the Carl D. Perkins Vocational and Technical Education Act. Both Acts, passed in 1998, make reference to each other and seek program compatibility and the avoidance of incompatible policies and procedures.

WIA, which overhauls the federal job training and welfare to work programs, will have a major impact on vocational education services offered in K-12 adult and ROPC programs. Unlike its predecessors, the Manpower Development and Training Act (MDTA), the Comprehensive Employment and Training Act (CETA), and the Job Partnership Training Act (JTPA), WIA gives the K-12 education a primary role in the delivery of youth and adult education and employment and training activities at the state and local level. At stake are approximately $1 billion dollars of education and job training resources.

Implementation of the Act requires the establishment of a State-level Workforce Investment Board to develop a state plan, develop recommendations and provide policy oversight, and facilitate the coordination among the various segments of the state's employment and training system. Some of the more significant changes WIA makes are:

1. Establishment of Individual Training accounts to provide vouchers for adults to choose the certified training provider of their choice.

2. Designation and expansion of One-Stop Career Centers as the primary delivery system for adult services at the local level.

3. Mandatory inclusion of adult education and Carl Perkins postsecondary programs as One-Stop partners.

4. Required performance evaluation with specific measures for all Titles of the Act, and require substantial changes to the data collection and reporting systems at state, county and local levels.

Under the JTPA, the CDE administered the 8 percent funds which provided $19 million in state and federal funding to local areas to support School-to-Career partnerships, work-based learning, and Cal-WORKs (welfare-to-work) employment and training programs. Under WIA, the CDE has positioned itself to assume a leadership role in administering all youth activities in addition to providing education and training services to adults. These are major changes that will face many challenges at all levels when WIA becomes fully operational following a transition period through June of 2000.

Vocational Student Organizations

One of the more significant and rewarding aspects of vocational education are the efforts and activities of vocational student organizations.

Vocational education has been the beneficiary of having some of the most dynamic student organizations in education. They are unlike any other student organization in the schools. This can be observed by what and how student learn as well as their business like attire which distinguishes them from the rest of the crowd wherever they are seen. They represent an ideal role model for America's youth.

Vocational student organization programs are organized around the subject matter career fields of agriculture, home economics, business and distribution, industrial technical, and health. They are an extension of the curriculum and are an integral part of the instructional process. Regional, state national, and international competition where students demonstrate vocational skills learned in the classroom as well as leadership skills are examples of how the learning process is enriched in these programs. The skill and leadership competitions fully involve corporate America who participate and support the programs financially as well as in judging student competition.

Although vocational student organizations are supported in the State Plan for Vocational Education, not all high schools offer an opportunity for students to participate in these organizations. However, while vocational education enrollments have declined, participation in vocational student organizations has generally increased over the past 25 years. This is a tribute to the quality and educational value of these student-centered programs.

In 1979, AB 8 (Greene) was introduced to support vocational education student organizations. The Act appropriated $500,000 annually from licensing fees for conducting horse racing to the CDE to maintain and strengthen statewide vocational education student organizations. The bill recognized the value of vocational student organizations as a viable instructional strategy which equips students with competencies and leadership skills needed for employment. The CDE was charged to manage the statewide program, including the training of teacher advisors to conduct vocational student organization activities. By 2000, state support had increased to $560,000.

In 1988, SB 2943 (Waters) established in state law the following requirements regarding the conduct of vocational agriculture programs:

> *"the curriculum of school districts that choose to participate in the state program of agricultural vocational agriculture shall include all of the following components:*
>
> *(1) organized classes of study in agricultural science and technology*
>
> *(2) a student-supervised occupational experience in agriculture*
>
> *(3) a program of leadership, organization, and personal development"*

The Legislature also said that *any learning activity developed to supplement these components shall be considered as a curricular activity and contribute to the grade received by the student.* Thus, state law recognizes the activities of vocational student organizations. In this case it was FFA, but it is the same for all vocational student organizations.

Future Farmers of America

As early as 1920, vocational agriculture students were forming school-based clubs. In 1928, the California Future Farmers of America (FFA) was formed in California. FFA is the "granddaddy" of all vocational student organizations. FFA was chartered by an Act of Congress in 1950. Membership in FFA includes all students enrolled in vocational agriculture.

In 1974-75 there were 297 chapters of FFA with an enrollment of 20,091 students. The number of chapters grew to a high of 323 in 1980-82 but enrollment dropped to a low of 18,240. However, this trend changed during the time statewide educational reform got underway and enrollments increased even though there was a slight drop in the number of FFA chapters. With the passage of AB 2943 in 1988, the growth pattern continued upward. In 2000-2001 there were 308 chapters with an enrollment of 55,448 students.

The success of FFA is due, largely in part, to the efforts of the CDE which sponsors the program. CDE agriculture staff provides on-going leadership and advice to the program. They work with local agriculture teachers/advisors and students to conduct a state program of leadership and interpersonal skill development. The State Program Manager for Agricultural Education serves as the State FFA Advisor. All other state agriculture staff serves as FFA advisors to the student officers teams in six geographic areas in California. However, FFA is operated by the students themselves.

Industry support for FFA is extensive and long term. The Agriculture Council of California, for example, annually provides instructional materials and conducts area and statewide competitions for members based on these materials. FFA chapters and members compete, are recognized, and awarded cash prizes for their accomplishments by the Agriculture Council of California.

The California Farm Bureau Federation is another organization which provides support for many FFA activities. They sponsor and coordinate a public speaking competition for FFA members at a "Discussion Meet." FFA members demonstrate their knowledge of issues facing the agriculture industry and their ability to exchange ideas regarding these issues with other FFA members. Annually, the Farm Bureau

Federation provides financial support to the State FFA Leadership Conference and the State Career Development Event competitions.

Future Homemakers of America

The next organization that was formed was the California Association of Future Homemakers of America (FHA). The organization was chartered in 1946. FHA went through a gradual transition of school-based home economics clubs to a formalized, statewide association operating through local chapters. With the passage of the Vocational Education Act of 1963, the scope of home economics expanded preparing students for occupations other than homemaking. FHA incorporated a sub group known as Home Economics Related Occupations, HERO. The first FHA-HERO chapters were chartered around 1970. In 1975 there were 2000 members. Currently there are some 4350 members.

On the national scene FHA has taken on a new name, Career and Community Leaders of America. California members voted to retain the name FHA-HERO to retain an identity which reflects the two types of programs that are under the umbrella of Home Economics Careers and Technology Education: Consumer and Family Studies and Home Economics Related Occupations.

California FHA-HERO is unique in that it was the first state association in the nation to establish competitive recognition events for members. There was opposition across the country and at the national level. However, California FHA-HERO prevailed. Now, all FHA state associations in the nation conduct competitive events.

Like other vocational student organizations, FHA-HERO conducts a leadership program for students. They have a strong leadership program for regional officers and teacher advisors who assist state staff in coordinating regional activities. Also, they have instituted an in-service activity for the students. It provides training on how to effectively utilize FHAHERO as an effective teaching strategy that is integral to classroom instruction.

Major business organizations that have a close working relationship with FHA-HERO include Total Communications, Inc.; California Restaurant Association; Hospitality Business Alliance; JoAnne Fabrics; Save Mart Stores; Johnson and Wales University; and Fashion Institute of Design and Merchandising. These organizations provide financial support to graduating senior members. In addition, business and industry representatives serve as judges for the competitive recognition events as well as speakers for leadership development activities.

Future Business Leaders of America

Another business oriented vocational education organization is the California Association Future Business Leaders of America (FBLA). It was formed in 1947 when many different school-level business education clubs were incorporated. The purposes of FBLA have been to augment classroom and laboratory instruction with opportunities for student members to develop those competencies not traditionally developed in the regular instructional program, such as leadership skills. FBLA also conducts skill competition where students demonstrate the occupational skills they have learned in the classroom.

In 1975 there were about 2400 members in 122 chapters of FBLA. Even though business education programs have been curtailed in the secondary schools, FBLA membership has increased to approximately 7,000 students in 2000.

The State Advisory Foundation for Education (SAFE) was established in 1987 by the California FBLA Advisory Board for the purpose of making additional funds available to deserving members and advisors of the California State Chapter of FBLA. Industry support for FBLA comes from a broad base of industry sectors with strong and important information technology functions. Companies that have provided significant support to California FBLA through the FBLA Advisory Board include: Bank of America, Pepsi, Chevron Petroleum, Xerox, Southern California Edison, Beatrice Grocery Group, southwestern Publishing and GESCO Corporation.

Distributive Education Clubs of America

The California Association of Distributive Education Clubs of America (DECA) was chartered in 1951. This organization was an outgrowth of federal legislation which recognized that occupational training was needed in distribution and retail merchandising. In today's job market there is a high demand for trained personnel in these career fields. However, occupational programs designed to meet those job needs are lacking. In spite of declining vocational enrollment in these programs, DECA increased its membership from 1,200 in 1975 to nearly 4,000 students in 2000. Student occupational competencies are assessed annually through competitive events at the local, district, state, and national levels. The competitive event assessments are holistic, standards and competency based, and are administered and evaluated by industry personnel.

Industry support for DECA comes from a broad base of industry sectors with strong and important marketing functions. Long term support has been provided by Miller's Outpost/Levi Outlets, the Rich Company, Bed, Bath and Beyond, Sketchers, Mervyn's, and Eddie Bauer. Industry support provides judges for student occupational assessment, staff development for teachers/advisors, scholarships for students, career orientation materials and speakers for students, and program direction.

SkillsUSA-VICA
(Formerly Vocational Industrial Clubs of America)

After many years of interest, students in industrial education formed California's Vocational Education Clubs of America, VICA in 1967. The national association, formed three years earlier, was delayed in its formation due to the objections of organized labor. The reluctance was based upon the reservations stemming from a concern that that such an organization might have a negative effect on the apprenticeship system.

Four chapters of VICA were started in 1967 with a total membership of 40 students. In 2000 there were approximately 4,000 members in spite of many industrial and technology programs being eliminated from the secondary schools.

In 1999, VICA took on a new name, SkillsUSA-VICA. The change was made at the urging of business and industry. Industry knew that their future of staying competitive in the world marketplace was vested in our youth and the skills that they develop in school programs, which includes participation in vocational student organization activities. Their rationale for the change was that the name VICA, in and of itself, did not represent the real spirit or mission of what VICA's programs were all about.

One of VICA's major accomplishments was the development of their Skills Olympic Competition program. It is the highlight of the year which includes leadership skill development for all students. In the Skills Olympics, students compete on a regional, state, national, and international level by demonstrating the job skills they have learned in the classroom. Judging for the competition is done by industry people, who also supply the awards to student winners. It is a major event and has stimulated other vocational education student organizations to strengthen competitive events for their organizations.

Some of the private sector companies that work closely with SkillsUSA-VICA include True Form Industries, Ford Motor Car Company, General Motors Corporation, Snap On Tool, Inc., Toyota Corporation, Briggs and Stratton Engines, Universal Technical Institute, Wyoming Technical Institute, Journal of Construction, Bosch Tools, and Columbia Steel Corporation.

Health Occupations Students of America

The Health Occupations Student of America (HOSA) is the most recent vocational student organization. It was established in 1987. Formerly, health career students were served by VICA and had a total health careers membership of 100 students. Membership has grown to over 1700 students and professional members in 2000.

HOSA is a national organization which serves secondary, adult school, ROCP and postsecondary (community college and university) students enrolled in a health career education program. Its purpose is to enhance the delivery of compassionate quality health care by providing opportunities for knowledge, skill, and leadership development of all health care education students. HOSA is a voluntary program that provides leadership development, interaction with health care professionals, career and employment preparation and physical, mental and social enhancements through integral activities in the health careers instructional program.

Students may participate in local, regional, state and national events and activities such as the competitive events program, public speaking opportunities, serving on committees and/or local, state or national HOSA officers.

Through the involvement of Judi Hansen, Director of Workforce Analysis and Transition for Kaiser Permanente Medical Group, scholarship funds have been made available to students who successfully accomplish one of the top three places at the State Leadership Conference competitive event program. Kaiser has contributed over $75,000 in donations plus many hours of in-kind support at meetings, projects and competitive event judging. Other health care providers and professionals that have been involved include Sutter Memorial Hospital in Sacramento, and Anaheim General Hospital, the California

Association of Health Career Educators, and the California Association of Medical Assistants Instructors.

Summary

The last quarter of the 20th century has been truly volatile for vocational education. Vocational education careened through an extended period of major changes in education and federal policy. This can be likened to being a proverbial pin ball on a steep slope, out of control, bouncing and missing one opportunity bumper after another, coming perilously close to dropping off the edge and not making a lot of big points.

Vocational education faced many big challenges and took its bows and lumps over the past quarter of a century. There were missed opportunities for which it had to pay the price in more ways than it bargained. A state level dynasty in the 1970s, vocational education leadership was reduced to a mere shadow of its former prominence in the CDE by the year 2000. Vocational education became a major victim of Proposition 13. At the local level, a large portion of its capacity to provide opportunity for students to gain the skills needed for entry-level employment were severely diminished with the loss of nearly half of its teachers, a large majority of it administrative leadership, and many of its programs, classrooms, and laboratories were put to other use. It may be unaffordable to rebuild this capacity if and when there is a rebirth of vocational education in the K-12 system in the next millennium.

The Legislature, which had been supportive during the 60s, took away some of the financial incentives which made it possible to expand vocational programs throughout the state. Vocational education leadership failed to heed the direction of the Legislature to develop a planning mechanism that would ensure coordination, articulation of programs, and delineate who was responsible in providing a particular program in an area among all training providers. Vocational education has probably been studied and restudied more than any other field of education in California. Throughout the 1970s and 80s, various attempts were made to organize vocation education to make more effective use of its resources, avoid duplication of programs and services, and ensure programs offered were geared to meet individual and labor market needs. The Arthur D. Little Report, RISE Report, and Commission on Vocational Education all provided opportunities for vocational education to take a leadership role and become a major benefactor in educational reform. However, vocational education never capitalized on these studies to ensure its future. There was no effective leadership or vision to advance the programs, policies, strategies with a support base to make it happen. Vocational education remained a federally driven program which provided a financial stimulus to maintain a federal rather than a California direction.

On the heels of these reports was the most promising of missed opportunities, the Career Education movement. Current reforms and federal policy are virtually a mirror of what was attempted by Sidney Marland with his concept of Career Education. Vocational education would have been the vehicle, the main driving force, for educational reform in the 1970s. The emphasis would have been on integrating practical vocational applications, concepts, and career guidance into the entire K-12 curriculum at all grade levels. All students would have benefited from an enriched curriculum that would have been relevant to the real world rather than simply the academic world. In time, Marland will be proven to have been right.

During the height of the civil rights equal opportunity for employment movement, vocational education was asked to assume new responsibilities. A large portion of its federal support was redirected to serve the needs of special targeted populations: the handicapped, disadvantaged, single parents, displaced homemakers, and the limited English speaking. It rose to the challenge, did a good job, but paid a heavy price. Valuable resources previously earmarked to keep vocational education current with industry standards for job preparation were redirected to ensure access to these special targeted groups. Further, it drove the limited resources available to small and rural school districts into large urban districts which served large numbers of disadvantaged students. State level services to the traditional vocational education subject matter areas were curtailed. This led to a major governance battle which has yet to be resolved.

Vocation education had measured success in addressing the needs of special populations and in sex equity efforts. However, once the targeted resources were removed from federal law, the state and local school districts moved on to new program requirements which focused on integrating academics and vocational education, and building on private sector linkages to improve vocational education.

The Partnership Academy program is an excellent example of a successful program of building linkages with the private sector. It is a model program targeted primarily for at-risk students utilizing a team approach involving vocational and academic teachers and private sector involvement throughout. This includes planning, mentoring, providing work experience opportunities, and job placement.

Another is the Tech-Prep program which involves the private sector which is similar to the Partnership Academy program. Tech-Prep programs are articulated from the high schools to the community colleges and pay particular attention to academic skill attainment as they relate to the industry the program is geared to. However, due to changing federal law the promising Tech- Prep Consortia model used by California may have to be abandoned.

Project Workability was another program that, due to its demonstrated success, was institutionalized into state statutes. The program continues to serve handicapped students who would have never experienced the opportunity to gain skills for a real job other than those previously offered to them in selected sheltered workshops.

In the 1980s, vocational education took a back seat in the state educational reform movement. It was not by choice. Vocational education was hindered from implementing the alternative means provisions of SB 8 13 which provided a mechanism to allow vocational education classes to satisfy academic graduation requirements. It was the first to prepare model curriculum standards needed to measure academic excellence in vocational education. Although the Legislature directed the State Board of Education to adopt model curriculum standards for vocational education twice, none have been officially approved by the State Board of Education. The CDE reportedly has scheduled to present the vocational education curriculum standards for State Board of Education adoption in 2002.

Reluctant to advocate support for the alternative means provision to satisfy graduation requirements, the Legislature directed $150,000 to the CDE to pilot test the alternative means provision in six school districts and report its finding to Legislature by November 1993. A check of records found no evidence that funds were expended or that reports were filed by the districts receiving the grants.

Near the turn of the century, it was federal policy that presented vocational education its biggest challenge, to experience an education reform of its own. However, this time it would not be to add vocational education to the public school curriculum as was the case in the early 1900s. Rather, it would be to utilize vocational education as a change agent by integrating academics into vocational education to improve academic performance of students. Vocational education resources and programs were to be utilized to repair the failure of the academic program to teach basic skills needed by business and industry.

The accountability focus of the 1998 Carl D. Perkins Vocational and Technical Education Act was primarily on quantifiable results without adequately assessing or certifying that vocational education students have acquired the job skills needed for employment. The major emphasis in vocational education at the turn of the century is more on succeeding in acquiring academic competencies and successfully completing high school than it is on acquiring job skills.

Vocational education's success is primarily being measured on how well it improves academic competence and high school graduation rates. This is being done at the expense of many students and has contributed to the decline of vocational education.

Students who choose to take vocational education participate in an enriched curriculum which has always emphasized the application of academic skills while learning job skills - rightfully so. One of the goals of vocational education has been to be a curricular vehicle to enhance academic learning through real world of work applications. On the other hand, students who choose to go the academic route without taking any vocational educational courses are asked to achieve academic competence in the basic academic core curriculum which has no direct practical relationship to the world of work. There must be a balance. It is not enough to have acquired basic academic skills; if one is not able to apply them in a work setting, regardless when one enters the work force, it becomes costly to industry as well as to the individual. Those responsible for the core academic curriculum have not been asked to enrich their curriculum with vocational education applications so students can acquire applied academic skills for an occupation or career in core academic classes. Given that roughly 20 percent of high school graduates eventually earn a four-year college degree, it is only logical that all students could benefit from real world of work applications throughout the curriculum and not exclusively in vocational education. Reform efforts have been underway for over 15 years without the participation of vocational education as an equal partner.

Efforts to develop a statewide occupational system to measure educational supply with job demand never were able to be successfully implemented through the collaborative efforts of state agencies. However, once the functions of the system were separated, measured success was achieved. The COICC has had a positive impact in developing career development and guidance information using technology to deliver it to students. Job demand information has become more reliable through the efforts of the State-local Cooperative. Job survey information is formatted in a manner which provides guidance information to students including needed skills and career paths to employment.

Another attempt was undertaken in the 1990s to develop a coordinated and integrated career vocational education delivery system in the state. Again, these efforts would be directed by federal policy initiatives, namely the School-to-Work Opportunity Act and the Regional Workforce Preparation Economic Development Act. These programs have brought together collaborative efforts of state agencies to effect an integrated, effective, and efficient statewide delivery system of career and vocational education programs and services. Time will tell if these efforts were worthwhile.

After nearly 30 years of operation, CACVE or as it was known in later years, SCOVE, the State Council on Vocational Education, no longer exists. Moving into the new millennium, there will be no third-party citizen oversight of vocational education in the State. Vocational education is left on its own to find its way. Interestingly, vocational education has as one of its basic principles for program development and improvement, the mandatory use of advisory committees. Advisory committees are of primary importance and required in both federal and state statutes. No one in vocational education stepped forward to advocate the need to retain the State Council on Vocational Education. Time will tell if this was a wise decision.

Finally, with the help of the California Legislature, stability and growth was sustained in several vocational education subject matter areas and vocational student organizations. Agriculture and home economics both were established in statute as state programs along with financial support. Both benefited from these statutory provisions which included incentive grant funding for both programs. The most sizable of these was for agriculture which receives approximately $4 million each year to strengthen its programs. The same was true for vocational education student organizations. Statutory provisions recognized the value of vocational student organizations as viable instructional strategies where students can learn leadership skills, compete, and demonstrate their skills learned in the classroom. Again, financial support was given to the CDE to provide leadership to sustain these valuable vocational education programs.

O'Lawrence, H. (2013)
The Historical Critique of Career and Technical Education in California from 1900 – 2000 and the
Status of California Community Colleges in the 21st Century
Santa Rosa, California: Informing Science Institute

Chapter Four

Technical Education is the Pathway to Social and Economic Stability

In March 15, 1969, the then governor of California, Ronald Reagan, presented a powerful speech to the 40th Annual Convention of California Industrial Education Association held in Fresno. He said that one of the heaviest demands for a share of the tax dollar is in the field of education by way of providing educational opportunities for all people of the state. This concept stems from a conviction of nearly over 200 years old that we could not have a government of the people, by and for the people, unless we have a literate and well-educated citizenry; the heavy emphasis on education in the allocation of public resources arises from a basic belief that life is dynamic and that to be fulfilled, one must grow. It is the function of education to help individual students fulfill their greatest personal potential and to help them discover themselves as individuals to the greatest extent that is consistent with law and order. The greatest resource of America is not necessarily only the tremendous wealth but rather the ability to utilize effectively human potential.

The task for providing opportunities for personal fulfillment and personal growth over a wide range of human experience is both formidable and urgent. Indeed we are becoming more technical, certainly in our industrial and our work life; technology and technological innovation are becoming more and more important in our day-to-day existence, more important to our economic well-being, more important to cultural enhancement, and more important to national survival. Can we proudly and appropriately describe our educational efforts to equip our young people with the skills and knowledge necessary for tomorrow's jobs – to employ a new phrase – "technical education" or as we may call it in 21st century, "workforce education and development"? This includes those programs which, over the years, have been developed in the area of industrial arts, vocational training, and industrial education. It is appropriate in today's technical world, and it is significant to repackage and revitalize to give a new impetus and a new style to the total program.

Indeed, we do need a new trust and new package to help in the important task of developing a new public attitude toward the entire field of technical education. Technical, industrial, or vocational education (whatever we may want to call it) must be seen as an open road to success and an opportunity for a new generation to be competitive in the global economy; it is an opportunity which will provide youth and the dislocated worker with a better understanding of sense of belonging in the world of work, and change will "reach" those students who are slow in learning and hard to teach. Education programs for industrial educators are an integral part of California's State College and University system. These programs are quite diversified, and they encompass hundreds of different occupational areas.

It is important in the 21st century workforce to redirect our efforts back to programs of CTE that prepare student entrance into the world of work. The CTE program must be strengthen for out-of-school youth and adults who are improperly prepared, imperfectly prepared, and unprepared for the world of work. Indeed as Reagan stated, we have answers to all our problems if we do the right thing; the answer to poverty is income and not handouts, the answer to unemployment is employment and not politics, and a great part of the solution is a technical program which prepares individuals for jobs that are available now and in the future. For the war on poverty to be won, we must go back to basic in training and retraining the dislocated workers.

Today American business and industry need a highly skilled workforce to compete in a global economy, and community colleges and other two-year postsecondary institutions are in the best position to fulfill that need. For those at the higher institutions, we need to teach in classrooms the transfer from school to work that requires a greater variety of educational preparation for work and the new levels of integration of general and technical knowledge and skills. Urgent demand and new ideas, innovation, and experimentation are needed if we are to survive the economic uncertainty that the nation is going through. These must be the cornerstones of a revitalized technical education program in our schools from elementary all the way to the university level. California has the largest program of career technical education in the United States and is an integral part of California's State College and University system.

Implications for the Future of
Career Technical Education

Writing a historical review would not be complete without some analyses of trends to gain insights for the future. Such analyses should be helpful to policy makers and career vocational leaders in setting a course of direction in the 21st century. As evidenced in this review, there were some interesting trends that evolved over the past quarter of the 20th century. These are outlined below.

Trend One

The first trend is the changing mission of career technical education through the integration of academics into CTE curricula.

Vocational education's primary mission to prepare people for gainful employment has changed dramatically over the last two decades of the twentieth century - most of these changes have been to respond to educational reform efforts to integrate academics into vocational education. Vocational education's mission has been modified from teaching job skills to helping teach basic academic skills and improve high school graduation rates. Less emphasis is being placed on specific job skill development. Rather than serving as means to reinforce basic academic skills through practical job applications, vocational education now assumes a much larger role of serving as a vehicle to improve student outcomes in acquiring academic basic skills as measured by local and state curriculum performance standards. These state standards are generally void of practical work applications which are taught in vocational education.

To some degree, educational reform is being done at the expense of vocational education. Declining vocational education enrollment, a reduced capacity to deliver instruction, and persistent school dropout data support this conclusion. Vocational education accepts the responsibility of supporting reform efforts with the understanding that it is an equal partner in the process. However, this has not been the case as evidenced in this review. In spite of the barrier of being granted equal partnership in the process, vocational education has done an exceptional job in educational reform efforts and will continue to do it better than anyone expected. Unfortunately, vocational education still impacts very few students, comparatively speaking. All students could benefit from taking vocational education, but are not afforded that opportunity for all the reasons previously discussed in this review.

Trend Two

The second trend is that the status of CTE as an integral part of public education has been diminished.

An elitist attitude prevails within the educational community that the primary mission of the K-12 system is to prepare students for the next level of education - postsecondary. The connection between school and work is predicated on the assumption that a 4-year postsecondary education holds the only key to one's success in the world of work. Yet, the number of jobs requiring four or more years of postsecondary education represents no more than 20 percent of the jobs, with the largest number of these being in the field of education. The statistics on the number of students entering high school that go on to complete a 4-years degree have not changed appreciably over the past quarter of a century.

No one disputes the fact that today's jobs require greater technical skills, knowledge, and abilities. The mission of educational reform should be to teach skills needed for success in a career or occupation. Every student should have the opportunity to develop a career plan, and take relevant and sequential classes that move them along a career path to achieve their career and educational goals. In many cases some or a full and complete postsecondary education will be an absolute necessity. However, most students will require continuing education throughout their lifetime in order to adapt to changing job requirements, or to change jobs. This is an appropriate role for K-12 adult vocational education programs. School reform efforts should be directed at making career and occupational preparation available to all students who want or need it as prescribed in SB 812.

The private sector should demand a change in the focus of reform efforts, but appear to be caught up in the idea that the return to basics is the answer to getting better qualified workers. On the international scene, 19 European and Asian countries already require technical reading, math, and applied science skills for high school graduation. In 14 of these countries, technical skills are required to enter the 9th grade. These countries are gearing up for global competition which was the main reason the private sector got involved in California's reforms in the first place.

In California and the nation, vocational education is being measured on how well (raw numbers) it's contributing to improving academic achievement and if students are successfully graduating from high school. Basically, there are no measures in California's school accountability system on how well students have acquired basic technical reading, math, and applied science skills, nor if they have acquired job competencies required for employment. The system is virtually void of such measures, and functions under the assumption that attainment of basic academic skills and a high school diploma are the exclusive and primary mission of the public schools. Former Secretary of Education John W. Gardner best expressed what vocational education faces today within the context of educational reform in California and the nation:

> *"An excellent plumber is infinitely more admirable than an incompetent philosopher. The society which scorns excellence in plumbing because plumbing is a humble activity and tolerates shoddiness in philosophy because it is an exalted activity will have neither good plumbing nor good philosophy. Neither its pipes nor it theories will hold water."* (California Advisory Council on Vocational Education (5th annual report), 1984)

Vocational education is caught up in the vortex of reform and is being swept along to achieve academic excellence and is not positioned within the educational power base to say much about its own destiny. Reflecting on the work of the National Commission of Vocational Education, Chairman Harry F. Silberman said:

> *"We concluded that some of the methods being used to achieve reform were incompatible with the goal they were intended to reach-namely, increasing the competitiveness of our economy by enhancing the capability of our labor force. The school reform movement had tended to ignore or dismiss the role of vocational education in promoting excellence and equity in education. We did not think that adding more of the same academic courses without changing the way they are taught would improve our educational system."*

Trend Three

A third trend is that CTE has a diminished capacity to deliver instructional programs needed to contribute to the career needs and aspirations of students and to satisfy the skills needed to keep California competitive in the global economy.

Since the passage of Proposition 13 and SB 813, vocational education has suffered tremendously. Over half of the secondary teachers were lost in the process, vocational classrooms, shops and laboratories were closed and converted to some other use by the schools. Many new schools are being built today without shops and practical arts classrooms and laboratories. In addition, many teacher training programs no longer exist to prepare and upgrade vocational education teachers. The end result is that California may have "tossed the baby out with the bath-water." The state may never be able to recapture that capacity to deliver vocational instruction to students. If and when state policy makers have a revelation that there needs to be a resurgence of vocational education in the schools, it will be unaffordable to recapture the infrastructure capacity, nor will it be possible to train teachers to teach these programs. Unfortunately, no one person is being held personally accountable for allowing this situation to occur, but all fingers point toward Sacramento. Californians are paying the price for the mismanagement of our schools, especially our youth who are our future and tomorrow's workers.

Trend Four

A fourth trend is that the justification for federal support of CTE has changed from maintaining our national defense to ensuring our nation's ability to compete in a global economy.

Federal support and funding for vocational education was initiated in 1917 as an outgrowth of World War I when the need was fueled by the war effort. Justification to provide federal support was based on the need to maintain a national defense. This justification served the country well and held for the better part of the century. However, after the end of Cold War, this justification was modified to address global competition due to the explosion of technology and social change. In order to meet the technical skill needs of industry, federal aid was directed to the schools to improve education and training programs. Also, massive federal and state efforts were undertaken to train the unemployed and the under employed, to provide equal opportunity for the disadvantaged, to remove people from welfare, and to provide general training for special need populations so that all people in the nation could be contributing members of society. Vocational education played a pivotal role in that effort. It also paved the way for other federal programs to aid education and job training efforts.

It is very apparent that federal and state efforts have not been all that successful over the past 30 years. Expenditures for job training, for example, have increased dramatically as has the system it supports. Yet, the problems of unemployment, under-employment, and unequal opportunity still exist. If any of these programs had been successful, they would no longer be needed. Instead, they keep getting bigger. The problem has and will continue to be that federal support is misdirected. Funding priorities should be changed to support capacity building at the K-12 level so that everyone has the opportunity to gain the basic job skills along with a career plan needed for successful entry and progress in a career and occupation, or to continue their education at the postsecondary level. Policy makers need to attack the problems at the front end and not try to repair the failures of the existing education system to prepare people for the world of work with job training programs which are, at best, politically expedient and costly short term solutions. Remediation has always been more costly than prevention programs.

Trend Five

A fifth trend is that there is an increased use of leveraging the participation of the private sector in vocational education to increase financial and programmatic support as well serving as proactive change agents to get the schools to employ new approaches to organizing and delivering vocational education instruction to students.

State and federal policy has been instrumental in creating an active role for the private sector in vocational education. The Partnership Academy, Project Workability, and Tech Prep are prime examples of such efforts. Not only do the students who participate in these programs benefit from the active participation of the private sector, but so do the schools. Ultimately, the employer benefits by getting employees who possess the necessary basic academic and job skills to be successful employees. Rather than spending excessive and unnecessary resources to train unprepared employees in basic skills, they turn relatively small investments into a positive return.

The cost benefits of helping attack the problem at the front end is a much more efficient way of doing business. Unfortunately, the number of students being served in vocational education programs using the collaborative efforts of business and industry is limited. State and federal resources are primarily being directed to serve students who are failing academically or are disadvantaged. This effort is laudable, successful, and should continue. However, additional effort is needed to expand Partnership Academy and Tech Prep programs to all students who wish to pursue their career interests, which requires participation in such programs in high school. Until business and industry realize that they are only attacking the pool of potential workers at the tip of the iceberg, the problems of not having enough qualified workers will persist.

Trend Six

A sixth trend is that federal and state efforts are being directed to develop an articulated and coordinated delivering system for CTE and job training programs.

This is a major trend which has been occupying policy makers and agency directors at the state level since the early 1990s. Collaboration is the name of the game to develop an articulated, coordinated, and accountable delivery system to address the training needs of the state. The need for such a system has been obvious for better than 30 years as first evidenced in the Arthur D. Little Report, then by CACVE and the California Legislature. Several legislative efforts were made but failed, no thanks to ineffective leadership from the CDE and vocational education. In 1994, when the Governor and Legislature initiated a new work force preparation system for California, it was determined that there were at least 23 state operated programs dealing with vocational and job training. As new federal laws were passed by Congress in the mid to late 1990s, this set the framework and financial support to implement such a system in the state. This was the capstone of California's One-Stop Career Center System and the various elements that support it. However, just as past efforts have gone, it is not an easy task and there are many obstacles with some possibly being insurmountable to overcome.

Trend Seven

A seventh trend is that there is a growing interest by higher education in CTE programs as a source of future students who will be able to succeed in 4-year academic setting.

Higher education has a major stake in educational reform outcomes. It is and will continue to be the major benefactor of educational reforms that successfully prepare more students to attend postsecondary education at the University of California or the State University system. The livelihood of academic faculty is dependent on having their classrooms and laboratories filled with a steady stream of students from the public high schools. The very stature of the University, and the public's support of higher education, demands that everything be done to assure University classrooms are filled.

An interesting phenomenon has occurred over the later part of the past decade. There has been a growing interest in vocational education by University leaders. This has evolved out of vocational education's success in integrating academics into their curriculum and local school districts successfully submitting vocational education courses for approval to meet University A-F entrance course requirements. Vocational education has demonstrated that it can offer courses with the same vigor as academic classes. Second, recent research by University personnel have found (rediscovered) that students who learn through practical application teaching methods do as well or better than students taking traditional academic courses. The students are more motivated, see a relationship of what they are learning to their future goals, and have more confidence in themselves than their academic counterparts. Vocational educators have known this for a long time and the idea of "learning by doing" has been a guiding principle of vocational education instructional methodology. A potential outcome of university research could lead to the utilization of applied learning methods as the preferred method to teach students at all levels of education.

Trend Eight

An eighth trend is that program survival depends on the ability to successfully advocate its need and institutionalizing the program in state statute.

There are at least five or maybe six programs that have been successful in this regard. These include vocational agriculture, home economics, Workability, the ROCP, and the Partnership Academy. There is a lesson to be learned by vocational education. Without state policy support in statute, survival is much more difficult. Efforts to establish a comprehensive policy structure for vocational education under the leadership CACVE was not seen as essential or needed at the time it was advanced. Possibly because it was so complex to be understood or that CACVE lacked the political savvy on how to advance it through the legislative process. However, in the long run, it was a missed opportunity that cannot be recaptured. Timing is ever so important, and to attempt such an effort again may be next to impossible for a number of reasons already outlined in this review.

When it comes to timing, one program that stands out is agriculture. It not only had the know how and political clout to institutionalize its program in state statutes as part of statewide educational reform efforts, but also got funding to keep the program current with industry. Another is the ROCP which was institutionalized by the Legislature in the 1960s and has been successful in strengthening its position through legislative actions over the years. Although somewhat limited in its capacity to expand program delivery, it has a major funding base to support programs. However, due to the lessening of options for high school students to take vocational education in school or the ROCP, the ROCP is serving a larger number of adult students.

Trend Nine

A ninth trend is that current educational reforms are following a traditional pattern of roughly 30 year time periods to implement.

Current efforts to reform California's public schools have been underway for over 20 years. One of its elements, supported by federal policy and funding, is to integrate academics into vocational education. In many ways, this effort is a revisit of the educational reforms attempted and abandoned in the early 1970s. Those reform efforts were initiated by Sidney Marland with the Career Education movement. A reverse strategy is being employed in present day reforms. Rather than infusing vocational education strands throughout the curriculum, academics are being infused into vocational education. Vocational education's failure to embrace the Career Education movement in the 1970s was a missed opportunity from which it has suffered the consequences.

If the public fully understood how difficult it is to implement change in education, they would know why the improvement of student outcomes has been so dismal. In 1967-68, the California Association of Secondary School Administrators Association Subcommittee on Applied Arts issued a report titled, "Issues in Occupational Education." The report, written by secondary school administrators, was a condemnation of the public school system. Some of the findings are applicable to today's reforms and problems facing their implementation.

The report made the following observations:

- There is a 30-year lag between innovation in education and widespread adoption of the innovation. In fact, it takes about 15 years for the first 3 percent of schools to make any given change. Yet, there are estimates that as much technical knowledge will be developed in the next 30 years as has been accumulated in the entire past history of mankind.

- There are too many constraints to change in our secondary schools today which result in failures to meet advancing needs of children and youth in a time of social and technological revolution.

- The secondary schools tend to deal with conventionalized forms of knowledge and with highly conventional approaches to scheduling, providing units of credit, and measuring progress. It can be expected to reflect patterns of inclusion and exclusion, emphasis, and subordination, which support its conventions.

- Schools tend to withdraw from society and favor a sheltered secure position in which school practices perpetuate themselves in terms of staffing, courses, organization and time.

- Teachers tend to reflect attitudes toward children and youth based on high grades as a basis for acceptance and on low grades as a basis for rejection, both based on a college-oriented, academic curriculum.

- School districts and their educational leadership tend to confine themselves to small, insignificant, internal management problems rather than attack the major national, state, and local needs expressed by societal groups.

- Schools and their personnel have been willing to manipulate change in material things, but somewhat reluctant to assess the needs of children and youth as basis for planning instructional activities that might require changed behavior on the part of staff or to "rock the organizational boat."

- The system of counseling and directing students toward careers has been inadequate. Parents, teachers, and counselors themselves are simply not informed about what students' options are, and they try to force them into slots, which high school and college curricula reinforce.

Although this report was written over 30 years ago it is applicable today. It should give the reader some insight into why it takes so long for schools to change. In vocational education, the direction of change is predicated on federal policy which has changed often over the past quarter of a century. By the time schools get moving in a particular direction, new requirements take them into another direction. Also, there hasn't been a problem to repackage the policy and to try it again and again with different requirements and adding more money. It is not a very cost effective use of public funds. Congress is not alone; the state Legislature does the same thing. Programs that come up for sunset review are continued without having the benefit of a full assessment. This is especially true when the author has his or her name in the statute, e.g., Unruh Reading Program.

Unfortunately, vocational education doesn't stand alone when it comes to reacting to policy changes. The same can be said for education as a whole, which must respond to ever changing state and federal policy requirements. California probably has more laws governing education than any other state. The public is not getting its bang for the buck and is troubled because there is no easy answer to the problem. However, the Legislature continues to pass more statutes each year adding more mandates, categorical programs, educational requirements, etc. and often funding them with federal funds that are the responsibility of the State Board of Education. Vocational education funds have been a major resource to both the Legislature and the Superintendent of Public Instruction to achieve a variety of purposes, not all of which have been directly related to existing vocational education policy. It has been an easy cookie jar to raid.

Conclusion

These are the trends identified based upon this historical review. Creative leadership will be needed in the 21st century to create and implement a vision for vocational education. As noted throughout this review, there were numerous missed opportunities which vocational education failed to capitalize on. Vocational education can no longer fail to take advantage of every opportunity presented to it to strengthen and improve the program. It can no longer afford to be an island unto itself totally relying on federal funding and policy direction. Rather, it needs to become an active participating partner within the entire spectrum of public education coupled with clearly defined state policy direction and fiscal support. If vocational education is to continue to be a viable program in the public schools, then it needs proactive leadership to ensure its future. Hopefully, this historical review will provide some insight into developing that vision and leadership.

Bibliography for Chapters 1-4

American Vocational Association. (1998) *Official guide to the Perkins Act of 1998*. Alexandria,

Area VI County Office Assistant Superintendents Vocational Education Committee. (n.d.). *Balancing the curriculum with vocational education a strategies handbook*. (Working Papers)

Arraez, C. (1984). *Conditions of Education in California: 1984*. Stanford, CA: Policy Analysis for California Education.

Arthur D. Little, Inc. (1970). *A policy and system study of California vocational education*. A report prepared for the California State Board of Education. Sacramento.

Assembly Bill 576 Task Group. (1980). *Vocational education and youth employment training programs in California*. A report to the California Legislature. Sacramento.

Bancroft-Whitney Company. Statutes of California. San Francisco: 1900-1901.

Bancroft-Whitney Company. Statutes of California. San Francisco: 1916.

Berrnan, Weiler Associates. Restructuring California Education. Berkeley: 1988.

Bogetich, T. M. (1978). *A historical perspective: Conditions leading/contributing to the issues of vocation education governance and state-level services in California*. Sacramento

Bogetich, T. M. (1984). *Vocational Education in the High School*. Prepared for the California Coalition on Occupational Education. Sacramento.

Bogetich, Thomas M. (1984). *Vocational Education in California State of the State*. Presentation to the California Vocational Education Association.

Bogetich, T. M. (1985). *The value of experience in the world of work for students*. Presentation at the Work-Ability II Luncheon. San Francisco.

California Advisory Council on Vocational Education. (1973). *Fourth annual report: Toward equal opportunity*. Sacramento

California Advisory Council on Vocational Education. (1975). *Review of the development and management of manpower and related in California vocational education*. Sacramento

California Advisory Council on Vocation Education. (1976). *A survey of the effects of the five percent budget limitation on adult and vocational education programs and services.* Sacramento.

California Advisory Council on Vocational Education. (1977). *Barriers and bridges: Overview of vocational education services available for handicapped Californians.* Sacramento.

California Advisory Council on Vocational Education. (1977). *A study of the governance of vocational education: Issues related to SB 1028.* Working Papers. Sacramento.

California Advisory Council on Vocational Education. (1978). *Vocational education in California: A focused study of progress toward statewide goals.* Sacramento.

California Advisory Council on Vocational Education. (1978). *Ninth annual report.* Sacramento.

California Advisory Council on Vocational Education. (1979). *A study of the impact of Proposition 13 of vocational education technical report.* Sacramento.

California Advisory Council on Vocational Education. (1979). *Tenth annual report: Vocational education in California: A focused study of progress toward statewide goals FY 1978-79.* Sacramento.

California Advisory Council on Vocational Education. (1980). *Eleventh annual report: vocational education in California A focused study of progress toward statewide goals FY 1979-80.* Sacramento.

California Advisory Council on Vocational Education. (1981). *Twelfth annual report.* Sacramento.

California Advisory Council on Vocational Education. (1983). *Fourteenth annual report: A call for action! Comprehensive policy for vocational education.* Sacramento.

California Advisory Council on Vocational Education. (1984). *Fifteenth annual report: Opportunities for vocational education in the Educational Reform Act of 1983 alternatives that satisfy graduation requirements.* Sacramento.

California Association of Vocational Education. CAVE News Exchange. Mt. View: 1972 through 1978.

California Business Education Association. *Advocate.* Vol. 1. Number 1, 1983, through Vol. VIII, Number 2, 1990. Los Altos.

California Business Education Association. *CBEA Bulletin.* Vol. XVIII, 1987 Number 1 through Vol. XXI, Number 3, 1991. Los Altos.

California Commission for Reform of Intermediate and Secondary Education. (1975). *The Rise Report.* Sacramento.

California Department of Education. (1985). *California Agricultural Vocational Education Incentive Grant Report of Expenditures 1982-84.* Sacramento.

California Department of Education. (1990). *Focus on Excellence Implementing the New. Curriculum Annual Performance Report for Vocational Education in California. 1988-89.* Sacramento.

California Department of Education. (1999). *California Agricultural Vocational Education Incentive Grant Report of Expenditures 1997-98.* Sacramento.

California Department of Education. (2000). *California Agricultural Vocational Education Incentive Grant Report of Expenditures 1998-99.* Sacramento.

California State Auditor. (1999). *Perkins Vocational Education Program: The State's Use of Funds to Administer Other Programs Reduced Its Ability to Provide Effective Administration and Leadership.* Sacramento.

California State Department of Education and Chancellors Office of the California Community Colleges. (1990). *California Plan for Career-Vocational Education Part I: Policy Directions.* Sacramento.

California State Department of Education and Chancellors Office of the California Community Colleges. (1990). *California Plan for Career-Vocational Education Part II: Implementation Strategies.* Sacramento.

California State Department of Education and Chancellor's Office of the California Community Colleges. (1994). *Annual Performance Report 1992-93 Submitted to the United States Department of Education.* Sacramento.

California State Department of Education and Chancellor's Office of the California Community Colleges. (1995). *Annual Performance Report 1993-94 Submitted to the United States Department of Education.* Sacramento.

California State Department of Education and Chancellor's Office of the California Community Colleges. (1996). *Annual Performance Report 1994-95 Submitted to the United States Department of Education.* Sacramento.

California State Department of Education and Chancellor's Office of the California Community Colleges. (1997). *Annual Performance Report 1995-96 Submitted to the United States Department of Education.* Sacramento.

California State Department of Education and Chancellor's Office of the California Community Colleges. (1998). *Annual Performance Report 1996-97 Submitted to the United States Department of Education.* Sacramento.

California State Department of Education and Chancellor's Office of the California Community Colleges. (1999). *Annual Performance Report 1997-98 Submitted to the United States Department of Education.* Sacramento.

California State Department of Education and Chancellor's Office of the California Community Colleges. (2000). *Annual Performance Report 1998-99 Submitted to the United States Department of Education.* Sacramento.

California State Department of Education and Chancellor's Office of the California Community Colleges. (1991). *California State Plan for Carl D. Vocational and Applied Technology Education Act Funds 1991-94.* Sacramento.

California State Department of Education and Chancellor's Office of the California Community Colleges. (1994). *California State Plan for Carl D. Perkins Vocational and Technology Act Funds: 1994-96.* Sacramento.

California State Department of Education and Chancellor's Office of the California Community Colleges. (2000) *California State Plan for Vocational Education: 2000-2004.* Sacramento.

California Department of Education Standards High School Development Division High School Initiative Office. (2001). *Program Overview and Operational Handbook.* Sacramento.

California Occupational Information Committee. (2000). *California Career Planning Guide.* Sacramento.

California Occupational Information Coordinating Committee. (2001). *Grant Application and Budget: 2001-2003.* Sacramento.

California Postsecondary Education Commission. (1977). *Proposed Resolution - Adopting Governance of Vocational Education: A Proposal.* Sacramento.

Commission on Vocational Education. (1979). *A Unified Approach to Occupational Education.* A report prepared for the California State Board of Education. Sacramento.

Council on California Competitiveness. (1992). *California's Jobs and Future.*

Farmer, E.I & O'Lawrence, H. (2002). Differences in Characteristics of Postsecondary Technical Students in Pennsylvania Community Colleges and Two-year Proprietary Institutions. Journal of Career and Technical Education, Volume 18, Number 2.

Eastin, D., Hatamija, L., Johnson, G., & Nusbaurn, T. (1998). *California Workforce Development: A Policy Framework for Growth.* Sacramento.

Ferri, C. M. (2001, May). *Memorandum to High School Principals District Staff.* University of California: Berkeley.

Gardner, J. W. (1984). *Excellence.* New York: Harper & Row.

Governor's School-to-Career Task Force. (1994). *California's Preliminary School-to-Career State Plan.* Sacramento.

Hemsley, R. (1998). *East San Gabriel Valley ROP 1997 Evaluation Technical Report.* University of California, Riverside: California Educational Research Cooperative.

Home Economics Careers and Technology Advisory Committee. (1998). *Final Report for SB 1454 Home Economics Careers and Technology Vocational Education.* Sacramento.

Home Economics Careers & Technology Unit, California State Department of Education and the Home Economics Professional and Curriculum Development Project. SB 1832 Incentive Grant Sites Take Action. California State University, Fresno: 2000.

Hoyt, H. E. (1968). *Report of CASSA Curriculum Subcommittee on Applied Arts 1967-68 Issues in Occupational Education.* Northern San Joaquin Counties Supplementary Education Center.

Hoyt, K. B. (1972). *Career Education: What It Is and How to Do It.* Salt Lake City: Olympus Publishing Company.

Hull, D., Parnell, D. (1991). *Tech Prep Associate Degree A Win/Win Experience.* Waco: Center for Occupational Research and Development.

Legislative Analyst. (1977). *Vocational Education in California.'* Sacramento.

McCormick, J. G. (1986). *'Vocational Education Reorganization Proposal Review and Report.* Executive Planning and Management Analysis Unit, California State Department of Education. Sacramento.

National Commission for Secondary Vocational Education. (1984). *The Unfinished Agenda: The Role of Vocational in the High School.* Information Series No. 289. Columbus: Ohio State University.

Peters, P. (1974). *AB 1331 and AB 1486, Individualized Instruction with Integrated Vocational Education.* California Department of Education. Sacramento.

Peterson, P. E., Rabe, B. G., & Wong, K. K. (1986). *When Federalism Works.* Washington, DC: Brooking Institute.

Price, B. (1984). *The Effects of Funding and Graduation Requirements on Vocational Education in Secondary Schools.* Research Study for Superintendent Honig. Sacramento.

Porter, S. (1976, October 17). *Column by Sylvia Porter.* Los Angeles Herald Examiner.

Quinlan, C. (1989). *Vocational Education Squeeze, by Academics.* California State Department of Education. Sacramento.

SB 1832 Advisory Committee. (2000). *Final Report for SB 1832 Home Economics Careers and Technology Vocational Education.* Sacramento.

Silbetman, H. F. (1988, October). The Unfinished Agenda Revisited. *American Vocational Education Journal.* Alexandria.

Slayton, A. T. (1997). *Sex Equity is Happening in American Schools: Institutionalization of Sex Equity Promotion in Vocational Education.* Cambridge: Harvard Graduate School of Education. Doctoral Thesis.

Smith, W. P. (1979). *A History of Vocational Education 1900-1975.* Sacramento.

Special Education. "Workability I Briefing Document." California State Department of Education. Sacramento: 2001

State Job Training Coordinating Council. (1998). *Road Atlas for Preparing California's Workforce.* Sacramento.

Stem, D., Dayton, C., & Raby, M. (2000). *Career Academies: Building Blocks For Reconstructing American High Schools.* University of California at Berkeley.

Stern, D., Raby M., & Dayton, C. (1992). *Career Academies: Partnership for Restructuring American High Schools.* San Francisco: Jossey-Bass Publishers.

Tech Prep Resource Consortia. (1993). *Marketing Communication Plan.* State Center Tech Prep Consortium: State Center Community College District.

United States Congress. (1963). *Vocational Education Act of 1963.* Washington, DC: U.S. Printing Office.

United States Congress. (1968). *Vocational Education Amendments of 1968.* Washington, DC: U.S. Printing Office.

United States Congress. (1976). *Educational Amendments of 1976.* Washington, DC: U.S. Printing Office.

United States Congress. (1984). *Carl D. Perkins Vocational Education Act.* Washington, DC: U.S. Printing Office.

United States Congress. (1990). *Carl D. Perkins Vocational and Applied Technology Education Act of 1990.* Washington, DC: U.S. Printing Office.

Warren, E. (1998). *Four-Year Report on the Effectiveness of California Partnership Academies 1992-93--1995-96.* Sonoma State University.

West Publishing Company. (1992). *West's California Codes: Education Code.* St. Paul.

William T. Grant Foundation Commission on Work, Family and Citizenship. (1988). *The Forgotten Half: Non-College Youth in America.* Washington, DC.

Wilson, P. [Governor]. (1996). *School-to-career Grant Application.* Sacramento.

Wright, C., & Kim, Y. (1980). *An Assessment of the Development and Maintenance the California Occupational Information System.* A Study Prepared for the California Advisory Council on Vocational Education. Sacramento.

Section 2: Career Technical Education and the Community College – 2000 to the Present

Chapter Five

The Status of CTE and Community Colleges in California

The influence of Career Technical Education on the 21st century workforce reported in this review of the literature aligns with curriculum, instruction, and occupational experience, the current changing workforce, and the postsecondary technical education. In community colleges, vocational education is unique in a number of ways; it treats students as practitioners, preparing them for skilled entry-level jobs not requiring a baccalaureate; and it offers training in specialized skills such as technology. Evidence of research reported shows that there are many factors that contributed to the development of today's workforce education and development.

Under the authorization of the Smith-Hughes Act of 1917, the Vocational Education Act of 1946 (referred to as the George-Barden Act) and supplementary legislation enacted since 1917, Federal funds became available for allotment to the States and insular and territorial possessions for vocational education in agriculture, distributive occupations, home economics, trade and industry, practical nursing, and all area of vocational educations programs. Since 1917 the primary objective of vocational education has been to prepare students for jobs in order to meet the labor market needs of the American economy. Beginning in 1960, vocational education became increasingly concerned with meeting the needs of its students and of society (NAS, 1976).

The achievements under programs of Smith-Hughes and George-Barden are matters of public record. For those who are able to look beyond the immediate future to, say, 10 years from now, it is obvious that every dollar we spend on CTE programs will yield a tremendous return in savings to our economy. The returns will be twofold: savings in reduced welfare cost, and increases in income tax returns. CTE should be available to every student in all schools as specialized training regardless of college degree focus.

In addition, the Area Redevelopment Act of 1961 authorizes assistance to the States for the provision of assistance for needed facilities and services to meet the occupational training and retraining needs in redevelopment areas. The Federal Vocational Education Acts require that in order to benefit from the provisions of the acts, each State shall, through its legislative authority, designate or create a State Board consisting of not fewer than three members and having all necessary power to cooperate with the Federal Office of Education in the administration of the acts. The State Board for Vocational Education is the State agency responsible for carrying out the provisions of the Federal acts in the State and for the expenditure of Federal funds allotted to it.

Vocational/Career Technical education programs provide training for young persons in regular day schools and for out-of-school youth and adults, both employed a temporarily unemployed. This Federal-State cooperative endeavor is based upon the fundamental ideas that vocational education is in the national interest and is essential to the national welfare, and that Federal funds are necessary to stimulate and assist the States in making adequate provisions for such training.

Career Technical Education in a Changing Economy

Modern science and technology have opened new fields of endeavor and have liberated many from routine toil, but they have also created economic and social problems. New technologies have also emerged to create clusters of new occupations. Many traditional jobs have disappeared; including some which long had served as labor market entry positions for youth and provided employment for those with minimum skill and education. The workforce has gone through many changes in the last century; at the beginning of the previous century, wages were low, and the Nation did not even measure unemployment. Today, the Bureau of Labor Statistics (BLS) measures almost every aspect of the American labor force. The 21st century promises to be even more exciting and enterprising for the American workforce; due to all of the changes, the 21st century workforce needs to do more than simply adjust to the new economy and to succeed in the 21st century, California particularly must be prepared to embrace the changes in our economy on how we work, where we work, and how we balance the professional and family lives.

This pattern was common throughout industry – greater demand for skilled workers and less call for the unskilled and semiskilled as the American system of career vocational education was created to meet the National's changing manpower needs. The systems have supplied a steady stream of millions of trained workers since the Smith-Hughes Act of 1917 established it. As conditions changed through the years, the basic principle of local-State-Federal cooperation embodied in that act remained, but the program was modified and expanded by a series of subsequent statutes.

As the pace of economic and technological change quickened in the early 1960s, it became apparent that another look at vocational education was needed. President Kennedy called for a Panel of Consultants on Vocational Education; the panel surveyed the status of public vocational education and, in November of 1962, submitted its report. The panel noted that by 1970 the American labor force – those working or seeking work at any time during the year – will total 100 million people. The group considered the educational needs of all nonprofessional workers and concluded that the local-State-Federal vocational and technical education program can provide appropriate training and retraining for the Nation's workforce.

Vocational and Technical Education for a Changing Economy

Vocational and Technical Education is America's answer to the cries of business and industry for skilled workers. It qualifies persons for gainful employment in occupations that do not require a baccalaureate or higher degree. It conserves and develops our resources, prevents a waste of human labor, and increases the wage-earning power and productivity of individual workers. Over the years of technological and occupational change, the basic principle of local-State-Federal cooperation embodied in the Smith-Hughes Act has remained. Subsequent statutes, such as the George-Barden Act and National Defense Education Act have provided Federal financial assistance, advice, and counsel to the Status to support vocational programs designed to meet evolving conditions.

The last decades have opened new fields of science and technology. Almost every occupation now requires some degree of technical preparation. The amount of preparation has steadily increased; as society has become more complex, demands upon all workers have become greater and their tasks more complicated. Progress in business and industry has been accompanied by a trend toward specialization of workers. Today's knowledge is outdated tomorrow; skills in demand today may be obsolete next year. Occupations are constantly disappearing and being replaced by new ones not previously recognized.

These new demands on vocational education, reflecting a changing economy of industrial dislocations, declining opportunities for unskilled in productions jobs, decreasing opportunities in small-scale farming, and an influx of new workers into the job market, led to the passage of two short-term, far-reaching measures to provide the unemployed with opportunities for learning new skills. The Area Redevelopment Act of 1961 provides for short-term training programs for the unemployed in areas designated for redevelopment. The Manpower Development and Training Act of 1962 offers training for the unemployed and underemployed. Under both laws most classroom training is arranged through public vocational education agencies, although private institutions conduct part of the training. On-the-job training is done by direct contact between the Department of Labor and private industry. Both the Manpower and ARA training programs provide 100% Federal financing of training costs and pay allowances to trainees.

The Federal Vocational and Technical Education Acts

The Smith-Hughes Act of 1917 provided for the promotion of vocational education by a permanent appropriation of $7,161,455 annually. It appropriates allotment to the States for agricultural education, trade, home economics, and industrial education, and the training of teachers of these subjects. The act served as the base for the cooperative Federal-State-local program of vocational education (Public Law 347, 64th Cong.) 39 Stat. 929, 20 U.S.C. 11-15, 16-28. The act of March 3, 1931, extended the provisions of the Smith-Hughes Act to Puerto Rico and authorized an annual appropriation of $105,000 (Public Law 791,71st Cong) 46 Stat. 1489, 20 U.S.C. 30.

The Vocational Education Act of 1946, usually referred to as the George-Barden Act, provided for the further development of vocational education and authorized an annual appropriation of $29,310,823. This act authorized increased appropriations, use of funds for administration, vocational guidance, and training in the distributive occupations (Public Law 586, 79th Cong.) 60 Stat. 775, 20 U.S.C. 2 m, o-q. The Act of March 18, 1950, extended the benefits of the George-Barden Act to the Virgin Islands and authorized an annual appropriation of $40,000 (Public Law 462, 81st Cong.) 64 Stat. 27, U.S.C. 31-33.

The Vocational Education Act of 1963

The Vocational Act of 1963 was signed into law by President Johnson on December 18, 1963, to confirm the determination of the United States to provide person of all ages and ability levels in all communities with training which will qualify them for gainful employment in virtually all the recognized nonprofessional occupations, from the least skilled to the most highly technical, and including, for the first time, office occupations. The act offers increased financial support through a permanent program of allotments to states to assist them in the improvement of existing programs and the development of new ones. It also authorizes work-study programs to provide part-time employment for youths who need the earnings to continue vocational schooling on a full-time basis.

A Look Back at Tech Prep Academic Course Integration in Post-secondary Institutions

The level of support and the resource investment that tech prep consortia enjoy across the nation through states, the federal government, and the private sector comes about after stakeholders are convinced, via empirical studies, that tech prep is working. The results of such studies also guide tech prep coordinators and administrators toward designing programs intended to achieve a technologically improved workforce with greater career skills. The need for empirical data is critical to sustaining support for tech prep programs, especially in the future. Sooner or later, stakeholders want to see some accountability and concrete indications of how beneficial tech prep initiatives have been for postsecondary institutions, supporting agencies, students, career and technical education programs, and workforce quality (Farmer & Honeycutt, 1999).

Perkins Title II review. Perkins Title II funds partnerships of Local Educational Agencies (LEAs), BOCES, and postsecondary education institutions for the development and operation of CTE programs consisting of at least the last two years of secondary education and at least two years of postsecondary education. Secondary level Title II programs provide technical skills education that prepares students to transition to postsecondary studies. Title II programs are also designed to:

- strengthen curricular and other linkages between secondary and postsecondary institutions;
- develop CTE programs of study in high-skill, high-wage, high-demand areas;
- align school, college and community systems in these programs of study;
- support strong academic performance;
- promote informed and appropriate career choice and preparation; and
- ensure that students gain the knowledge and skills needed for careers in emerging fields.

Secondary students who complete programs of study are able to receive postsecondary credit for college and are better prepared to transition to associate or baccalaureate degree programs.

Title II programs are required to have accountability systems that are able to

- meet the new performance reporting requirements of the law and,
- document program impact

Title II technical preparation education can begin as early as ninth grade. Planned sequences of study in grades 9-12, 10-12 or 11-12 are closely aligned with two years of postsecondary study in a technical field, in associate degree or apprenticeship programs. All Perkins Title II funded programs are required to have seven key elements:

1. an articulation agreement between secondary and postsecondary consortium participants;
2. an instructional design that aligns a grade 9-12, 10-12 or 11-12 sequence of study with two years of postsecondary instructional design with a common core of proficiency in math, science, communication, and technology;
3. a specifically developed Perkins Title II curriculum;
4. joint in-service training of secondary and postsecondary teachers to implement the Perkins Title II curriculum effectively;
5. training of counselors to recruit students and to ensure program completion and appropriate employment;

6. equal access for special populations to the full range of Perkins Title II programs; and

7. preparatory services such as recruitment, career and personal counseling, and career assessment.

Part of the Perkins II goals is to conduct studies on tech prep and disseminate results nationwide (Public Law 105-332, 1998). This would mean, therefore, that all of the models in practice have to be studied to identify those that meet national, regional, and local needs and standards. It is very important to note the original master plan that the California district Board of Trustees in August 1986 adopted - a five-year master plan of which the purpose was to establish a high-school articulation agreement which will encourage and facilitate the transition of students from high school to community colleges, resulting in a coordinated curriculum between these two levels. It was also intended to gain strong board leadership and support for an articulated 2+2+2 (two years secondary, a two years associate degree, then completion of baccalaureate degree) model. For instance, there are the 2 + 2, 4 + 2, and 2 + 2 + 2 models, plus several other combinations in between; it is in the national interest to determine which of the models would be most effective in attaining national goals. The answer lies in further studies which would generate results that could be used to determine levels of achieved goals. Separate models need to have their own studies, since perceptions of each model's successes in practice vary, depending on who one talks to and which model is being referenced. Then, stakeholders seem to know, generally through available empirical data and by intuition, how tech prep initiatives are attaining the goals for which the donated time and resources are earmarked.

Several studies conducted seem to focus more on overall tech-prep initiatives that use a 2 + 2 model and show promising signs of success (Bragg, 1995). Those studies done on planning, development, and implementation of tech prep initiative model 2 + 2 have provided rich information and resources to use in determining how the model is performing in a general sense. However, more studies need to be done beyond what are known, in terms of models of tech prep activities and the effectiveness of different parts of each model. Focus has to be placed on different parts of the 2 + 2 as well as other models'. There are at least several reasons why empirical studies should be available on each model and each component of tech prep initiatives:

1. The need to develop a set of guidelines for a tech prep national standard that meets global workforce skills needs;

2. Information for funding agencies and stakeholders on an on-going and regular basis, showing the effectiveness of tech prep for a given period so that they may assess whether their investments in time and resources are worthwhile;

3. Provide administrators and educators associated with tech prep with the empirical data they need to decide on the tech prep's worthiness; and

4. Scrutinize tech prep concepts to determine areas that lack effectiveness in the initiatives based on empirical data available for each model and component of tech prep initiatives.

Sustained funding for tech prep in the future may very well hinge on the results of studies supporting tech prep's perceived accomplishments. Even the committed stakeholders (Bragg, 2000), such as states, Congress, and federal agencies that are committed to tech prep, also need to be assured that supporting tech prep initiatives on a long-term basis is a worthwhile investment in the future of education and the preparedness of the nation's workforce. CTE is a product of tech-prep and the question here is what are the differences between them; or why don't we stick with tech-prep philosophy and let CTE be blended with it.

It is therefore necessary to focus on conducting more studies on different parts of tech prep programs that have not been focused on and that are outcome-based. One such area which needs to be revisited is the 'academic course integration' component of tech prep initiatives, which is designed to integrate the academic courses in career and technical education programs and outcome-based. This will allow for the determination of the levels of academic integration already achieved so far in career and technical education.

Determining the effectiveness of specific national goals of tech prep/CTE programs is not easy to do because of different tech-prep/CTE models or designs currently in practice and the differences in levels of academic course integration attained to date. Therefore, more studies are needed to generate discussions, pro- and con, in professional circles about tech-prep programs and their impact on career and technical education. Findings would help to identify what resources are needed to fuel current successes in CTE activities into the future. Key areas to study include:

- Academic, career, and technical course integration, outcome-based;

- Models used in the initiatives, particularly 2 + 2, 4 + 2, or 2 + 2 + 2; and

- Make-up of local consortia and their curricula.

Determining the Effectiveness of Tech Prep

The ultimate goals of tech prep initiatives can be fully realized only by determining the effectiveness of different academic integration levels in the old tech prep initiatives in comparison to today's CTE. If the academic courses are appropriately integrated with career and technical courses and the pre-set standards maintained or raised, the overall effectiveness of initiatives may yield benefits worthy of the efforts and resources being invested in the initiatives. Studying some components of tech prep initiatives would help us to address parts of the overall purposes for CTE existence. However, complete studies to justify sustained existence of each part of initiatives may be needed to identify tech prep as a realistic vehicle and an educational reform method needed in career and technical education. Requiring applied academics in classroom learning through integration in career and technical education programs increases the need for advanced academic courses as an integral part of tech prep's goals (Bragg, 1992).

As stated by Bragg, Layton, and Hammons (1994), the decision by Congress to fund tech prep in the Perkins II, TITLE IIIE, 1990 provisions redirected national attention and focus onto the tech prep concept, even though similar concepts had been debated across this great nation for over a century. For instance, John Dewey (Wirth, 1992) believed that it was essential to combine career and liberal arts learning in order to provide students with education appropriate to the technological age. John Dewey's idea fits into the tech prep's well! Other efforts made, including those by Parnell, who was convinced that tech prep was an improved form of career and technical education, pointed to similar needs for tech prep programs.

All across the nation, tech prep initiatives continue to gain in both popularity and number among education, business, industry, labor, and community leaders. With such interest and enthusiasm being generated in tech prep, it would be counter-productive to not assure stakeholders of tech prep's effectiveness and that it is meeting the set goals. When efforts are focused on each of the different components of initiatives and findings are available to support perceptions then and only then would it be proven beyond a doubt, one way or another. Findings from studies would increase levels of participation by all parties involved once empirical data are available to support tech prep effectiveness at all levels in career and technical education programs. The information also would generate new support and needed resources in the form of funding for further improvement in tech prep effectiveness in the future. Studies would assist in identifying needs for reconfigurations of the make-up of consortia, in terms of partner participation and depth of commitment, as the parts played by and effectiveness of each component become increasingly known to stakeholders.

Based on available studies on tech prep thus far, it is perceived to be effective in career and technical education reform efforts and it may very well be a catalyst in raising academic levels in career and technical education programs (Bragg & Layton, 1995). A study by NCRVE (Bragg, 2000) points to tech-prep's great potential as a change agent, but also points to some uncertainties and troubled areas at local, regional, and national levels. There have been several studies on some of the models being used in tech prep initiatives across the nation, but knowing the effectiveness of each model should be a focal issue, if some form of a national standard is to be established based on those models that work.

For many years now, career educators have sought to identify working formulas that would help to raise the academic levels of courses in career and technical education programs and have been less successful at doing so. However, the good news is that efforts continue to be made toward that goal and, more than any other approach, the tech prep concept seems to capture the professional and philosophical imagination and interests of community and education leaders by its applied academic contents and its prospects of raising academic levels to new heights in career and technical education. A crucial component of tech prep initiatives is its integrated curriculum development, which it establishes within secondary and post-secondary education curricula. The integrity and effectiveness of the curriculum in meeting set standards in tech prep programs also must be determined.

Academic Course Integration

While the tech prep initiatives are being recognized as means to achieve academic course integration goals, educators should create more awareness for the need to test the effectiveness of the integrated academic courses in career and technical programs through empirical studies. These efforts by career and technical educators must be extended to their academic counterparts (the liberal arts teachers) as well. Once it is empirically determined that tech prep's academic course integration (and any other component) is effective, it would then be easy to determine the skills levels of students in tech prep programs in postsecondary institutions. Graduates would be academically competent and highly skilled for today's academic rigor, based on outcomes. The students who graduate from the program would be able to meet employable skills levels needed in career and technical education as a result of effective integration of academic courses in some form, to improve their chances in both academic and career programs by using the educational options created by the integration, and to be much more marketable in their chosen fields. Students who are academically competent, competitive, and skilled for the workforce in their chosen careers also make reliable and productive employees since they become lifelong learners by virtue of their being tech prep graduates which make them re-trainable for today's changing technological workforce environments. Therefore, the tech prep approach gives students more than empowerment; it allows them the flexibility and latitude to be well rounded in learning and challenges them to attain marketable academic and career skills. Regardless of which path(s) they choose (academic or career) to take in their pursuit of further career or academic goals, postsecondary tech prep graduates should be able to succeed in an academic environment, enjoy gainful employment, or become productive citizens through the lifelong learning skills gained.

Farmer and Honeycutt (1999) contend that community colleges would have to account for changes in their tech prep curricula to achieve set goals outlined in Perkins II legislation and that "community colleges will before long, issue a tech prep national report cards to American taxpayers …" (Bragg, 1995, 22; Farmer & Honeycutt, 1999, 724). Partnerships between community colleges and other Tech Prep Academic Course Integration stakeholders such as business, industry, and labor groups need more commitments in order to offer students and their communities the needed outcome-based career and academic rewards that will provide lifelong academic and career opportunities. With encouraging and effective tech prep practices being experienced in career and technical education programs in some places in the nation, there is still the need to determine how and which components of the models in practice are working. For example, is it or is it not necessary to determine whether or not more students who graduate from career and technical education programs are transferring to four-year colleges and universities than before, and whether a significant number of those students who transfer there are from community college tech prep programs?

Conclusions

Engaging in research on different components of tech prep is the appeal that has been echoed throughout this paper because it is the one critical element that would respond to the professional calls dedicated to the betterment and effectiveness of career and technical education programs. As Bragg stated (1993), the only way to know if tech prep is working is through studies. The future of tech prep may seem on a firm foundation and holding steady because all indicators are perceived to be positive in terms of its educational benefits. As many as 860 consortia were at the implementation stage in 1992, according to Bragg (1992). Such a huge number of consortia being in existence and recorded in such a short time tends to speak favorably of tech prep programs now and in the future.

The high levels of interest shown in tech prep initiatives over the years may or may not make a case for the need for further studies a matter of urgency. However, the lack of sufficient studies on tech prep initiative components may lead one to ask questions, slanted to reflect the need and call for more studies on tech prep. For instance, when will studies be done on different models other than 2 + 2 or 2+2+2? Is there a need to have appropriate studies conducted on other models of tech-prep, in order to measure achieved set goals across the nation? Why have not more studies been conducted to determine which models and components are making significant advances in reform efforts so far? The key point is that all models in practice across the nation are having an impact and the empirical studies should be done on all of them in order to identify and separate those to model national standards after.

In the meantime, the general perceptions of experts, coupled with available studies, may continue to guide us, indicating that tech prep initiatives are meeting identified needs of localities, states, and the nation. Whatever our perceptions, however, stakeholders' faith, coupled with existing studies, needs to be sustained and expanded. For whatever reasons, the level of optimism in tech prep initiatives remains high, at least in the form of support and investment of time, energy, and resources. There is little doubt among those in career education that tech prep is the reform approach needed to advance the academic level of career and technical education thereby making learning much more relevant, rewarding, and accessible to all students who desire to have a variety of educational options.

The role of community colleges in tech-prep implementation is a determining factor in the levels of success the initiatives will attain because of community colleges' defined leadership roles in the Perkins II provisions (Public Law 105-332, 1998). In their concluding statement, Farmer and Honeycutt (1999) challenged career and technical educators in community colleges to be aware of the fact that they (educators) may have to account for the outcomes of tech prep initiatives in their communities, one by one, all across the nation. In fact, all those who are associated with tech prep initiatives may have to account for their roles in creating outcomes in their localities at one point or another.

Through taxpayer funding, community college tech prep initiatives continue to gain prominence and significance. However, one question that still lingers in many minds has to do with an acceptable national standardization of academic course integration in community college tech prep programs. Again, a thorough study of components would help to identify those variations in the areas of initiatives in postsecondary institutions. The major challenge would be for community colleges to develop score cards through empirical studies to support their basis and justification, so that taxpayer funding will continue making financial and community resource investments in tech prep initiatives in the future.

There is a need for tech-prep concepts to be revisit for the purpose of finding which system work best for revamping unemployment among college graduates. Tech-prep would create globalization, technological change, and restructuring of institutions from major corporations to governments at every level that will transform State's economy to be strong with low levels un unemployment and strikingly small increases in inflation and several small businesses been opened. A new tech-prep program in our schools will meet employer demand for skills, changes in labor supply and in the acquisition of skills, the structure and organization of work; and changes in wages and compensation.

References

Bragg, D. D. (1992). *Planning and implementation of tech prep by local consortia. Implementing tech prep: A guide to planning a quality initiative.* National Center for Research in Vocational Education. Berkeley, CA: University of California, Berkeley.

Bragg, D. D. (1993). Leadership strategies for planning and implementing tech prep. *Community College Journal of Research and Practice, 17*(6), 519-532.

Bragg, D. D. (1995). Tech prep: Where are we now? *Vocational Education Journal, (April)*, 18-23.

Bragg, D. D. (2000). Tech prep: Winning ideas, challenging practices. *Techniques, (April)*, 14-17.

Bragg, D. D., Hammons, F. T., & Layton, J. D (1994). *Tech prep implementation in the United States: Promising trends and lingering challenges.* National Center for Research in Vocational Education, University of California Berkeley. MDS-714.

Bragg, D. D., & Layton, J. D. (1995). Tech prep implementation in the United States: The once and future role of community colleges. *Community College Review, 22*(4), 3-15.

Dykman, A. (1995). What school-to-work means to tech prep. *Vocational Education Journal, (April)*, 24-25, 44.

Farmer, E. I., & Honeycutt, F. D. (1999). Community college administrators and faculty opinions of tech prep. *Community College Journal of Research and Practice, 23*, 717-725.

Grubb, W. N. (1999). *Edging toward effectiveness: Examining postsecondary occupational education.* National Assessment of Vocational Education

Public Law (105-332, Dec. 31, 1998). Carl D. Perkins Vocational and Applied Technology Education Amendment of 1998. United States Congress, Washington, DC.

Wirth, A. G. (1990). *Education in the technological society: The vocational-liberal studies controversy in early twentieth century* (Reprint). Virginia Tech, Virginia: Department of Vocational Education.

Chapter Six

Strengthening Career and Technical Education in the California Community College System: An Implication for Workforce Development in the 21st Century[1]

This chapter is written by Renah Wolzinger, from Golden West Community College, and Henry O'Lawrence in order to understand the differences in Career and Technical Education (CTE) programs offered in California community colleges. Data from all CTE programs in five colleges were analyzed and the top 17 programs were chosen for their significantly higher number of enrolled students during the past three years. Only programs that were identified as vocational by the California Community College Chancellor's Office were included and this chapter identifies the core strengths of CTE programs that provide preparation for a state licensure exam. The results were used to develop a profile of strong CTE programs and to recommend ways of strengthening CTE program offerings in a single college environment.

Keywords: California Community Colleges, CTE vocational programs, Certification, CTE skills model, workforce.

Introduction

California has the largest community college system in the country, with 72 districts, 110 colleges, and more than 2.9 million students. There are more than 270 occupational programs, leading to certificates or licenses based on industry standards (California Department of

---

1 This chapter was previously published as Wolzinger, R. & O'Lawrence, H. (2011). Strengthening career and technical education in the California community college system: An implication for workforce development in the 21st century. *International Journal of Vocational Education and Training, 19*(2), 23-33 and is reprinted here with permission.

Education, 2008). The colleges range in size from small to large, from 1,500 students to 36,000 students, with one college in Northern California being one of the largest in the country, with more than 100,000 students.

California community colleges offer more than 175 degree and certificate programs. The certificate system is designed to provide workforce skills in certain areas, with the opportunity to obtain additional certificates leading to advanced job skills or advancement in employment. There are many exit points in Career and Technical Education (CTE) programs, where students either enter the workforce or continue their education. Some CTE programs also may be combined with general education to obtain an Associate's degree, and prepare a student to transfer to a 4-year university program (California Department of Education, 2008).

The field of Career and technical programs has evolved into a broader definition of workforce preparedness education, which is critical in today's high-tech work environment (Rojewski, 2002). The dynamic and increasingly global nature of work and the workforce, the evolving patterns of family and community living, and the need for career and technical educators to revise and update curricular contents so that constituent groups are adequately prepared to meet the emerging challenges encountered in the work place, family, and community have always been major issues that have substantially impacted CTE.

Currently, there is policy and financial support at the state and national level to increase STEM (Science, Technology, Engineering and Math) education in secondary and postsecondary institutions. The current national focus on increasing STEM education is an opportunity to demonstrate to students how disciplinary content areas, such as algebra or physics, can be applied to real-world situations and problem solving (Brand, 2008).

Educators and employees in California agree that the CTE system must focus on preparing students for higher-order-skill, high-wage, and high-demand occupations (California Department of Education, 2008). Fifteen sectors have been identified and two to seven career pathways have been identified within each sector. The CTE sectors for California as identified by the California Department of Education are:

1. Agriculture and Natural Resources

2. Arts, Media, and Entertainment

3. Building Trades and Construction

4. Education, Child Development, and Family Services

5. Energy and Utilities

6. Engineering and Design

7. Fashion and Interior Design

8. Finance and Business

9. Health Science and Medical Technology

10. Hospitality, Tourism, and Recreation

11. Information Technology

12. Manufacturing and Product Development

13. Marketing, Sales, and Service

14. Public Services

15. Transportation

In 2007, the California Community College Chancellor's Office developed ten committees to study the relevance of curriculum, responsiveness to industry, funding priorities, emerging industries, industry partnerships, and program development needs. The goal of these committees is to improve CTE education in the ten identified areas, which are: 1) Agriculture and Natural Resources, 2) Business Education, 3) Family and Consumer Sciences, 4) Health Careers, 5) Industrial and Technical, 6) Public Safety Education, 7) Career Development, 8) Research and Accountability, 9) Special Populations, and 10) Work-Based Learning and Employment Services.

The 2008–2012 California State Plan for CTE is designed to advance California's economic growth and global competitiveness through improved education including increased use of technology, continuous workforce development, and analysis of workforce needs and trends. All new programs are required to be submitted to the district and state for approval, based on labor market needs. New and emerging areas are sent to the California Postsecondary Education Commission for approval. The California Employment Development Department has listed the following industries as most critical for the California economy: automotive, biotechnology, construction, energy, financial services, aerospace, health care, hospitality, information technology, manufacturing, retail, transportation, agriculture, arts, media, and entertainment (California Department of Education, 2008).

In order to measure the strength of a CTE program, California has developed guiding principles for CTE planning and implementation. CTE is accountable by means of measuring and reporting student course participation, completion of CTE courses and pathways, student and program certification, transition to postsecondary education, completion of postsecondary certificates and degree programs, short-term and long-term employment outcomes, and other measures necessary to ensure program quality (California Department of Education, 2008).

The state also has identified 15 elements of a high-quality CTE system. These characteristics are leadership at all levels, high-quality curriculum and instruction, career exploration and guidance, student support and student leadership development, industry partnerships, system alignment and coherence, effective organizational design, system responsiveness to changing economic demands, skilled faculty and professional development, evaluation, accountability, and continuous improvement, CTE promotion, outreach, and communication (California Department of Education, 2009). Under the Carl D. Perkins Career and Technical Education Improvement Act of 2006 (Perkins IV), states and local programs will be required to report on separate core performance indicators for secondary and postsecondary students and provide an increased focus on the academic achievement of career and technical education students, strengthen the connections between secondary and postsecondary education, and improve state and local accountability. The above elements are also aligned in the Perkins IV legislation to determine funding levels for CTE programs, as well as in the defined career pathways for California students. The Perkins Act has been a critical component in funding college programs related to Career and Technical Education.

In an analysis completed by the U.S. Department of Education, the persistence and completion of occupational students entering 2-year institutions were reported. Students entering college seeking a credential had a 60% completion rate nationally. This rate is lower than for baccalaureate students, who have an 82% completion rate. There were no statistical differences between students seeking an occupational certificate or an associate degree. Students who completed an occupational program had a better chance of employment in their field than those who did not complete their program. The highest success rate in employment related to field of study was 74.5% for students who completed an occupational program and achieved an associate degree. The lowest rate of success was 42.6% for occupational students who did not complete the associate degree requirements (U.S. Department of Labor, 2008).

As labor market trends shift and financial support policies for CTE programs change over time, it is inevitable that certain CTE programs require updating, merging, or even elimination in order to fit into the current needs of the college, the students, and the community. CTE programs are one of the major tools that the federal and state governments are relying on to impact positively the unemployment situation in America. Many jobs that workers were trained for no longer exist and, therefore, job retraining has become a priority to bring people back into the workplace.

We wanted to verify the profile for strong core CTE programs that strengthen and provide preparation for a state licensure exam as defined by the California Department of Education (2008). This will show whether the profile continues to produce higher success rates for students. Identifying strengths and weaknesses in these programs aids the strengthening of CTE program offerings in a single college environment. We also examined several CTE programs, targeting representative California community colleges in order to develop a model of strong CTE offerings at an individual institution. Program statistics relating to characteristics of a strong CTE program were collected and analyzed.

California community colleges have a large number of CTE programs that have been in place since the 1960s. However, the broad spectrum of CTE offerings is not sustainable in the current funding environment. The programs in the community college system that prepare students for state license exams are among those that have historically been the most successful. This study examined several traits of strong programs under the CTE umbrella that prepare students for a state license examination. These programs are a foundation of a strong CTE division. This study will show that strengthening CTE in the California community college system during the current financial and labor market crisis can be accomplished by supporting and expanding programs, for which employment prospects is dependent on government or professional certification, and reducing programs in those areas that do not require certification for employment.

Data used from this report include credits, degrees, and certificates awarded statewide by program, and ratings of the top vocational programs in the state. Data are also provided on individual colleges on achievement and persistence rates of students. The National Center for Education Statistics (NCES) was also used to collect data. Data used from NCES include program completion by community college, including one-year certificates, one to two-year certificates, and associate's degree awards. The Bureau of Labor Statistics was also used to collect data regarding occupational outlook for jobs by job type, salary, and expected employment growth. The main data source is the California Community College Chancellor's Office, which is the direct reporting agency for educational data from all California community colleges.

Data were combined by year for each program by college and sorted for highest success rates as defined by successful course completion and achievement of a certificate or degree awarded by the college. Data were analyzed over a five year period from the California Chancellor's public data. We looked into students enrolled in postsecondary technical education programs in community colleges in California. Enrollment data were obtained by also using courses that were identified as having Vocational Education Status. Data pertaining to certificates and degrees awarded were cross-referenced to the same data provided by the NCES to insure accuracy by college and program. Data collected were statistically analyzed on a computer using Microsoft Excel and SPSS software. The data were sorted into tables by academic year to evaluate trends in the last three academic years, and then analyzed to evaluate program trends in enrollment; awards obtained, and program success defined by successful course completion, and certificate or AA completion.

Our focus is based on students seeking postsecondary technical degrees and certificates from community colleges institutions in California, and the students were identified by Full-Time Equivalent Student (FTES) data for vocational programs in each college. We identified major factors in three major areas: (a) the enrollment of students in each program using FTESs by semester, TOP code (Taxonomy of Programs for the State of California), and Vocational Education Status; (b) success rates by college and program (Number of enrollments with grade of A, B, C, CR, P); and (c) student program awards (AA/AS awards, Certificates of Achievement 30-60 credits and 18-30 credits, Certificates of Specialization 6-18 credits). Table 1 demonstrates enrollments in all programs of CTE in Southern California for the past 3 years. The table also shows programs that are in higher demand with their FTES, awards, and success rates. This table represents the overall growth in programs that prepare students for state or professional license exams over programs that do not require a license in order to obtain employment.

Table 1. *Major CTE Programs, FTES, Awards, and Success Rates in All Sample Schools Combined*

Program	FTES	Awards	Success Rate %
Year	2008-2009		
Accounting	1610.79	135.00	68.90
Admin of Justice	451.87	214.00	79.00
Appl Photo	406.52	25.00	67.25
Architecture	373.64	68.00	77.33
Auto Tech	440.71	172.00	74.67
Child Dev	669.81	73.00	77.00
Comp Inf Sys	732.26	18.00	64.63
Comp Software	748.06	28.00	60.30
Cosmetology	779.11	132.00	79.75
Dig Media	621.11	50.00	63.80
Film Studies	427.55	39.00	74.50
Graph Art/Des	245.81	30.00	70.80
Nursing	1154.3	615.00	88.17
Nutrition	521.28	151.00	75.00
Office Tec/Comp	449.21	31.00	55.88
Radiology Tec	315.73	75.00	91.00
Radio/TV	293.67	13.00	75.33
Year	2007-2008		
Accounting	1528.34	96	67.03
Admin of Justice	535.27	177	78.85
Appl Photo	492.49	21	58.75
Architecture	350.54	72	75.85
Auto Tech	483.64	314	74.98
Child Dev	527.34	75	76.78
Comp Inf Sys	282.75	6	67.02
Comp Software	389.65	25	61.01
Cosmetology	809	166	88.80
Dig Media	110.48	38	92.32
Film Studies	115.22	22	66.75

Program	FTES	Awards	Success Rate %
Graph Art/Des	196.26	26	70.73
Nursing	542.91	575	87.71
Nutrition	254.31	192	72.34
Office Tec/Comp	416.5	21	55.77
Radiology Tec	376.48	74	89.31
Radio/TV	256.12	9	75.40
Year	2006-2007		
Accounting	1417.89	87	68.89
Admin of Justice	214.27	212	79.46
Appl Photo	500.28	8	57.62
Architecture	351.81	31	75.93
Auto Tech	356.81	138	77.59
Child Dev	467.75	57	77.41
Comp Inf Sys	286.41	15	67.59
Comp Software	321.26	32	62.51
Cosmetology	716.18	48	93.01
Dig Media	120.73	32	63.32
Film Studies	119.81	15	72.28
Graph Art/Des	187.1	22	77.76
Nursing	829.58	417	87.95
Nutrition	234.12	108	73.65
Office Tec/Comp	403.8	20	56.08
Radiology Tec	361.49	99	89.98
Radio/TV	208.25	8	74.96

Note: This data was compiled from the Chancellor's Office Data Mart in the California Community Colleges Chancellor's Office

New Discovery

To answer the first question regarding strengthening CTE in the California community college system, data were compiled looking at the top 17 programs in community colleges in Southern California. Future studies could analyze smaller programs, or programs that are more prevalent in different California regions. Data included enrollment numbers by FTES and program awards. Awards included Associate degrees, Certificates of Achievement, and Certificates of Specialization.

Success rates were also evaluated to show whether the difficulty of courses in a program impacted program completion. There were several programs with high enrollment that also had a high number of awards, denoting that students successfully completed the program. Group 1 of programs evaluated by FTES and awards are Accounting, Administration of Justice, Automotive Technician, Cosmetology, Nursing, and Nutrition. In addition, these six programs grew each year in enrollment and awards between the years 2006 and 2009. The FTES for these programs (colleges combined) ranged from 440 to 1610, and the awards given were between 132-615 for the academic year 2008–2009.

Group 2 of programs evaluated by FTES and awards are Architecture, Child Development, Digital Media, Film Studies, and Radiology Technician. These five programs did not grow at the same rate as the previous group; however, Digital Media and Film Studies grew significantly in enrollment. The FTES for these programs (colleges combined) ranged from 315 to 669, and the awards given were between 39 - 75 for the academic year 2008–2009.

Group 3 of programs evaluated by FTES and awards are Applied Photography, Computer Information Systems, Computer Software Development, Graphic Art and Design, Office Technology/Office Computer Applications, and Radio and Television. From these six programs in Group 3, Computer Information Systems and Computer Software Development had tremendous growth in FTES. The FTES for the programs (colleges combined) were 245–748, and for the academic year 2008–2009 between 13-31 awards were given.

Success rates were highest for Radiology Technician, Nursing, and Administration of Justice (69%–91% success rate); however, they had smaller number of awards. Success rates were lowest for Office Technology/Office Computer Applications, Computer Software Development, Computer Information Systems, and Digital Media (56%–65%). These programs fell in Groups 2 and 3 for this study.

In order to strengthen CTE program offerings at a single campus, the goal would be to provide programs that lead to higher matched employment rates. Group 1 programs as listed above satisfy all of these requirements. Each of the programs in Group 1 (Accounting, Administration of Justice, Automotive Technician, Cosmetology, Nursing, and Nutrition) has a strong demand in the workplace (Table 1). Each of these programs prepares students for a state license or professional exam, which is required for employment in these areas. Group 1 completion rates may be correlated to programs that prepare students for their license or professional exams.

Table 2. Fasted Growing Occupations with Most Opening in California

Occupation Title	Average Annual Job Openings
Registered Nurses	9,900
Elementary School Teachers	9,320
Executive Secretaries	7,400
Bookkeeping & Accounting	7,140
General and Operations Managers	6,630
Accountants and Auditors	5,820
Secondary School Teachers	5,700
Child Care Workers	5,470
Computer Software Engineers	5,380
Managers of Office and Admin Support	5,160
Computer Systems Analysts	2,950
Lawyers	2,900
Police and Sheriff Patrol Officers	2,730
Automotive Technicians and Mechanics	2,700
Middle School Teachers	2,600
Licensed Practical and Vocational Nurses	2,580
Medical Assistants	2,570
Electricians	2,460
Computer Software Eng/Systems Software	2,230
Preschool Teachers	1,990
Network & Computer Systems Administrators	1,720
Correctional Officers	1,660
Cosmetologists	1,580
Multi-Media Artists and Animators	1,540
Graphic Designers	1,490

Note: Compiled from EDD Top 100 Jobs with the Most Openings in California (2006–2016)

Programs that were selected for Group 2 (Architecture, Child Development, Digital Media, Film Studies, and Radiology Technician) are already strong but have the potential to grow more. These programs are growing year to year, but could have a higher number of awards given. In addition, programs that are related could be combined to create a new environment of shared facilities, resources, and technology. Programs lacking a state licensure or professional license component could combine with programs that have that element in order to help them grow in FTES and program completion.

Programs that were selected for Group 3 (Applied Photography, Computer Information Systems, Computer Software Development, Graphic Art and Design, Office Technology/Office Computer Applications, and Radio and Television) had a good enrollment and steady growth; however, they had a relatively low number of awards compared to Group 1 and Group 2. These fields have a retraining element in common. Some students from industry attend these programs to get up to date on computer software and equipment used in the workplace. In fields involving cameras, video, or audio, the change from analog formats to digital and high-definition formats has altered dramatically those areas in the past three years. Software has changed to accommodate those new digital technologies. Another component of these programs is that they do not lead to state license exams, but could lead to professional exams. For example, software certification in Adobe, Avid, or Final Cut software could be incorporated into some of these programs. In order to strengthen CTE offerings at a single college environment, it may also be possible to combine programs to make them stronger. Using the programs from this study, the recommendations follow.

Stand Alone Programs

The Accounting, Criminal Justice, Architecture, Automotive Technician, Child Development, Cosmetology, Nursing, Nutrition, and Radiology Technician programs are unique and strong, and prepare students for a state or professional license exam. It would not be necessary to combine these programs with other programs. Combining programs might only be effective when there are many similarities and where the workplace requires a worker to have multiple skills for one job. These programs do not fit into that category. However in the case of Radiology Technician, it may be advantageous for one campus that offers other smaller Medical Technology certificates to share resources and combine with the Radiology Technician program.

Programs that can be strengthened by combining with strong programs are (a) Applied Photography, Digital Media, Film Studies, Graphic Art/Design, Radio/TV, and (b) Computer Information Systems, Computer Software, Office Technology/Office Computer Applications. These programs are broken into two groups, as they could share resources in these groups or could combine to be one large group. Group A may have different computer requirements than Group B. The second research question was: Can a model be developed based on strong CTE programs to aid in the reformulation of current CTE offerings in California community colleges? To answer this question, it is important to examine what qualities make a program strong in enrollment, completion, and student success. According to the data, one single attribute that all of the strong programs have in common is that they prepare students for a state or professional license exam.

Recent studies show that CTE programs in California are a vital contributor to the workforce. The Research and Planning Group (RPG) (RPG, 2009) for California community colleges states that California will suffer major shortages of available workers with bachelor's degrees in the next decade unless there is an increase in available workers, especially from CTE disciplines. This study suggests increasing the transfer rate of CTE students from community colleges to four-year institutions. RPG also states that the workforce shortages are forecasted to be in STEM disciplines.

The Employment Development Department in California has reported the Orange County industry projections from 2006–2009. Half of all new jobs in California are projected to be in the following sectors: professional and business services, leisure and hospitality, education, health care, and social assistance. The fastest growing industry sectors are projected to be education, health care, and social assistance. The top 100 jobs with the most openings in California are listed by the Employment Development Department. Occupations related to this are listed in Table 2.

References

Bragg, D. D. (1992). *Planning and implementation of tech prep by local consortia. implementing tech prep: A guide to planning a quality initiative.* National Center for Research in Vocational Education. Berkeley, CA: University of California, Berkeley.

Bragg, D. D. (1993). Leadership strategies for planning and implementing tech prep. *Community College Journal of Research and Practice, 17*(6), 519-532.

Bragg, D. D. (1995). Tech prep: Where are we now? *Vocational Education Journal, (April)*, 18-23.

Bragg, D. D. (2000). Tech prep: Winning ideas, challenging practices. *Techniques, (April)*, 14-17.

Bragg, D. D., & Layton, J. D. (1995). Tech prep implementation in the United States: The once and future role of community colleges. *Community College Review, 22*(4), 3-15.

Bragg, D. D., Hammons, F. T., & Layton, J. D (1994). *Tech prep implementation in the United States: Promising trends and lingering challenges.* National Center for Research in Vocational Education, University of California Berkeley. MDS-714.

Brand, B. (2008). *Technical education through federal and state policy.* American Youth Policy Forum.

California Department of Education. (2008). *2008-2012 California state plan for career and technical education.* Retrieved from http://www.schoolsmovingup.net/cte/downloads/cteplan_1228 08.pdf

California Department of Education. (2009). *ARCC 2008 Report.* California Community Colleges System Office, Sacramento, CA.

Dykman, A. (1995). What school-to-work means to tech prep. *Vocational Education Journal, (April)*, 24-5, 44.

Farmer, E. I., & Honeycutt, F. D. (1999). Community college administrators and faculty opinions of tech prep. *Community College Journal of Research and Practice, 23*, 717-725.

Grubb, W. N. (1999). *Edging toward effectiveness: Examining postsecondary occupational education.* National Assessment of Vocational Education.

Gray, K.C., & Herr, E. L. (1998). *Workforce education: The basics.* Boston, MA: Allyn and Bacon.

The Research and Planning Group for California Community Colleges (2009). *CTE transfer research project.* Retrieved from http://www.rpgroup.org/documents/CTEPhaseISummary.pdf

Rojewski, J. (2002). *Preparing the workforce of tomorrow: Conceptual framework for career and technical education.* Department of Occupational Studies, University of Georgia. Retrieved from http://136.165.122.102/mambo/index.php?option=com_content &task=view&id=168

U.S. Department of Labor. (2008, May). *The employment situation.* Bureau of Labor Statistics. Retrieved from http://www.bls.gov/ces/

U.S. Department of Labor. (2006). *America's dynamic workforce 2006.* Retrieved from www.dol.gov.

Public Law (105-332, Dec. 31, 1998). *Carl D. Perkins Vocational and Applied Technology Education Amendment of 1998.* United States Congress, Washington, DC.

Wirth, A. G. (1990). *Education in the technological society: The vocational-liberal studies controversy in early twentieth century* (Reprint). Virginia Tech, Virginia: Department of Vocational Education

.

Chapter Seven

California Community Colleges[2]

This chapter discusses the status of postsecondary occupation/technical education students in California. Both technical and vocational education are used interchangeably. This discussion is based on data collected from the California Technical Students Profile Survey. The unique nature of the community college, a result of the diverse makeup of the student body, its continued growth in a constantly changing educational and social environment, and its leadership role in providing training for advanced technological skills to the state workforce, has prompted research designed to gather more data on students enrolled in postsecondary Career technical education (CTE), and to determine the success of California's community colleges.

This chapter establishes the importance of continued support for AB1725. AB 1725 validates the articulated programs for career technical training by K-12 districts, community colleges, and the 4-year institutions. Just as it is important for the community colleges to continue to offer vocational-oriented associate degrees that prepare students for careers, it is as well, very important to make sure that graduates' of CTE programs are not discriminated against for further education within the CSU system, as established by AB1725.

According to Kasper (2003), today's comprehensive community college is both a principal provider of academic instruction and a major provider of vocational preparation. It is also serves as workforce development through adult training programs, the offering of vocational preparation, career training, and academically oriented education. All these factors led to a surge in enrollments that outpaces the enrollment growth of educational institutions offering bachelor's degree.

---

[2] This chapter was previously published as O'Lawrence, H. (2007). A case study report of a comprehensive benchmarking review of the status of vocational education students in California: Building a new relationship between community colleges and California State University System. *Journal of Career and Technical Education, 23*(1), 85-96 and is reprinted here with permission.

The promotion for continuation of such programs for these students at the bachelor and master's level will also trigger the same surge in enrollments at all the California State University system.

At one point in the lives of this population, there will be a need for them to obtain their bachelor's degree, master or even doctoral, and we must not close that door of opportunity on them totally at the higher institution level for them to achieve their goal. It has now even become real to some of them that have been teaching for long time that for them to keep their job at both high school and community college, they must obtain a bachelor's degree.

As a result of this, the number of application for admission to Professional studies at California State University Long Beach has increased dramatically since Fall 2004. Students were beginning to really understand the value of the Senate Bill 752 in California. The Senate Bill 752 was introduced into the California Legislature by Senator John Harold Swan and enacted into law in 1943 to abet in the professional development of trade and industrial teachers. The legislation established a procedure by which such teachers may be allowed college credit for work experience, thus enabling them to enter a state college and pursue the required studies leading to the Bachelor of Vocational Education degree.

Businesses' demand in the 1980s for entry-level workers who could think critically and had analytical skills brought new thinking about education from the federal level that eventually led in 1988 to House of Representatives Bill HR7 and subsequently the Carl D. Perkins Vocational and Applied Technology Education Act of 1990. This legislation encouraged articulation agreements between secondary school and community college curricula, that later was called "Tech-Prep" (O'Lawrence, 2000).

One of the major purposes of the Perkins Act of 1990 also was to make the United States more competitive in the world economy by developing more fully the academic and occupational skills of all students and to improve educational programs leading to the academic and occupational skill competencies needed to work in a technologically advanced society (Public Law 101-392, 1990, sec. 2). This law is a standards movement in vocational technical education, as the Act requires all states receiving federal funds to develop and implement an accountability system of core performance standards and measures. This includes:

(1) Measurement of learning and competency gains, including student progress in the achievement of basic and more advanced academic skills; and

(2) One or more measures of performance, with each state developing a system of different standards and measurement for both secondary and postsecondary program (sec. 115).

Unfortunately, with funding reductions reducing access to higher education in California, the students' fee increase has also reduced access to CTE programs across the state; with some programs phased out at all level especially the continuation of such programs at the CSU level. In most cases, access to education has been most compromised in the community colleges.

There is a need to establish an accurate database of the status of students in career technical education programs in California who may be considering furthering their education through CSU systems in the future. Based on national data from previous studies, many highly skilled career and technical positions do not require a four-year college degree, but they do require more than a high school education. In fact, 65% of jobs in the new millennium require only some training beyond high school but not a four-year college degree (Farmer & O'Lawrence, 2002). However, in spite of the statistics, a majority of these people are coming to four-year institutions to complete a bachelor's degree, even a master's degree. In addition, and due to changes in legislation and teacher preparation requirements, many high school and community college occupational education instructors now have to further their education (obtain bachelor's and/or master's degrees) to remain employed in their current jobs.

How important is career technical education to California? Very important indeed! According to Mark Drummond and formal Chancellor of the Los Angeles Community College District (2005), California's community colleges received more than $49 million in fiscal year 2004 through the Perkins program to improve vocational programs, career pathways, help support students attending the career technical programs at community colleges, and help the prospective students to achieve academic knowledge, vocational and technical knowledge, and skills necessary to attain employment, further their education, and to be competitive in the workforce.

This chapter provides legislators and educational leaders with adequate and appropriate information to make intelligent decisions on the growth and development of occupational education in California. Occupational educators, policymakers, and directors of strategic planning will also find this report important especially in the area of program outcomes and follow-up measures, types of training provided, and employment trends on a region-by-region basis.

The demand for technical training workers has rapidly increased since the new millennium and is projected to rise much faster than employment as a whole. Educators are beginning to realize that Information Technology is here to stay and the expansion of jobs in the computer technology and system analysts' areas appears to grow and more training is needed in those areas. Industry are contending that we are facing shortages in thousands of IT works, and for quick response to this need, community colleges can serve as a supplier of low and semi-skilled workers for those jobs that do not required BA/BS degree. There is no doubt that community colleges could provide or produce the in-depth training necessary for high-tech jobs and skills necessary for our youth to be competitive in today's global economy.

Historical Background of California Community Colleges

The California Community College system is comprised of 109 colleges, serves about 2.5 million Californians, and is known to be the largest system of higher education in the world (CCCO, 2004). Developing the California economy depends on a skilled workforce and academic preparation; such academic preparation will provide education and economic opportunity that will keep our youth and adults stay competitive in today's global market. The growth of market economics and the wealth of a nation are largely dependent on buying goods and services, but it is commerce that leads to jobs, independent wealth, and a high standard of living especially when capitalizing on natural resources, technology, and human capital (Grey & Herr, 1998; O'Lawrence & Martines). Capital and technology are very valuable in today's global economy, and to become a major leader in a global market, California's human capital must be completely skilled and effective.

The changing role of community colleges, especially toward vocational education and job training, has made California's community colleges a force to be reckoned with as a workforce preparation centre that provides technical skills for skilled positions, grants associate degrees under a timely (2 years of full-time study to complete) and vocationally oriented degrees that prepare our youths for competitive careers. A competitive global workforce must first start at the local level in which community colleges serve the important needs of local businesses, rural areas where career training are difficult to obtain, and communities at large.

It is important for program evaluation and assessment of each curriculum at the community college system in the state to determine the academic outcomes of those in different areas of career programs, i.e., if it actually prepared them for the workforce to be competitive. It needs to be known to the public how effective the programs are and how prepared the students are when they graduate. There are 109 community colleges in California serving over 1.5 million students and it is the largest institution of higher education in the globe. The Fiscal year 2005 budget proposed by President Bush on Community-Based job Training Grants strengthens the role of community colleges in promoting the U.S. workforce's full potential. The competitive grant program builds on the High Growth Job Training as a national model for community colleges to train workers for the skills required to succeed in high growth, high demand industries (Bush & Bush, 2004).

Due to large flocks of immigrants coming to California for a better life, education and training became a necessity through community colleges as the only institutions with an open door policy that quickly molds, trains, teaches, and guides them to be competitive and self-dependent and productive and useful to the society. So, career technical education in California is the vehicle for supply and demand, economic success and provider of quality of life and for global competitiveness.

Rapid changes due to the scientific and technological revolutions, demographic changes, industrial reorganization, and the interplay of social forces forced community colleges to rethink new strategies for postsecondary technical education; students must gain the necessary skills not only to find or keep their jobs but also to compete in the global economy (O'Lawrence, 2000).

There is a need for a comprehensive plan in California on how vocational and technical education at the community colleges could contribute to the economic future that will reflect on industry needs, economic structure, availability of training resources and ability to train workers for the skills required to succeed in high growth, high demand industries for global competitiveness. Today's students' at the community college will need to be exposed knowledge economy and be flexible by understanding that the skills they were trained for at present may be outdated the following year and must understand the importance of vocational education and training as being indispensable to economic success and quality of life.

For the community college system itself, there is a need for rigorous curriculum and updated regularly to meet the economic demand in the workforce. According to the Executive Summary of the 2000-2004 California State Plan for Vocational and Technical Education, "...delivery of vocational and technical educational services must be driven by the needs of both our populace and our rapidly-changing economy and must take into account the major demographic and educational forces that operate within that economic context" (Haywood, 2001, p. iii).

CTE plays a key role in improving economic and industrial problems in the State of California by better preparing students for skilled labor and by allowing them to become economic contributors in the state, and must be viewed as a principal centerpiece in attracting industry and preparing the workforce for existing and new industries. As was cited in O'Lawrence (2000), the Hudson Institute, in its Workforce 2000 report examined the skills levels in occupations projected to grow and it concluded that the fasted growing jobs will require more reasoning skill, language, and math.

The executive summary of 2000-2004 California State Plans for Vocational and Technical Education by Hayward (2001) indicated the importance of all students in California gaining advanced literacy and mathematics skills as well as being experienced, technically competent, and having the ability to understand the interdependency among all aspects of an industry. The vocational technical education must be able to (a) integrate theory and application, (b) combine technical, computational, reasoning, and communication skills, (c) incorporate school-and work-based learning experiences, (d) better connect secondary and postsecondary educational opportunities, and (e) strengthening connections among educational, business, labor, and government.

Due to the current world trend of globalization such as world market economies, free trade and the out-sourcing of American jobs that were once considered safe from foreign encroachment, there is a need for vocational educational students to have academic foundations necessary for world competency of work, and be able to obtain the ability to deal with issues of daily life and skilled for global competitiveness.

The demand for white-collar work will increase, and executive, administrative, and professional specialty occupations will comprise 30% of all employment of those with at least four years of college. The projections of the Bureau of Labor Statistics as reported in the Monthly Labor Review indicated that occupations requiring training leading to an associate degree are expected to increase by 1.5 million jobs by year 2008

An analysis of postsecondary technical education programs in California community colleges and their impact on the American job market is important to improving the number of qualified entry-level workers joining the labor market in this state. We need to make sure that California is flexible and diversified, that business are equipped to compete in the global market place, and that our workers have the skills needed to occupy and exceed in the jobs of the future (O'Lawrence, 2000).

For our students to be competitive and able to keep their jobs in the 21st Century, the community college will need to continue with short-time on-the-job training (OJT) that will develop needed workers' skills after a short demonstration or up to one month of on-the-job experience or instruction, moderate term on-the-job training that will develop needed skills for about a year of combined on-the-job experience and informal training, and log-term on-the-job training or combined work experience and classroom instruction that will require completion of vocational training and passing an examination after completing the training.

A gradual shift toward vocational education, job training, and programs catering to the community and the students in those programs desiring career advancement and advance degree of higher learning has made it necessary to continue building the relationship between the California State University System and the Community Colleges by promoting continuation of college education and higher degree for vocational education students. This chapter sheds light on Community College system and students regarding the use and benefit of AB1725 in the Professional Studies Department since 1947 at California State University in which vocational career students could benefit from their work experience that would allow then to earn college credit towards their bachelor's degree.

Conceptual Framework

The conceptual framework for this report was based on a benchmarking review of the status of postsecondary technical and occupational education in Pennsylvania conducted by O'Lawrence (2000). The benchmarking concept as discussed by Ellibee and Mason (1997) was used to guide the study, thus providing a baseline from which the effectiveness of new programs can be evaluated. This concept generates a shared in-depth understanding of postsecondary technical students and practices by identifying specific objectives, strengths, and weaknesses to focus its discussion on specific areas needing improvement.

This is a three-phase pilot study to plan, implement, and examine a benchmarking review of the status of Postsecondary-technical and occupational education in California by using a convenient population in Southern California to determine future overall study of the whole of California. There were three objectives in the planning and organization phase of the study: (1) to develop a plan of action to collect and disseminate useful data on the existing conditions of postsecondary technical and occupational education in California, (2) to gather written material from certain institutions relevant to the study and then to conduct a series of on-site observations at those institutions, and (3) to develop a report and disseminate it to a select group of stakeholders.

The pilot study only served for development of action to collect information from students and looked into the existing conditions of postsecondary technical and occupational education in the community colleges in California. A plan was developed in collaboration with participant institutions who provided and gave permission to allow their students to participate in the study. According to Mazzarol and Soutar (2001), the increased demand for education in higher education particularly was driven by the expectation that it would raise the status of the graduate economically and socially.

The overall purpose of this study was to determine (a) the differences among the personal, situational, and outcome characteristics of students in California community colleges and (b) the nature of and the relationship among them. Most importantly, the study findings provide a better understanding of students in postsecondary vocational education technical programs in California. Particularly, little has been done to this point to involve community colleges in postsecondary technical education and participation by these types of institutions will change this lack of involvement and undoubtedly make a valuable contribution to workforce education by providing quantitative data on postsecondary technical students in community colleges in California.

Target Population, Study Sample, Instruments and Procedure

The population for this study included students enrolled in postsecondary technical education programs in community colleges in Southern California. Survey research procedures were used to collect data for this study. A 19-item questionnaire (a total of 100 copies each) was randomly mailed to all participating 6 community colleges selected based on geographical location, to be distributed to each school's vocational technical degree students. These students were asked to complete the questionnaire by May 6, 2005.

In total, 600 questionnaires were sent; a total of 480 were returned for a response rate of 80%. Out of that 480 (80%), 80 (13%) were unable to be processed because those participants did not answer almost 90% of the questions in the survey. Also 44 (11%) out of the total sample responses were classified missing, leaving 386 (89%) of sample responded for analysis. Out of the six schools that received the survey only one did not return any of the surveys sent to them.

The gender breakdown was as follows: 201 (51.9%) women and 185 (47.8%) male. One individual (.3%) out of the respondents did not identify his or her gender status while about 13 (3.3%) were identified as missing number – meaning participants did not provide enough information to be analyze. The total percentage for women reflects the fact that more women are now entering nontraditional career occupations.

The survey instrument used in the study contained 19 items divided into five domains. The five domains comprising the questionnaire were (1) demographic factors, (2) personal circumstances, (3) personal goals/aspirations, (4) institutional participants (the school they are attending), and (5) perception of/satisfaction with current institution.

Data Collection/Analysis

A survey research design was used in this study, a method widely used to investigate educational issues. The data collected were statistically analyzed by computer, through consultation with an expert from the Institutional Research Department at California State University Long Beach (CSULB). The statistical analysis for this study was done through SPSS (Statistical Program for the Social Science, Version 13.0 for Windows).

The researcher used descriptive, two-way ANOVA and log-linear model to analyze study data. With the log-linear approach, researchers develop cell counts in a contingency table in terms of associations among the variables. The two-way ANOVA model was used for continuous responses whose values may be affected by two factors; the log-linear model is a technique for categorical data because it describes association patterns among categorical variables and best describes the relationship among other factors (Agresti, 1990).

The data for this study were drawn from the California Technical Students Profile Survey (described earlier). The study focused on two research questions: (1) what are the differences and relationship between postsecondary technical students in community colleges on selected personal, situational, and outcome characteristics? (2) What are the primary educational goals upon completion of their program? The researcher utilized all of the returned survey questionnaires. For this particular question, four hundred students answered the question.

Findings/Analysis

The demographic information revealed differences between students' ethnicity. Indeed, racial and ethnic minorities made up an increasing number of students enrolled at community colleges. There are twice as many Latino students compared to African-American and American Indian/Alaskan Native while there is no major significant difference between Asian/Pacific Islander and Caucasian (see Table 1). It should be noted that the results are limited only to the data reported by survey respondents.

Table 1. *Gender and Ethnic Background by Respondent in the California Vocational Education Student Profile Survey (CVESPS) Study*

Ethnicity	Gender (n) Male	Total (%)	Gender (n) Female	Total (%)
American Indian / Alaskan Native	5	1.4	1	0.3
Asian/Pacific Islander	39	11	41	11.5
African-American	16	4.5	21	5.9
Latino	57	16	76	21.3
Caucasian	47	13.2	42	11.8
Foreign	5	1.4	6	1.7

| Total | 169 | 47.5 | 187 | 52.5 |

Note. N =356

As shown in Table 1, the sample of males was 169 (47.5%), compared to 187 (52.5%) females. Even though there is no major significance difference between gender, the number of women slightly reflect the national report by the American Association of Community Colleges database that overall, more females (58%) than males (42%) enrolled in the 1,132 community colleges in the United States (Farmer & O'Lawrence, 2002).

The percentage of students in each age group in the study describes the population of students in the vocational program. About 121 (31.7%) are considered traditional students who just recently finished high school, 84 (22%) are between 23 to 28 years old while about 93 (23.3) are above 40 years old (see Table 2). There is no significant relationship between gender and age; the average mean age for male students was 28.98 compare to female 30.69 which means that females in the program are older than men. Also, the median for male is 25.0 compared to 26.0 for women; overall, the mean age for students at these community colleges is 29.85. According to Kasper (2003), enrollment of women overtook of men in 1980s with women accounting for 55% of community college students and which during the 1990s held steady at about 57%. The national center for educational statistics also reported that the participation rate of young woman outnumbers that of young men, and that by 2003, 51% of young women had entered and/or completed postsecondary education compared to 41 percent of young men; while Whites continued to have higher participation rates than both Blacks and Hispanics (NCES, 2005).

Table 2. *Age Breakdown of Respondents in California Vocational Education Student Profile Survey (CVESPS) Study*

Respondents Age Group	n	%
Between 17 -22	121	31.7
Between 23 - 28	84	22
Between 29 - 34	48	12.6
Between 35 - 39	35	9.2
40 and above	95	24.3
Total	382	95.5

Note: 18 (4.5%) respondent did not identify their age

With regard to students' primary educational goal, Table 3 clearly revealed the largest portion of the students (about 28.3%) are attending school to prepare for their first job or career compared to 20.4% that are exploring a new career area or different focus/track of educational goal. About 12.8% are in school to update or improve their skills for their current job while a total of 23% plan to transfer to a four-year college. 23% is a very significant number when we are talking about continuing education through professional studies program utilizing the AB1725 (an application for swan bill) (see Table 3 for complete results).

Table 3. *Respondents' Primary Education Goal While Attending This College in the California Vocational Education Student Profile Survey (CVSPS) Study.*

Primary Goal	N	%
To prepare for a first job / career	108	28.3
To update / improve skills for current job	49	12.8
For self-enrichment / personal interest	32	8.4
To improve my basic skills	6	1.6
To explore a new academic / career area	78	20.4
To prepare for transfer to 4-year college	22	23
To cope with a major change in life	21	5.5
Did not respond to questions	18	4.6
Total	400	100

On the question of students' plans after completing their course of study, it is noteworthy that most students at the community college wanted to work somewhere in California or in their home area. About 41.7% indicated that they will work somewhere in California compared to 26.9% who preferred to work in their home area. Also 22.2% indicated that they would like to continue their education in four year institution (see Table 4).

Table 4. *Respondents Plans after Completing Their Course of Study in the California Vocational Education Student Profile survey (CVESPS) Study*

Description	n	%
Work in my home area	100	26.9
Work in another State	14	3.7
Retirement	7	1.8
Work somewhere in California	158	41.7
Continue education	84	22.2
others	14	3.7
Did not respond	21	5.3
Total	400	100

Conclusions

The findings of the data set used in the study serve as a major step towards providing information regarding California's postsecondary technical education students. In part, these could serve as data for further research. This study led to many insightful and useful findings, including students' responses regarding their major objectives after graduating. Several feedbacks were also provided, some students planned to prepare for their first job, work in their home area/or in California; while some want to explore a new career, improve skills for their current job, get their associate degree, and then transfer to a four-year college.

This finding provides additional information to legislators and educational leaders in the state so that they may make further intelligent decision on the management of postsecondary technical education in California. Further development of vocational education programs in community colleges to meet the expanding needs may be hampered by external agencies both within an outside the government that do not fully understand the purpose of those programs.

Thus, the state's postsecondary technical education institution and program must aim to assure that students achieve clearly defined learning outcomes, including the skills, values, and perspectives as well as knowledge needed in the 21st – century workplace. Community Colleges must also continue to ensure their reputation for high standards and academic quality as the region's colleges of choice for the first two years of college and for career education.

Implications/Recommendations

Several implications may be drawn from the results of this study for education leaders and policymakers to consider when planning, managing, and delivering postsecondary technical programs. In terms of planning future programs, the results may provoke a debate for more diversity in student enrollment and overall goal upon completion of their studies in community colleges technical fields of study. At present, the most significant is accountability and the need for more managing and delivering quality programs that would set a stage for global competitiveness among the nation's best and the global competition in the marketplace for technical skill workers. Flexibility of curriculum will help the community colleges to react quickly to technological changes and increase the ability to quickly train student for latest skills necessary at a job.

Academic challenges in all disciplines must be major and rigorous programs will be the key for successful careers for new graduates. The State Boards in partnership with local businesses must develop strategic plan that will chart the statewide course in administering every aspect of a workforce development program by designing and implementing new critical training that foster programs for consortiums of small, medium-sized employers, offer a support system between local community, corporation and the community college in the area to provide workforce training. Providing classes that give exposure to the fields of study that become vocations allow these students when enter college to have an idea of their skills, interests, and how they can continue to develop their talents; this vocational experience is what provides unique opportunities for academic success when they finally decided to further their education.

For the institution itself, there must be continuing efforts in the state and the localities in developing challenging academic standards, promoting the development of services and activities that integrate academic, vocational, and increase state and local flexibility of providing services and activities; disseminate national research and provide professional development and technical assistance that will improve vocational and technical education programs as intended by the Perkins III. Perkins III supports the preparation of individuals for nontraditional training and employment, and Section 3(17) of Perkins III defines "nontraditional training and employment" as occupations or fields of work, including careers in computer science, technology, and other emerging high skill occupations, for which individuals from one gender comprise less than 25% of the individuals employed in each such occupation or field of work. It is recommended that universal access to postsecondary technical and occupational education must be designed in the state to meet the needs of the economy; the state needs to offer a more organized system of technical education to meet the need for technical workers through effective coordination with its labor markets and with total coherence to the system of providers. More focus is needed to understand the essential technical skills and efficient delivery of postsecondary technical education and training to allow the economies of various regions of the state and its skilled workers to flourish.

This report points to and would help frame the following recommendations for further follow-up research in the area of postsecondary-technical and occupational education in California to ensure the availability and accessibility of high-quality postsecondary technical and occupational training to the citizens of California. Further research that the author will undertake will include systematic tracking systems with agreed-upon components of excellence in postsecondary technical and occupational education for students as agreed-upon by all postsecondary technical institution's presidents. Also further investigation about the status of postsecondary technical education and students in the state is needed by obtaining grants to fully involve all California postsecondary institutions in the study in order to properly determine where California stands among other states in the United States; and to determine if students are getting jobs in their area of specialization upon graduation.

References

Agresti, A. (1990). *Categorical data analysis.* Wiley series in probability and mathematical statistics. A Wiley-Interscience Publication, NY.

Bush, E. C., & Bush, L. V. (2004). Beware of false promises. *Community College Journal,* pp. 36 – 39.

California Community College Chancellors Office (2004). Retrieved August 10, 2005, from http://cccco.edu

Drummond, M. (2005). *House and Senate committees pass vocational education bills.* Retrieved August 10, 2005, from http://www.orangecoastcollege.edu/about_occ/news/Pages/default.aspx?d=03-17-2005&newsId=6773

Ellibee, M. A., & Mason, S. A. (1997). Benchmarking for quality curriculum: The heart of school-to-work. In E. I. Farmer & C. B. Key (Eds.), *School-to-work systems: The role of community colleges in preparing students and facilitating transitions.* San Francisco: Jossey-Bass.

Gray, K. C., & Herr, E. L. (1998). *Workforce education. The basics.* Needham Heights, MA: Allyn & Bacon, The Viacom Company.

Farmer, E., & O'Lawrence, H. (2002). Differences in characteristics of postsecondary technical students in Pennsylvania community colleges and two-year proprietary institutions. *Journal of Career and Technical Education, 18*(2), 47-65.

Hayward, G. C. (2000). *Executive summary of the 2000-2004 California State Plan for Vocational and Technical Education.* California Department of Education.

Kasper, H.T. (2003). The Changing Role of Community College. Occupational Qutlook Quarterly Winter 2002-2003. The Office of Occupational Statistics and Employment Projections, BLS, (2002) 691-5696.

Mazzarol, T., & Soutar, G. N. (2001). *Education as a global industry. The global market for higher education.* Massachusetts: Edward Elgar Publishing.

NCES. (2005). *Postsecondary participation rates by sex and race/ethnicity: 1994-2003.* U.S. Department of Education, Institute of Education Sciences; NCES 2005-028. March 2005 Issue Brief.

O'Lawrence, H. (2001). Characteristics of students in Pennsylvania community colleges and two-year proprietary institutions. *Workforce Education Forum, 28*(1).

Public Law 101 – 392. Carl D. Perkins Vocational and Applied Technology Education Act Amendments of 1990

Chapter Eight

The Influence of Workforce Education and Development on the Growth of Today's Economy [3]

Introduction

This final chapter investigates and reports on the status and influence of Workforce Education and Development and its importance on the economy. This report relies almost exclusively on data from the U.S. Department of Labor Statistics. This study also establishes that the skilled workforce depends on career and technical programs for skill training as the recipe to the success of economic growth in the U.S. The report also emerged from analysis of many other studies, especially the Labor Bureau Statistics, on the state of the economy, unemployment rate, the labor force, employment growth, and the importance of education and training as key to promoting economic growth in the country. The report also justifies and validates the author's notion on the importance of workforce education and development in the 21st century as a way of developing economic growth and providing learning to make individuals competitive in the global economy.

What is not known to many in our society and academia is that workforce education and development is the key to promoting individual learning and skill training. Career and technical educators throughout the nation are affected by what goes on globally because of new developments, improved communication, faster travel, and increased commerce, which lead to global competition. What makes some nations rich, with their citizens enjoying a high standard of living is commerce, that is, producing, selling, and buying goods and services

---

[3] This chapter was previously published as O'Lawrence, H., & Martinez, L. (2009). Influence of workforce education and development on the growth of today's economy. *Online Journal of Workforce Education and Development, IV*(1), 1-14 and is reprinted here with permission.

that lead to jobs, individual wealth, and a high standard of living. For a nation to be competitive in a global economy, its human capital (workers) must be trained and educated to develop its natural resources and able to improve technology (Gray & Herr, 1998; Gordon, 2008, O'Lawrence, 2008b).

Natural resources, technology, and human capital workers are important strategic economic advantages. Human capital is the most important of the three; the most important elements in the quest for a competitive advantage in commerce are the skills and initiative of a nation's workforce. Technology is only as good as the ingenuity of those who can both maintain and use it to its fullest potential (Gray & Herr, 1998; Thurow, 1992). According to Gray and Herr (1998), those who have a workforce that can use the technology to the fullest will have the advantage over those who cannot, and those with the highest skilled labor force will be able to adopt technology faster and use it to produce the best quality at the lowest price. (p. 44).

Lack of workforce education for both professional and nonprofessional workers is a major concern. Even though the United States has the best-educated professionals or salaried workforce in the world, still the country lags in global commercial competition. Indicators suggest that the U.S. has the worst-educated unskilled nonprofessional/hourly workforce among the major economic powers because of a lack of investment in workers' training and retraining (Chao, 2006). The postsecondary education system in the nation represents the greatest intangible legacy ever established, which represents a large, productive, and diverse country as America. Higher education has been a principal means of social mobility for many acculturating immigrants and for empowering minorities (Allen, 2002). Vocational education, increasingly known as career and technical education, is a longstanding program whose place in American education continues to evolve. The broadening of its goals, the ongoing diversity of participants, and the changing education and labor market climate in which it operates suggest vocational education programs are a flexible option for colleges and students (Silverberg, Warner, Fong, & Goodwin, 2004).

This chapter identifies (1) major factors that influence the nation's economy, (2) how well the unemployment rate is controlled, (3) the labor force, (4) employment growth, and (5) how committed the nation is to educating the labor force. These five areas prove in the analysis that they should be considered seriously, as they lead to global competitiveness. History also tells us that no society dedicated to intemperance can long survive unless the society as a whole becomes aware that meaningful work, done well, and dedication are essential aspects of a worthwhile life. This should be made known in our classrooms and should be one of the major goals of education. It is important in the 21st century to examine once again, and debate the importance of workforce education and education – corporate training and human resources development – on our economy: globally, federally, statewide, regionally, and locally. As we continue to review the current status of the economy, we should be concerned with unemployment, especially why college graduates can secure only mediocre jobs or nothing at all, and why our veterans are on the streets, homeless, jobless, and unwanted (O'Lawrence, 2008b).

When thinking about these issues, we ought to consider the importance of workforce skill and retraining programs that will benefit individuals seeking training for employment. As a result of these issues being raised, this chapter proposes that those in authority and in control of educational policy should anticipate the nation's changing employment needs and facilitate better fits among high school graduates, college graduates, veterans returning from war, and jobs. Workforce development programs allow students to acquire the special competencies associated with a particular vocation after they have learned something about their own special aptitudes and capacities, the range of work specializations available to them, and the requirements and rewards associated with different occupational pursuits.

To make this chapter more easily understood, the analysis is divided into four different sections: unemployment rate, labor force, employment growth, and the importance of career and technical education programs. Today's generation has realized the impact of information technology on society, the global phenomenon of world of competitiveness brought about by new characteristics of mass communication, and the potential for bringing remote parts of the world to the forefront of economic development. Indeed, the world is becoming flatter every day. The influence of technology on education includes developments designed to provide communication from one geographical area to another. It is a way of social life, frequently linked with communication and motivation for social change (Friedman, 2007). These information technologies tend, in different ways, to both accelerate and retard social change. Information technology has brought rapid transmission of news, and events create consequences that are immediately considered by other nations, such as creating business-industrial mechanisms that cannot be reversed.

In international relations, the art of diplomacy has been affected in various ways by the use of information technology, which has given us exposure to third-world countries and the other parts of the world. The world is overwhelmingly different in this regard from what it was and the universal tool of today—computer technology—is a global tool that has come to stay. If technology does not break us, it will eventually make us a better society. Information technology brought educational reform to a changing society with the anticipation that today's education would be much better than the past. However, there is tremendous concern among both politicians and educators that we may be heading toward the collapse of education structures if precautions are not taken. The question remains whether technology will make us or break us in the global economy, help us maintain our status as a superpower, and, of course, make us competitive. What would break us is our refusal to acknowledge the importance of career technical education, skill training, and retraining of citizens (O'Lawrence, 2007).

One must wonder why change occurs so slowly in our attitudes toward the value and necessity of vocational or occupational education, career technical education, and workforce development. Those in this field are held in highest esteem, and their work ethic is fundamental to the value system that prepares us for the meaningful work that our economy, community, and society deserve. Workforce development education trains the mind, inculcates values, and strengthens the individual's capacity for responsible citizenship. It is important to recognize that workforce competence is the ability to use one's talents constructively toward productive ends and is an important aspect of responsible citizenship (O'Lawrence, 2008a).

The response of our schools to changing needs and opportunities can be viewed in the context of today's three fundamental educational tasks: socialization, social mobility, and individual self-realization. Our task is to educate, leading to the ability to participate constructively in the global economy, engage in policy, and advance the social-civic life of society by using information technology to produce a flexible labor force that will react effectively to the labor market. We have to be able to help today's generation identify the things that make its members unique through the education we provide. It is important to continue to find ways to develop curricula appropriate to students with special interests and abilities so that they can succeed. It is important to continue business and government support for higher education to help colleges and universities meet the challenges of a new economy (Barrow, 2000). Higher education administrators also have to agree that curricula need to continue to focus more on areas that are significant to economic growth:

- Symbolic skills (conceptual, mathematical, and visual), not only specialized disciplinary content.

- Research skills, rather than established expertise, and

- Communications skills (oral and written), rather than mere "self-expression" (Barrow, 2000, p. 67).

The only way these can be achieved is when higher education institutions can produce a workforce that is highly educated and trained. Workforce 2000 called attention to the skills gap. As capital becomes globally mobile, the only way for high-wage developed nations to attract private capital investment will be the skills and productivity of its domestic workforce. The 21st century workforce and higher education must be positioned to respond to the global challenge to our economy and human resources. They must ensure that our students identify early their vocations and the type of education and training that goes with such vocations in order to be prepared and competitive. There is a need for articulation agreements among business, government, colleges, and universities to help promote and coordinate coursework that will lead to real jobs and sustainable growth (Barrow, 2000).

The Unemployment Rate

As reported by U.S. Department of Labor, in the first half of 2006 the unemployment rate averaged 4.7%, lower than the 5.1% average of 2005 and a full point lower than the 5.7% average unemployment rate of the 1990s. A comparison of France and Germany shows that both countries have persistent unemployment rates nearly double that of the U.S. and their long-term unemployment of 12 months or more is nearly triple that of the U.S. By June 2006, the latest month for which data from this report were available, the United States had enjoyed 34 months of uninterrupted job growth. More than 5.4 million net new jobs have been created in the United States since August 2003. This level of job creation reflects the overall economic growth that the country has been experiencing. The U.S. economy grew at an average rate of 3.2% in 2005, and in the first half of 2006 real Gross Domestic Product (GDP) gains averaged a 4.1% annual rate. That is the best record among the major G-7 industrialized nations, and it's remarkable for a mature, industrialized nation (Chao, 2006).

Even though good jobs are still being created in large numbers, the majority of employment growth during the past 5 years was in occupations with above-average compensation. Most of the new jobs projected for the future are expected to be filled by persons with some kind of postsecondary education (Gray & Herr, 1998). Workers who bring to the labor market the knowledge and skills that today's competitive economy demands are finding good jobs and rising compensation; those who do not keep up in terms of knowledge and skills increasingly lag behind in employment and earnings. Provisions must be provided by the institutions of high learning to ensure that all students have access to the information, training, and resources that will help them get the skills they need to access the growing opportunities in our nation's 21st century economy (Chao, 2006). Table 1 indicates that despite the economic problems the nation is facing, the unemployment rate is still lower when compared with other major countries.

Table 1. *United States and Selected Other Nation's Unemployment Rates in 2005*

Country	Unemployment Rate (%)
France	9.5
Germany	9.5
Spain	9.2
Euro Zone	8.6
Italy	7.7
Canada	6.8
Australia	5.1
United States	5.1
United Kingdom	4.7
Japan	4.4
South Korea	3.7

Source: OECD main Economic Indicators, U.S. Department of Labor, August, 2006.

The May 2008 report of unemployment rates indicated an increase from 5.0% to 5.5% while employment continued to fall in construction, manufacturing, retail trade, and temporary help services, according to the Bureau of Labor Statistics of the U.S. Department of Labor. These are areas of major focus for career and technical education programs to train and retrain. Why this is so important can be answered by looking at the unemployment rates for individuals as recently as May, 2008. Unemployment rates for adult men were (4.9%), adult women (4.8%), teenagers (18.7%), whites (4.9%), and blacks (9.7%);

the jobless rate for Hispanics (6.9%), was unchanged, while unemployment rate for Asians was 3.8%. The number of persons who had lost their jobs increased by 260,000 during the month of May to 4.3 million, and during the year 2007, the number of unemployed who had lost their jobs had risen by 907,000 (U.S. Department of Labor, 2008). The questions remaining are: Where are our retraining programs? And where are the career and technical education programs? Why do we still refuse to acknowledge the importance of such programs in this country?

The Labor Force

The U.S. is known as a leader in workforce productivity; however, what distinguishes the United States from other productivity leaders, such as France, is that the U.S. workforce is also a leader in work effort, that is, hours on the job. Hours worked per capita is a single measure of the labor activity across the population—taking into account both the portion of the population that is employed and the number of hours people work. In 2004, per capita hours worked totaled 859 hours, placing the United States in the same neighborhood as Australia and Canada. South Korea easily surpassed these countries by posting 1,122 hours per capita. The gap reflected the 2,394 hours an average South Korean employee worked per year in 2004; in contrast, an average U.S. worker worked 1,808 hours. On the flip side was France's relatively low hours per capita. Here lies the difference between per capita GDP in the United States and France (U.S. Department of Labor, 2006).

In broad terms, the two countries' workers are similarly productive, but the French simply work fewer hours. With respect to the economic indicators just discussed, the United States generally has led most other Organization for Economic Cooperation and Development (OECD) nations since 2000. The same holds true across most labor market measures, and it reflects strength throughout the U.S. labor market. At 5.1%, the U.S. unemployment rate in 2005 was well below that of most of its European peers. Both Japan and South Korea benefited from even lower rates, continuing long-term trends for both countries. The United Kingdom's rate has hovered around 5% for several years, after trending down from more than 10% in 1993. The U.S. unemployment rate edged down further by mid-2006; by May in the same year, it reached a nearly 5-year low of 4.6% (U.S. Department of Labor, 2006).

When we look at the 2008 report in the U.S., we see that the labor force rose by 577,000 to 154.5 million in May 2008 and the labor force participation rate edged up to 66.2 %. Total employment was little changed at 146.0 million while the employment population ratio, at 62.6%, also was little changed during the month. The number of persons who worked part-time for economic reasons was 5.2 million in May, which is essentially unchanged over the month, but was up by 764,000 during 2007. These individuals indicated that they were working part-time because their hours had been cut back or they were unable to find full-time jobs (U.S. Department of Labor, 2008).

The latest report as of December 2012 indicated that the unemployment rate remained unchanged at 7.8% and nonfarm payroll employment rose by 155,000 in December while employment increased in health care, food services, construction, and manufacturing. Seasonally adjusted household survey data have been revised using updated seasonal adjustment factors, a procedure done at the end of each calendar year. Seasonally adjusted estimates back to January 2008 were subject to revision. The unemployment rates for January 2012 through November 2012 (as originally published and as revised).

The number of unemployed persons, at 12.2 million, was little changed in December. The unemployment rate held at 7.8% and has been at or near that level since September. Among the major worker groups, the unemployment rates for adult women (7.3%) and blacks (14.0%) edged up in December, while the rates for adult men (7.2%), teenagers (23.5%), whites (6.9%), and Hispanics (9.6%) showed little or no change. The jobless rate for Asians was 6.6% (not seasonally adjusted), little changed from a year earlier. In December 2012, the number of long-term unemployed (those jobless for 27 weeks or more) was essentially unchanged at 4.8 million and accounted for 39.1% of the unemployed. The civilian labor force participation rate held at 63.6%t in December.

The employment population ratio, at 58.6%, was essentially unchanged, and the number of persons employed part time for economic reasons (sometimes referred to as involuntary part-time workers), at 7.9 million, changed little in December. These individuals were working part time because their hours had been cut back or because they were unable to find a full-time job. In December, 2.6 million persons were marginally attached to the labor force, essentially unchanged from a year earlier. (These data are not seasonally adjusted.) These individuals were not in the labor force, they wanted and were available for work and had looked for a job sometime in the prior 12 months.

They were not counted as unemployed because they had not searched for work in the 4 weeks preceding the survey. Among the marginally attached, there were 1.1 million discouraged workers (dislocated workers) in December, little changed from a year earlier. (These data are not seasonally adjusted.) Discouraged workers are persons not currently looking for work because they believe no jobs are available for them. The remaining 1.5 million persons marginally attached to the labor force in December had not searched for work in the 4 weeks preceding the survey for reasons such as school attendance or family responsibilities (U.S. Department of Labor, 2013).

Employment Growth

The best route to low unemployment is strong employment growth. The labor markets of both the United States and the European Union (EU-15) are quite similar in size and make for interesting comparisons. Between 1990 and 2005, civilian employment in the United States rose 19.3%, while the comparable measure for the EU-15 rose 11.1%. Employment clearly has increased in both areas, but the EU-15 has outpaced the United States in employment growth for the period between 1900 and 2005; only 5 of the past 15 years, most notably during and after the last two U.S. recessions, 1990–1991 and 2001. Since 2003, the United States again has taken the lead, while a number of European countries have seen somewhat stagnant employment growth, most notably France and Germany (U.S. Department of Labor, 2008).

On the surface, Japan's very low unemployment rates belie its employment woes. The number of employed in Japan, in six consecutive years of employment declines between 1997 and 2003, fell by 2.4 million (3.7%). The subsequent recovery in Japan has boosted employment by only 400,000 persons (0.6%). In addition to tepid job growth, a common thread between Japan and Europe is the incidence of long-term unemployment, defined as a spell of unemployment lasting at least 12 months. In Japan, the long-term unemployed accounted for one third of the total in 2005; in the European Union, the figure was more than 44%. Even the United Kingdom's share doubled the roughly 12% seen in the United States. Despite its relatively higher unemployment rate, Canada's incidence of long-term unemployment was lower than that of the United States. South Korea enjoyed very low overall unemployment and a very low incidence of long-term unemployment (U.S. Department of Labor, 2006).

A look at the U.S. again thus far in 2008 shows payroll employment declined by 324,000 and job losses continued in construction, manufacturing, retail trade, and temporary services while health care added more 34,000 jobs and job growth during 2007 totaled 383,000. Elsewhere in the service-providing sector, food services and drinking places employment continues to trend up, but job growth in the industry has slowed recently. Employment gains averaged 12,000 per month from November through May, compared with 27,000 per month during the first 10 months of 2007 (U.S. Department of Labor, 2008).

Importance of Career and Technical Education

According to the Bureau of Labor Statistics report, many jobs required no more than basic literacy and physical skills largely learned through experience. As recently as 1970, a high school diploma was sufficient for most jobs, and 38.1% of the labor force (23.5 million persons) had completed no education beyond high school (12th grade). In 1970, 36.1% of the labor force (22.3 million persons) had not completed high school. The proportion of persons ages 25 to 64 years old with some college (or an associate degree) more than doubled between 1970 and 2005 (from 11.8% to 27.8%). The share with a bachelor's degree or higher also more than doubled during the period (from 14.1% to 32.3%). In contrast, the share of the labor force with less than a high school diploma declined markedly. In 2005, 32.3% (38.9. million) of labor force members ages 25 to 64 had earned a bachelor's degree or higher, 27.8% (33.4 million) had undertaken some college but had not attained a baccalaureate degree, 30.1% (36.3 million) had attained only a high school diploma (or GED certificate), and 9.8% (11.8 million) had attained less than a complete high school education (no diploma or GED certificate). The number of people ages 25 to 64 in the labor force with less than a complete high school education fell by nearly half (47.1%) since 1970. During that period the number of persons with some postsecondary education (some college, associate degree, bachelor's degree, or higher) increased from 16.0 million (25.9% of the labor force ages 25 to 64) to 72.4 million (60.1% of the labor force ages 25 to 64 (U.S. Department of Labor, 2006).

The relationship between educational attainment and wages is strong and positive. Among workers 25 years and older, the median weekly wage and salary earnings among workers who usually work full-time and are high school graduates are nearly 2½ times more than those who have not completed high school. The weekly difference of $604 in 2005 would amount to an annual difference of $31,408 if extended over a 52-week year. The trend toward higher educational attainment represents more than challenging opportunities and tastes for consuming education services. The trends in educational attainment are closely associated with the trends in the occupational and industrial structure of the labor market, especially the growth in the demand for workers who provide professional, technical, and managerial services (U.S. Department of labor, 2006). This trend is reflected in the demand for persons with at least a college degree compared with those who have not completed high school (See Table 2).

Table 2. *2005 Median Weekly Earnings of Full-Time Wage and Salary Workers Ages 25 and Older*

Level of Education	Average Weekly Salary ($)
Less Than a High School Diploma	409
High School Graduates and no College	583
Some College or Associate Degree	670
Bachelor's Degree and Higher	1,013

Source: OECD main Economic Indicators, U.S. Department of Labor, August, 2006.

Educational attainment is also associated with notable differences in labor force participation. For individuals ages 25 and older, the labor participation rate in 2005 averaged 79.5% for those with advanced degrees (master's degree, first professional degree, or doctoral degree), 77.4% for those whose highest degree was a bachelor's degree, 76.7% for persons with an associate (typically 2-year) degree, 70.2% for those with some college but no degree, 63.2% for those with a high school diploma only, and 45.5% for those without a high school diploma (U.S. Department of Labor, 2006).

To some extent the differences in labor force participation reflect the fact that educational attainment is generally lower among older Americans, whose lower labor force participation is the result of retirement or disability. For example, in 2005 the 35.1 million Americans ages 65 and older included 7.6% with advanced degrees and 11.4% with bachelor's degrees only, compared to 9.7% advanced degree holders and 18.2% bachelor's degree (only) holders for the total population ages 25 and older. At the lower end of the educational attainment range, individuals without high school diplomas accounted for 25.6% of the population ages 65 and older versus 14.7% of the overall population ages 25 and older (U.S. Department of Labor, 2006).

The demand for a highly educated workforce is expected to continue. The Bureau of Labor Statistics projections for 2004 through 2014 indicate that nearly two thirds (63.4%) of the projected 18.9 million new jobs will most likely be filled by workers with some postsecondary education. Prior to 2000, it was also predicted that the majority of jobs would require a postsecondary degree (Farmer & O'Lawrence, 2002; Gray & Herr, 1998). While most of the 18.9 million new job openings will be in occupations for which workers with higher educational attainment will be the most suited, there will also be many jobs available for those with less education. In addition to growth, the Bureau of Labor Statistics projections estimate openings because of net replacement need—replacement of workers who permanently leave occupations because of retirement or other reasons. The beginning of retirement of the baby boom generation throughout the next several years will contribute to replacement openings across occupations all along the spectrum of education requirements.

Between 2004 and 2014, the U.S. Department of Labor (2006) projections show that the number of net replacement openings will total 35.8 million and total openings for both growth and net replacement needs will be 54.7 million. In general, occupations in the high-school-or-less educational requirements cluster will account for a greater share of replacement job openings than growth job openings because many of those occupations have a high turnover, an aging incumbent workforce, and relatively large replacement needs despite slower relative growth. Within the projected job growth category, the projection for the high-growth, high-wage subgroup is particularly noteworthy. High growth, high-wage jobs are occupations that are in the top half of the 2004 Organization of Economic States (OES) earnings distribution (median annual earnings greater than $28,770) and are projected to experience higher-than-average job growth throughout the 2004–2014 horizon.

Among the 18.9 million new jobs associated with projected growth by 2014, 8.7 million fall within the high-growth, high-wage group. Among those occupations with high growth and high wages, 87.0% of new jobs are expected to be filled by workers with at least some postsecondary education. Within the high growth, high-wage group, 5.5 million jobs (62.8% of the total) will most likely be filled by workers with at least a bachelor's degree and 2.1 million (24.2%) by those with some postsecondary education, such as a 2-year community college academic program, a vocational certificate, or specialized formal training (U.S. Department of Labor, 2006).

Technology has played a role in spurring the demand for a more highly educated workforce. Many technological innovations require more educated workers to install, operate, and maintain equipment. This is particularly true for information and communications technology, which has led the dramatic rise in productivity during the past 20 years. Technological change has introduced new occupations that require new skills and education in new subjects, and it has changed the educational requirements and skill content of many traditional occupations. Another factor contributing to the growing demand for educational attainment is the pace of change in both technology and in the competitive conditions of global markets. The faster pace of change in the modern economy means that both employers and employees must adapt to new conditions more often than in the past. To remain competitive, employers introduce new products and new processes to produce goods or services. Employees need new knowledge and skills to maintain current jobs or to find new ones. The latest longitudinal survey data show that, in 2002, the average American worker between the ages of 37 and 45 had changed jobs 10.2 times between ages of 18 and 38. For workers who started a new job between the ages of 33 and 38, a total of 39% reported that they changed jobs again within 1 year and 70% changed jobs again within 5 years (Friedman, 2007; O'Lawrence, 2007; U.S. Department of Labor, 2006).

The commitment and investment in education that Americans have made to achieve higher levels of educational attainment reflect their realization of the present and future benefits of education for labor market success. The 101.1 million Americans ages 25 and older who had completed some post-secondary education in 2005 constituted a valuable national asset of knowledge, skill, and experience. Of these, 18.4 million were advance degree holders, 34.5 million had a bachelor's degree, 16.5 million had completed 2-year associate or vocational degree programs, and 31.8 million had some college education but no degree. The 21st century labor market seeks and rewards workers who can offer the educational foundation, technical skills, and creative flexibility that employers need to compete and to adapt to changing needs successfully. Higher educational attainment contributes to a worker's ability to absorb efficiently new knowledge and to learn new skills. Workers who can quickly move up the learning curve of a new job have a competitive advantage for economic success (U.S. Department of Labor, 2006).

Since one of the purposes of the Perkins Act of 2006 is to develop more fully the academic and career and technical skills of secondary education students and postsecondary education students who elect to enroll in career and technical education programs, by building on the efforts of states and localities to develop challenging academic and technical standards and to assist students in meeting such standards, including preparation for high skill, high wage, or high demand occupations in current or emerging profession, the Perkins Act of 2006 therefore holds community colleges and their governing agencies accountable for student outcomes. While the full impact of this legislation has yet to be determined, state agencies will continue to be required to develop methods to assess performance outcomes with some flexibility in determining how these indicators are measured (Carl D. Perkins Career and Technical Education Improvement Act, 2006).

One of the challenges to human capital theory is the philosophy of Karl Marx, which states that education has been taken over by capitalists for the purpose of controlling the labor force and keeping it from striving beyond its designated status in the workforce (Brown, 2001). While there may be some truth to the Marxian philosophy that occupational education keeps individuals in lower levels of education, the 21st century community college is working hard to counter this stigma by providing educational access to many. Community colleges and occupational courses specifically, have provided opportunity for advancement for many who have been unable to obtain access to the higher levels of education. Given that this is a capitalistic society in which class disparity continues, community colleges provide education and training to many individuals to provide economic and personal advancement for many who would be unable to achieve such advancement by other means.

Conclusion and Recommendation

In this new era, strong skills and lifelong learning should be rewarded, and the nature and impact of student experiences in vocational education could have important implications for the nation's workforce and America's place in the global economy. The federal government should continue to ensure efforts to improve the quality and availability of articulated vocational programs such as 2+2+2 and the Carl D. Perkins Vocational and Technical Education Act (Perkins III). These programs reflect both continuity with previous vocational legislation and some substantive departures, specifically in funding and accountability. Given the labor market value of college credentials, lifelong learning, and flexibility in skills, the role of vocational education is increasingly important especially in partnership with community colleges and 4-year institutions with services from which most participating students will benefit. An emphasis on degree completion may be at odds with the shorter-term training emphasized by the Workforce Investment Act (WIA). But, at least so far, integration of decision making and services between Perkins and WIA has been limited in most states but must be nurtured and embraced further by higher institutions in accomplishing the 2+2+2 articulation agreement (Silverberg et al., 2004).

The majority of all students attending community college are considered to be in postsecondary vocational programs. These students vary in age, income, work experience, and previous college activity and have different goals. Some intend getting an associate's degree or certificate and then transfer to 4-year institutions to pursue a bachelor's degree. Others want to enhance their job skills or to engage in personal enrichment activities; while older students are more interested in obtaining job skills, younger students are more likely to aim for a credential and bachelor's degree (O'Lawrence, 2005). The comparable completion rate for students entering 4-year postsecondary programs and seeking bachelor's degrees is 61.9%; that is, almost two thirds of students who enter these longer degree programs actually earn a credential of some kind (including less than a baccalaureate degree), compared with about half of students who enter shorter-term vocational associate degree programs (Silverberg et al., 2004).

The Perkins III suggests that effective technical skills rest on a strong foundation of academic proficiency. For the nation to be competitive in a global economy, institutions of higher learning must continue to be responsive to the needs and demands of our changing society. An excellent education will be required in the future because a complex society such as ours with an influx of immigrants would not exist without workforce education and development. It will be difficult to be productive, competitive, humane, and peaceful if we do not properly educate our citizens. New knowledge, skills, attitudes toward cultural awareness, training, social responsibility, and total commitment to social values are what the nation needs to remain a super power (O'Lawrence, 2007).

To remain an advanced corporate economic power we need the production of high levels of technical knowledge to keep the economic apparatus running effectively and to become more sophisticated in the maximization of opportunities for economic expansion. Globalization and technology change are transforming national economies, and the skills needed in the workforce and the ability to continue a dominant position depend on prepared workers who can learn and adapt to the continually changing demand of the world economy. It is requisite that learners have access to the necessary information, training, and resources needed to help individuals get the skills that will lead to the growing opportunities in our nation's 21st century economy.

Several factors are driving the demand for educated workers: the most recognized in the 21st century is technology. Technology has played a role in spurring the demand for a more highly educated workforce. Many technological innovations require more educated workers to install, operate, and maintain equipment. This is particularly true for information and communications technology, which has led the dramatic rise in productivity throughout the past 20 years. Technological change has introduced new occupations that require new skills and education in new subjects and it has changed the educational requirements and skill content of many traditional occupations. The most important qualitative consideration is that telecommunications, financial, and information services, while inherent parts of the rapid growth in trade and services, constitute key components of the infrastructure for the overall globalization process. That they are growing fast suggests that the current rapid pace of economic globalization may accelerate further during the 21st century (Preeg, 2000).

Another factor contributing to the growing demand for educational attainment is the pace of change in both technology and in the competitive conditions of global markets. The faster pace of change in the modern economy means that both employers and employees must adapt to new conditions more often than in the past. To remain competitive, employers introduce new products and new processes to produce goods or services. Employees need new knowledge and skills to maintain current jobs or to find new ones. An investment in our future is the commitment in career and technical education that Americans have made to achieve higher levels of educational attainment. This reflects Americans' realization of the present and future benefits of education for labor market success. The 101.1 million Americans ages 25 and older who had completed some postsecondary education in 2005 constituted a valuable national asset of knowledge, skill, and experience. Of these, 18.4 million were advanced degree holders, 34.5 million had a bachelor's degree, 16.5 million had completed 2-year associate or vocational degree programs, and 31.8 million had some college education but no degree (U.S. Department of Labor, 2006). The 21st century labor market seeks and rewards workers who can offer the educational foundation, technical skills, and creative flexibility that employers need to compete and adapt to changing needs successfully. Higher educational attainment contributes to a worker's ability to absorb efficiently new knowledge and to learn new skills. Workers who can quickly move up the learning curve of a new job have a competitive advantage for economic success.

References

Allen, H. L. (2002, Fall). The best of times, the worst of times: American higher education in the 21st century. *The NEA Higher Education Journal*, 91–102.

Barrow, C. W. (2000, Fall). The new economy and restructuring higher education. *The NEA Higher Education Journal*, 65–81.

Brown, D. K. (2001). The social sources of educational credentialism: Status cultures, labor markets, and organizations. *Sociology of Education, 74*, 19–34.

Carl D. Perkins Career and Technical Education Improvement Act of 2006, S. 250, 109th Congress (2006).

Chao, E.L. (2006). *Secretary's Message*. In America's dynamic workforce. U.S. Department of Labor, August, 2006. Retrieved July 2, 2008, from http://www.bls.gov/ces/

Farmer, & O'Lawrence, H. 2002). Differences in characteristics of postsecondary technical students in Pennsylvania community colleges and two-year proprietary institutions. *Journal of Career and Technical Education, 18*(2), 47-65.

Friedman, T. L. (2007). *The world is flat: A brief history of the twenty-first century*. New York: Picador.

Gray, K. C., & Herr, E. L. (1998). *Workforce education: The basics*. Needham Heights, MA: A Viacom Company.

Gordon, H. R. D. (2008). The *history and growth of career and technical education in America* (3rd ed.). Long Grove, IL: Waveland Press.

O'Lawrence, H. (2005). Vocational education teachers' preparation in California: A case study assessing students' perceptions and learning outcomes of distance education. *Workforce Education Forum, 32*(2), 58-71.

O'Lawrence, H. (2007). A case study report of a comprehensive benchmarking review of the status of vocational education students in California: Building a new relationship between community colleges and California State University System. *Journal of Career and Technical Education, 23*(1), 85-96.

O'Lawrence, H. (2008a). Workforce competencies: A comparison of U.S. and Jamaican experiences. In V. C. X. Wang & K. P. King, *Innovations in career and technical education: Strategic approaches towards workforce competencies around the globe* (pp.193-217).

O'Lawrence, H. (2008b). Comparative new trends in career and technical education around the globe. *International Journal of Vocational Education and Training, 16*(1), 95-118.

Preeg, E. H. (2000). *The trade deficit, the dollar, and the U.S. national interest.* Indianapolis, IN: The Hudson Institute.

Silverberg, M., Warner, E., Fong, M., & Goodwin, D. (2004). *National assessment of vocational education: Final report to congress* (Executive summary). Jessup, MD: U.S. Department of Education, Office of the Under Secretary, Policy and Program Studies Service.

Thurow, L. (1992). *Head to head: The coming economic battle among Japan, Europe, and America.* New York: Morrow and Company.

U.S. Department of Labor. (2006). *America's dynamic workforce 2006.* Retrieved July 16, 2008 from www.dol.gov.

U.S. Department of Labor. (2008, May). *The employment situation.* . Bureau of Labor Statistics. Retrieved July 2, 2008, from http://www.bls.gov/ces/

U.S. Department of Labor (2013). The employment situation. Bureau of Labor Statistics. Retrieved January 8, 2013, from http://www.bls.gov/ces/